Peace
Games

Also by Theodore Caplow

Managing an Organization
Toward Social Hope
Sociology
L'Enquête Sociologique
Two Against One: Coalitions in Triads
Principles of Organization

Peace
Games

Theodore
Caplow

Wesleyan University Press
Middletown, Connecticut

All inquiries and permissions requests should be
addressed to the Publisher, Wesleyan University
Press, 110 Mt. Vernon Street, Middletown, Connecticut
06457

Library of Congress Cataloging-in-Publication Data

Caplow, Theodore.
  Peace games / Theodore Caplow.—1st ed.
      p.   cm.
  Includes index.
  ISBN 0-8195-5230-5
  1. Peace. 2. Nuclear arms control. 3. Security, International.
I. Title
JX1952.C34   1989   89-9051
327.1′72—dc20   CIP

Manufactured in the United States of America

First Edition

First printing, 1989

Wesleyan Paperback, 1991

92 93 94 95 96   6 5 4 3 2

To Peggy with love

Contents

Peace
Games

Chapter 1

War Games and Peace Games

To imagine peace? How can that ever be made as
exciting as imagining war?
James Reston

In the entire postwar period, there has been
amazingly little analysis of the content of peaceful
coexistence—the avowed goal of U.S. national
policy in all administrations.
Henry Kissinger

We have in recent decades seen the almost total eclipse
of an intellectual tradition—planning for permanent peace—that
goes back to the year 1306 when a Norman named Pierre Dubois
circulated the first of innumerable schemes for keeping peace
among the warring powers of Europe. From then on, peace projects
abounded until after the Second World War, when the nuclear
confrontation between the United States and the Soviet Union,
which we will call the End Game, created so strong an obsession
with a third World War that it became almost impossible to imagine a lasting peace. In the presence of the End Game and the
smaller war games to which it gave rise, peace games went out of
style.

War games are not new. Chess itself is an ancient war game.
Battles were rehearsed with toy soldiers in the seventeenth century. The game called Kriegspiel, invented by a German tactician,
was used for military planning in the nineteenth century by the
general staffs of Prussia, Austria, France, Russia, Italy, and Japan.
A variant called American Kriegspiel was adopted by the Naval
War College at Newport in 1889, beginning a long tradition of
strategic war gaming between the invariably blue American fleet
and hypothetical opponents designated as red, crimson, black, and

3

orange. Great Britain, colored red, was the adversary of choice before 1914. Japan, colored orange, was the preferred enemy from 1919 to 1941.

After 1945, the possibilities of war gaming were enhanced by two developments: the introduction of computers and the invention of recreational war games based on historical campaigns. Computers, which initially augmented the information available to human players, eventually became the players in many war games, especially in the simulation of nuclear exchanges. Unlike human players, they do not balk at crossing the nuclear threshold. Some of the recreational war games, more flexible and sophisticated than the conventional *kriegspielen,* are used for advanced military training.

A recent book by Thomas B. Allen is entitled *War Games: The Secret World of the Creators, Players, and Policy Makers Rehearsing World War III Today.* The subtitle summarizes the argument. War games are played incessantly in the Pentagon and the Kremlin, and in planning agencies and staff colleges on both sides. At its Technical Center in the Hague, the North Atlantic Treaty Organization runs one of the largest gaming centers in the world where day in and day out the blue players simulate responses to anticipated red attacks. The scenarios created by thousands of replays of the End Game are known to every schoolboy. *Newsweek,* discussing the Intermediate Nuclear Forces treaty in December 1987, presented this "worst case scenario" of its possible consequences.

On a Sunday morning in August, 20 crack Soviet divisions slash across the border between East and West Germany. There is no warning. The West has been lulled by a Soviet "peace offensive," including radical new disarmament proposals and a planned visit to the United States by the Soviet leader. Under the cover of Warsaw Pact maneuvers, an invasion force has massed near the inter-German border. Soviet commandos have infiltrated the West. Now, as the offensive begins, the commandos blow up bridges across the Weser and Aller rivers and sabotage ferry boats on the English Channel; NATO's ability to reinforce itself is further sapped when Soviet warplanes bomb allied bases and civilian airports. Millions of refugees fleeing westward also prevent NATO defenders from reaching their positions after a belated mobilization. The Soviet spearhead batters the relatively weak British and Dutch forces on the northern end of the front and then swings south. A second echelon strikes from Czechoslovakia, driving through Austria and circling behind the strong U.S. and West German divisions on their southern flank. Their defenses crumbling, the Western allies have two options: to go nuclear, or to surrender.

Nuclear war gaming has not been confined to strictly military operations. In *The Day After World War III*, Edward Zuckerman tells the fantastic but factual story of government and corporate planning for the aftermath of a nuclear exchange. The General Services Administration, for example, has compiled a list of the fifty most important paintings in the country and tried to persuade the museums that own these masterpieces to store them underground. The Treasury has stockpiled huge supplies of currency in a Virginia cave to replace the cash destroyed in a nuclear attack. In the National Defense Executive Reserve, civilian executives train a few days each year for future roles in the Emergency Solid Fuels Administration and in other new agencies the government intends to set up after the nuclear war. Many public agencies and private corporations have furnished underground offices from which they plan to direct their postattack operations.

The argument of this book is that well-played peace games can discover feasible alternatives to the endless disasters envisaged by contemporary war games. It is remarkable how few efforts have been made in these war-haunted times to imagine a durable peace and to work out scenarios for reaching it. Peace games are potentially as interesting as nuclear war games—and much more winnable—although the rules of play may be harder to devise. The games are less boring than an avid war game player might suppose. Although they lack the illusionary concreteness of toy tanks on a terrain model, peace games present more intellectual challenge and allow more scope for inventiveness than war games do.

The object of the basic peace game is to go from the existing "war system of the commonwealth of nations," as Charles Sumner called it, to a new system that excludes industrialized war without passing through a nuclear exchange on the way. The hypothetical players, as in nuclear war games, are national governments, and their moves are restricted to acts that national governments and their agents can perform. Population, resources, terrain, the social and economic infrastructure, popular culture, communication networks, and technology are given as real data, although plausible modifications may be introduced in the course of play. Two limiting conditions are imposed to keep the games relevant to the real world: existing nations may not be removed from the board except by voluntary merger; existing conflicts may not be ignored.

Chapter 2

End Game—The Unfought Nuclear War

Deterrence is not a game played by two players
seated at a chess or poker table. It is played by
small groups of people embedded in enormous
complex organizations whose outlines they barely
discern and whose detailed operations they
scarcely control.
Bligh, Nye, and Welch

NATO has thousands of nuclear weapons on the central
front that stretches from the Elbe to the Danube, so many that it
is said to require the equivalent of an entire division to guard
them. The most numerous are artillery shells six or eight inches
in diameter. The largest is the warhead for the Lance missile, with
a range of seventy miles and about as much explosive power as
the Hiroshima atom bomb. There are nuclear antiaircraft shells
and land mines. The other side has them too.

According to the 1987 Report of the U.S. Secretary of Defense:

The primary threat to Europe comes from the Soviet Union and its Warsaw Pact allies. The Warsaw Pact confronts NATO with massive conventional forces, a sophisticated array of theater nuclear forces (including the
new SS-20), and strategic nuclear forces. In designing U.S. forces, it is
not enough to identify the general threat. One must consider specific
contingencies. Toward that end, the NATO allies examine a broad array
of possible Warsaw Pact attacks against Western Europe, from a limited
effort to cut off Berlin to a full-scale offensive.

Nothing quite like this unfought battle was ever seen before—
two great armies, drawn up on the field of battle, year after year,
immobile. Each side says that its own intentions are purely defensive. There was a time long ago when the huge Russian army
advancing from the east might have moved into Western Europe

7

to support revolutionary uprisings *if* the uprisings had occurred and *if* the American and British armies had not stood in the way and *if* the U.S. had not possessed all the atomic weapons then existing. And there was a moment in 1956 and another in 1968 when the whole Soviet empire in Europe might have crumbled before a NATO invasion. Those opportunities were noted, examined, and refused at the time because the risks were too great. The risks are much greater now, with the Communist parties of France, Benelux, West Germany, and Italy reduced to relative impotence, the resistance movements superseded in Hungary and Czechoslovakia, and all the cities of both sides defenseless against missiles.

Each of the armies on the central front is ready, willing, and able to fight a conventional war, if only the opposing army will consent not to fire any nuclear shells.[1] The sequences of attack and defense have been worked out in meticulous detail, the historic invasion routes are guarded, hundreds of tactical contingencies have been plotted, schedules of reinforcement and resupply extend for months and years after the initial engagement. But all these capabilities depend on mutual abstention from the nuclear weapons. The modest reciprocal employment of nuclear artillery to destroy bridges and motor pools might conceivably permit the war to continue in a normal fashion, but it would have to be very modest indeed. A nuclear exchange on a larger scale would make the battlefield untenable for both sides and ruin the war, even if it did not bring in the nation-smashing missiles poised offstage. No one so far has been able to think of a plausible reason why the losing party in such a conventional battle would refrain from using its nuclear warheads when all other hope was gone. Or how, if the high command of the losing side elected to accept defeat, it could prevent its artillery commanders in the field from firing their weapons independently.

It is virtually certain that sooner or later some unauthorized persons will provide themselves with a nuclear bomb and will threaten to use it. The likely target is a city. A mere threat will put the local authorities in a dilemma. If they make the threat public, they will have to organize a general evacuation or permit a spontaneous one. In either case, the cost will be very high. What is much worse, the incident will be imitated. The same city will be threatened again, and other cities, too.

The authorities will probably choose to disregard the threat, but if they do, they will pass some very uncomfortable hours. All things considered, this has probably happened already, even more than once. If the threat is made credible, say with the serial number of a stolen warhead or a sample detonation out in the country, the official dilemma will be almost unbearable. The public will have to be told. The authorities will announce the danger and urge people to stay calmly in place, or to get out fast; whichever directive is given will be followed by some people and ignored by others. If the threat is accompanied by simple demands for money or the release of a prisoner or a fleet of aircraft or television time, the demands will be promptly met. This is what governments do—while vowing the contrary—when small numbers of hostages are taken and the ransom demands are not too onerous. With a multitude of hostages at risk, the ransom might be higher.

If the threat is accompanied by political demands—nuclear disarmament, the immediate establishment of a Palestinian state, the president's resignation, the prohibition of abortion—the authorities may agree in principle and propose to negotiate the details later, hoping that the agreement can be disregarded after the threatening parties are identified.

The worst case has still to be considered—the mad bomber who explodes his stolen or homemade nuclear warhead in the center of a city without warning. Like the great physicist who quoted the Bhagavad Gita after the first atomic test: "I am become Death / the shatterer of worlds." Even if the explosion of a terrorist bomb was not misread as an opening shot by a hostile state and returned with greater force, many Americans (supposing the destroyed city to be American) would insist on holding the Soviet Union responsible for the anonymous blast. War would be close on one hand and civil disorder on the other.

To return to the End Game: a one-megaton nuclear weapon detonated about two miles above any city on a clear day would create a blast overpressure of five pounds per square inch and deliver about twenty calories of thermal energy per square centimeter at a radius of five miles from ground zero. Very few people would be left alive and very few buildings would remain standing within that circle. Dividing the same explosive force among a number of smaller bombs would greatly extend the area of destruction. Properly divided and carefully aimed, one megaton should be sufficient to level the largest city and to kill most of the inhabitants.

The United States has thirty-six metropolitan areas with populations over one million. A pair of Soviet Delta III submarines with sixteen SSN18 missiles, range 4,000 miles, each carrying seven 200-kiloton warheads, are theoretically capable of destroying every one of these from their patrol station off the Chesapeake Bay—every large place from New York City to Portland-Vancouver. The immediate death toll should be in the neighborhood of 80 million. The U.S.S.R. has only twenty-two metropolitan areas of a million or more. No problem at all for a pair of Ohio Class submarines each carrying sixteen missiles armed with eight 100-kiloton warheads, one firing from a position off the Norwegian coast and the other from the Sea of Okhotsk.

Note that these exercises would take about 25 megatons out of the U.S. inventory of more than 4,000 megatons and make no use of intercontinental ballistic missiles (ICBMs), cruise missiles, or manned bombers. The U.S.S.R., targeting more and larger urban centers, might need as much as 50 megatons out of its inventory of 8,000. Even if every missile was backed up by five others, the U.S. and the U.S.S.R. would use up scarcely 3 percent of their current inventories. That is what is meant by overkill. At the beginning of 1989, the U.S. was planning to spend about 70 billion dollars to enlarge and upgrade its inventory of nuclear warheads, despite severe problems of safety and environmental contamination at the major manufacturing facilities. The U.S.S.R. was more than keeping pace. The abandonment of intermediate range missiles and the proposed reduction of intercontinental missiles stimulated rather than discouraged this bilateral "modernization."[2]

The most encouraging feature of the unfought war is that it has gone unfought for more than forty years. At every showdown—Hungary, Berlin, Cuba, Czechoslovakia—the side challenging the status quo has given way. For twenty of those years, the nuclear forces of the U.S. were greatly superior to those of the U.S.S.R. As late as 1966, the ratio in warheads was 10 to 1. During the same twenty years, the Warsaw Pact ground forces were easily capable of overrunning Western Europe. Deterrence was asymmetrical. It no longer is. Since the 1970s, there has been approximate nuclear parity and—although the point is much argued—something like parity in conventional forces on the central front.

As long as deterrence was asymmetrical, the United States was dissuaded from provocative actions by the conviction that the Russians were eager to march across the Rhine and bring all Europe into the Communist empire. The Russians, for their part, seem to have found the threat of an American first strike very plausible. Each side had faith in the devil it knew and was cautious, but each had a plan for winning World War III if matters got out of hand.[3] Today's symmetrical deterrence is a less interesting game. They can kill us. We can kill them. To keep the game going, each side tries to develop the capability to take out so many of the adversary's weapons with a first strike that they will be forced to capitulate. It cannot be done, of course, because of those invulnerable submarines. And if some way were found to pinpoint the location of hostile submarines beneath the sea, it still couldn't be done because of the bombers and cruise missiles. Rather than give up the game, the players have agreed to disregard the existence of these other vehicles and restrict the play to ICBMs.

Missile guidance systems have improved dramatically in recent years. With the location of an enemy silo known, the newest guidance systems can bring a missile in on top of the silo every time. The first missile directed against a silo in a battery will presumably find and destroy its target. But what happens to later incoming missiles when they encounter the 400-mph winds and the electromagnetic turbulence of the earlier explosion? Once this phase of the game has been played out to the end and every rocket in a fixed silo is targeted by an enemy rocket, the play can be started over again by taking the rockets out of their silos and putting them on flatcars or giant trucks, which eventually can be tracked by satellite to keep them in the cross hairs. But then the satellites can be knocked out as the first phase of hostilities. The hypothetical moves and countermoves go on forever, and none of it would make much difference except for the fact that the most obvious defense against a first strike is to launch first.

A nuclear war might grow out of an international crisis, or start by accident, or be provoked by a third party. The first of these possibilities—an act of national policy in response to an international crisis—seems the least likely. It would amount to collective suicide. An accidental outbreak of nuclear hostilities is more probable. It might be caused by human or computer malfunction. It is easy to imagine a large-scale missile launch triggered by an erroneous warning of an incoming attack. The use of nuclear weapons by one of the minor nuclear powers—Britain, France, China, Israel, South Africa—might draw one of the superpowers in, in accordance with its treaty obligations, and thus attract the other by reflex. Or a malign third party—perhaps a terrorist state hostile to both superpowers—might attack Moscow or Washington with its lone nuclear weapon in the hope of setting off a nuclear exchange. It seems probable that if the End Game continues, one of these situations will occur sooner or later.

Since the End Game began, the travel time of nuclear warheads from base to target has been reduced from 10–12 hours to 25–30 minutes for ICBMs and 10–12 minutes for "theater" weapons. The submarine missiles aimed at the capital cities can be fired from positions less than ten minutes away.[4] If the Soviet Union decided to attack Washington with missiles from an offshore submarine during the President's State of the Union address, they could be sure that there would be no effective warning. Even if the attack was detected and verified during the few minutes of the missile's flight, there would not be time enough for officials to escape from the Capitol, and it would make no difference if some of them did, since everything for miles around would be wiped out. No one would know for a while which, if any, of the President's sixteen constitutional successors had inherited the office, or where to look for him.

Operational control of the nation's nuclear forces would pass to an airplane code-named Looking Glass (after Alice-in-Wonderland) which flies in random patterns above the Midwest. Looking Glass carries an Air Force general, his staff, and communication equipment. With Washington gone, that officer would be responsible for assessing the situation, and ordering a retaliatory strike by U.S. missile and bomber forces.[5] But according to Daniel Ford's 1985 study of "The Button," Looking Glass might have problems with both of these assignments. It is dependent on the North American Air Defense Command (NORAD) command center in Cheyenne Mountain near Colorado Springs for information about an incoming attack, and the Cheyenne Mountain installation itself is a vulnerable target, good for perhaps twenty minutes after Washington disappears from the monitor screens. In that brief interval, it might be nearly impossible for NORAD to determine what had happened before it went off the air.

Looking Glass can order missile firings by sending coded signals directly to Minuteman silos; by sending them through a fleet of launch-control planes, which take to the air on warning of a hostile attack; by launching a set of special Minuteman missiles which carry radio transmitters instead of warheads; and by relaying radio messages to Strategic Air Command (SAC) bombers and Navy submarines through intermediary aircraft. Each of these systems has some weaknesses, according to Ford. The launch-control planes and radio rockets are vulnerable to destruction on the ground, the direct radio communications might be knocked out by an electromagnetic pulse, and the indirect links could be severed by attacking the relay points. Moreover, Looking Glass flies at the same altitude as commercial airliners and under the supervision of civilian air traffic control. It would not be exceptionally difficult for an enemy to track and destroy it in the air.

So far as is known, the Soviet Union relies on a network of underground bunkers in and around Moscow to keep its leaders safe from attack. But, as in the reciprocal case, the leadership would not have time to reach the shelters, and if they did, the U.S. has developed earth-burrowing warheads to get at them. The Soviet command and control structure seems to be somewhat less exposed than the American, but that signifies only that cutting it to pieces would take a lot of missiles.

If there is to be a nuclear exchange, the side that strikes first will have an enormous advantage. In a crisis in which the outbreak of hostilities appeared imminent, launching a first strike should be a much more attractive option than enduring one, particularly since the leadership that launches first can arrange to survive. Ford theorizes that the almost comical defects of the U.S. command and control system—it relies heavily on ordinary telephone lines—do not indicate that our military planners are incompetent but that they have never taken seriously the idea of absorbing a nuclear attack and then retaliating. The advantage of a first strike is too great to be ignored.

When Howard Bahr, Bruce Chadwick, and I interviewed the officials in charge of civil defense in many localities, as part of a government study in 1984,[6] we found a few places where public shelters were still partially stocked and occasionally inspected, but most have been abandoned. It was not uncommon for a civil defense official to learn from us that the building in which he worked had a public shelter clearly marked in yellow and black. The air raid sirens have been inactive for so many years that nobody knows how to activate them. The backyard shelters became tool sheds long ago.

Here and there, the private survivalist can be found with his cache of preserved food, weapons and ammunition, medical supplies, construction tools, board games, and motorcycles for the entire family, ready to take to the hills at the first warning. Many localities—especially those with frequent flooding—have elaborate plans and facilities for emergencies. The heart of such systems is a command post stuffed with communications equipment, food, and medical supplies, protected to some extent against blast and radiation. These are designed to shelter local officeholders—and often their families—for an extended period. Since outsiders do not know these facilities exist, the problem of invading neighbors is not expected to arise.

Civil defense again became a political issue, in a small way, with the announcement in 1981 of a national Crisis Relocation Plan, intended to go into effect whenever the President judged a nuclear attack to be imminent.[7] It called for evacuating the population of every metropolitan area into nearby villages and small towns. Private cars would carry most of the refugee population, assisted by buses, trucks, and trains. The actual planning was carried far enough by 1983 for quotas to be assigned to reception areas, although no method was devised for assigning individuals to particular places. CRP, as it was called, provoked furious opposition from two quite different audiences: small-town officials appalled at the prospect of housing, feeding, and controlling hordes of uncouth city dwellers, and nuclear activists enraged by the premise that some large fraction of the population might survive a nuclear war by taking flight.

Crisis relocation seems to have been forgotten by its sponsors sooner than by its critics, as they became aware that (1) the evacuation of cities might be taken by the other side as an unmistakable warning of an impending American strike, and give them a sufficient incentive to strike first; and (2) the refugees would have no homes to return to after an attack, and the host communities, greatly outnumbered, would be unable to keep them indefinitely.

For many years, the Russians were more serious about civil defense than we were. The escalators down to the Leningrad subway descend so far that the bottom is not clearly visible from the top, and the stations, taken together, can accommodate the entire population. But it is not clear that people sheltered there would survive a nuclear attack on the city directly above or would have anywhere to go when the All Clear sounded.

The Strategic Defense Initiative was introduced by President Reagan in a March 1983 speech. "Let me share with you," he said,

a vision of the future which offers hope. It is that we embark on a program to counter the awesome Soviet missile threat with measures that are defensive. What if free people could live secure in the knowledge that their security did not rest upon the threat of instant United States retaliation to deter a Soviet attack; that we could intercept and destroy strategic missiles before they reach our own soil or that of our allies. . . . I call upon the scientific community who gave us nuclear weapons to turn their great talents to the cause of peace.

Both the U.S. and the Soviet Union played with missile defense systems in the 1960s, and each side built one local system before concluding that they could be easily overwhelmed by aiming more missiles at the defended target. Both sides then found it advantageous to prohibit missile defense systems by treaty. But forgoing the right to self-defense was an idea that rankled with defense enthusiasts.

The media nicknamed the SDI project Star Wars. The battle station in the original film of that name was protected by an invisible shield off which missiles bounced harmlessly. Weapons were energy beams—sword beams for dueling, bigger beams for aerial dogfights, giant beams to disintegrate planets. Technology rushed to imitate art. Within a year, a 21-billion-dollar development program was under way. Although a considerable number of the research scientists at major universities pledged themselves not to work on the project, colleagues stepped forward and took their places.

One current plan calls for hundreds of surveillance satellites crisscrossing Soviet territory in low orbit on the watch for the firing of ICBMs. When a missile is fired, the computers on these satellites will direct U.S. battle stations in permanent orbit to fire chemical lasers at the Soviet boosters during the burn phase. In the next phases, the missile buses coast quietly through space. Without rocket plumes, they are much harder to track, but the feat is accomplished anyway, and the buses are hit with beams generated on the ground and reflected from mirrors in space, or by X-rays produced by the timely explosion of a hydrogen bomb thrown up by a submarine. In the third phase, when the missile has separated into ten or more separate warheads and perhaps a hundred decoys, the battle stations pot away at all of them with particle beams and rail guns. In the terminal phase, as the warheads come down, we send up fighter planes to intercept them with a swarm of "smart rocks"—tiny, high-speed projectiles that destroy their targets by impact.

The specifications are challenging. To put the battle stations into orbit will require, by one estimate, the equivalent of 15,000 space shuttle missions and will cost more than the national debt. The computers that run the system without human intervention will have to have about one hundred times the capacity of the largest existing supercomputers, weigh practically nothing, and work perfectly without maintenance.[8]

Critics have a number of objections to the project, of which several seem persuasive:

• To be effective, the shield would have to be leakproof, but one supposes that it can be made so. Even a 2 percent penetration rate would entail unacceptable losses.

• SDI promises little protection against short-range submarine-launched missiles and none at all against cruise missiles, bombers, or land and sea vehicles. If the system were ever perfected, it could be bypassed immediately.

• The surveillance satellites and battle stations must be in low orbit in order to identify and hit their targets. Since their positions at every moment are predictable, they could easily be put out of action by lasers and rail guns and kinetic projectiles as an attack began.

• There are many known ways in which the target missiles could be made harder to fit, for example by having the boosters burn faster or by increasing the number of decoys. Other methods could undoubtedly be devised.

• The environmental consequences of these high-energy activities in space and the upper atmosphere are unknown but probably harmful.

President Reagan said on several occasions that after SDI was perfected, it might be shared with the Soviets. Some administration spokesmen said it would convince them to be serious about arms control. To the amazement of the project's critics, it seemed to do just that. As SDI research gathered momentum, the Soviet Union abandoned bargaining positions it had held for decades, offered and even demonstrated a moratorium on nuclear testing, accepted the principle of on-site inspection, and finally, at the Reykjavik meeting between Gorbachev and Reagan, the Soviet leader proposed a wholesale dismantling of the superpowers' nuclear arsenals in return for a delay in SDI research. Plainly, SDI was a most effective bargaining chip. There was something about the project that seemed to alarm the Soviet leadership more than any other American move in the long history of the End Game. It could not have been the threat that their missiles would be rendered ineffective. That threat was remote, implausible, and easily countered. But SDI *is* an expedition into unknown technological territory in search of new scientific weapons—death rays, disintegration beams, magnetic cannon—and new devices to aim them. The Soviet Union probably lacks the economic and scientific resources to match the effort and is apprehensive that some of the defensive weapons SDI proposes to invent would serve just as well for offense.

Another factor of instability in the End Game has been the spread of nuclear weapons to other states besides the U.S. and the U.S.S.R. The British staged their first nuclear test—in the Australian outback—in 1952, the French in 1960, and the Chinese in 1964. All three acquired hydrogen bombs in due course. Their warheads are numbered in hundreds, not thousands, but each of them could inflict grave damage on any adversary. Israel and South Africa are each thought to have a stock of nuclear warheads and means of delivering them. If they did not, it would be very strange, since both have nuclear reactors and sophisticated research programs, and are surrounded by a ring of hostile states. India exploded a nuclear device as far back as 1974, and either has a nuclear force or can put one together quickly. Pakistan is thought to have acquired nuclear weapons in 1988. Argentina, Brazil, and Taiwan may have a few. Iraq, Iran, and Libya have made visible efforts to get them.

As of 1985, there were 240 light-water-cooled reactors in twenty-four countries having electricity as their product and plutonium as a by-product. A typical plant in this category can produce enough plutonium for forty or fifty fission bombs in a year. The breeder reactors introduced by the French produce vastly greater amounts of plutonium. The experts seem to agree that a very good backyard mechanic could put together a weapon in the range of the Hiroshima bomb using stolen plutonium and information in the public domain. Any state, however backward, having a nuclear power station could presumably manage the same trick.

The United States and the Soviet Union were quick to perceive a mutual interest in discouraging the acquisition of nuclear weapons by third parties, and the Nuclear Non-Proliferation Treaty, signed in 1968, was negotiated with remarkable ease. It is a multilateral treaty including both nuclear-weapon states and non-nuclear-weapon states. The principal provisions are: the non-nuclear-weapon states promise to stay that way; the nuclear-weapon states promise to share nonmilitary nuclear technology with the non-nuclear-weapon states but withhold the technology related to weapons. The quid pro quo for the non-nuclear-weapon states is that each nuclear-weapon state "undertakes to pursue negotiations in good faith on effective measures relating to cessation of the nuclear arms race at an early date and to nuclear disarmament, and on a treaty on general and complete disarmament under strict and effective international control."

At the conferences held periodically to review the treaty, non-nuclear-weapon state delegates have been known to complain that the nuclear-weapon states have not met their obligations, but the complaints are muted. The non-nuclear-weapon states do not, for various reasons, regard themselves as deprived. Some of them, like the Holy See, Monaco, San Marino, Jamaica, Barbados, and Cyprus, are demilitarized. Others, including the five Scandinavian countries, Switzerland, Canada, Australia, and New Zealand, are opposed to nuclear weapons on principle. The Eastern European clients of the Soviet Union—Bulgaria, Czechoslovakia, East Germany, Hungary, Poland, Rumania—presumably have no choice. Nor would the United States wish the smaller Latin American countries to acquire such weapons, although Argentina, Brazil, and Chile pointedly abstain from the non-proliferation treaty, as do other states with a known interest in nuclear weapons—India, Israel, South Africa, and Pakistan.

Japan, West Germany, and Italy would not have been allowed to abstain in 1968. Nowadays, all three have large-scale nuclear establishments, and either have weapons or could manufacture them on very short notice.

Any state adhering to the non-proliferation treaty is entitled to withdraw on three months' notice.

The treaty authorizes the International Atomic Energy Agency, based in Vienna, to inspect the nuclear installations of non-nuclear-weapon states to make sure that no one is stealing plutonium or putting it aside to make bombs. As of 1984, the agency's small staff was inspecting a total of 884 installations in 102 countries.[9] The safeguards are not foolproof, and a good deal of plutonium is known to be lost, strayed, or perhaps stolen.

The principal use of a small stock of nuclear weapons is to discourage invasion of one's national territory by a non-nuclear-weapon state, and for that purpose it should be very effective, unless nuclear-armed third parties become involved. There are two small defects in this strategy, however. The first is that the potential invader, perceiving its disadvantage, has a powerful incentive to obtain a few nuclear weapons of its own. The other is the virtual certainty that nuclear-armed third parties will involve themselves in any conflict that threatens to go nuclear.

Another reason for having a few nuclear weapons is to be able to resist diplomatic pressure from one of the superpowers. That is the theory behind the French *force de frappe*: that France's ability to threaten European targets on its own gives it an indirect veto over American policy in any crisis arising from the End Game.

Quite apart from these elegant strategical calculations is the chance that a rogue statesman might vent his spleen on a foreign city without regard for the consequences. And if his murderous rage were tinctured by a sense of fun, he might manage to destroy New York or Moscow, or even New York *and* Moscow, without revealing himself as the perpetrator.

There is no way of telling how grave the damage of a nuclear exchange might be. By one calculation, the energy released by a Hiroshima-size bomb is roughly equivalent to the sum of simultaneous head-on collisions at sixty miles per hour of all the motor vehicles in the United States. Another piece of hyperbolic arithmetic tells us that the explosive power carried by a single Trident submarine is ten times that of all the explosives (including the Hiroshima and Nagasaki bombs) detonated in the course of World War II.

But the blast is only the beginning. About 35 percent of the energy released in a nuclear explosion is thermal energy. The temperature within the bomb is tens of millions of degrees. A one-megaton bomb will burn the retinas of viewers fifty miles away. At closer range, it melts stone and ignites sand. A nuclear explosion produces bursts of direct radiation in two kinds—gamma rays and neutrons—which kill humans and other organisms. Radioactive fallout of neutron-activated debris from a nuclear explosion rises into the atmosphere and falls to earth between twenty-four hours and three years later, still emitting alpha, beta, and gamma rays, and X-rays. Fission weapons yield more than three hundred radioactive products. About forty of them are "long-lived" with half-lives ranging from a few days to 800,000 years.

The electromagnetic pulse was the last major effect of nuclear explosions to be discovered. It has not been measured as carefully as blast and fallout, but it is claimed that a one-megaton bomb detonated high over the geographical center of the U.S. or the U.S.S.R. would wreck the power distribution grid, disable most of the telephones and computers, and damage most of the vehicles.

Finally, there are two speculative effects that, if real, may threaten the extinction of the human species. One is nuclear winter, the other is ozone depletion. Nuclear winter is a condition of semidarkness after a nuclear exchange caused by the lofting of smoke and dust from burning forests and cities into the atmosphere. On a smaller scale, something similar happens after large volcanic eruptions. According to one computer model, sunlight would be totally shut off after a 10,000-megaton nuclear exchange and no place in the world would be as warm as O° Celsius a year later.

Ozone depletion is a possible consequence of the copious quantities of nitrogen oxides released by nuclear explosions. Ozone absorbs enough of the ultraviolet radiation in sunlight to make life on earth possible; unshielded ultraviolet radiation weakens the food chains at their base by inhibiting plant growth on land and killing plankton in the sea. Nitrogen oxides carried into the upper atmosphere can deplete the ozone layer, which, according to the current theory, will eventually recover. But nobody is quite sure.

In government circles, two images of the end of a nuclear war are held concurrently. The tactical image is used for military planning. In it, our side does not win but we "prevail." After the last detonation, the enemy lies helpless, with no weapons left to counter the weapons we have kept in reserve. The tactical image guides nuclear decision-making in both the U.S. and the U.S.S.R., but its credibility is confined to the office. In the apocalyptic image, the war goes on for days or weeks or months, until all the warheads have been fired or disabled. Then history stops, because everybody is dead or dying.

This split image is made necessary by a pivotal quirk in the logic of deterrence. To be effective, the deterring threat must be so great that no reason could ever be found for defying it. The consequences of challenging the threat must be apocalyptic. But it is essential that the threat be plausible, which implies that the consequences of executing the threat must *not* be apocalyptic. Thus, both sides, in order to maintain mutual deterrence, are compelled to alternate the two images.

It is not easy to decide which of the imagined postwar conditions is more probable. Given the character of existing missile systems—easy alerting, short flight times, vulnerable targets, and command systems that devolve downward when disrupted—the apocalyptic outcome cannot be dismissed as improbable, but there are other possible outcomes:

• One side decapitates the other by destroying its high command without warning while they are assembled in their capital for a ceremonial occasion. They then show that their own high command is sheltered and operational and propose conditions for withholding a second strike.

• Both sides launch major attacks, but equipment failures on one side are so numerous that most targets remain intact. That side capitulates.

• One side carries out a successful first strike. The response is ineffective because of communication failures. The responding side surrenders.

• The two sides attack each other's capitals, successfully in both cases. Frightened by the destruction, their surviving commands arrange a cease-fire and a peace conference.

• An accidental attack destroys a city. The attacker offers to disarm to avoid reprisal.

• After a 200-megaton exchange, both sides are badly hurt but retain their government structures. A cease-fire is proposed and accepted to avoid further damage.

In every one of these hypothetical situations, the next order of business would be to replace the existing international order by a safer arrangement. There would surely be no incentive to restore the End Game as a means of keeping the peace.

The principal argument for the End Game is that, since it began, no nuclear weapon has been fired in anger. To some observers, it is essentially a peace game, but if so, it is surely too dangerous and unstable to be played indefinitely. Moreover, the End Game, as a device for preventing nuclear war, has stimulated a remarkable amount of conventional war. The first four decades of the nuclear age witnessed an extraordinary growth of military forces and expenditures throughout the world.[10] Shooting wars—more than two hundred of them by any estimate—broke out in many places for many reasons. On every single day since representatives of the fifty United Nations met in San Francisco in April 1945 to rid the world of war, soldiers and civilians have died in military actions somewhere. With the liquidation of the overseas empires of the Western European powers between 1945 and 1975, more than a hundred new states moved into the international arena. Most of them rushed to arm themselves as soon as their independence was declared. By 1984, fifty-three countries had annual military budgets of more than a billion dollars.[11]

Under the rules of the End Game, the U.S. and the U.S.S.R. have viewed all the international and civil conflicts arising in and among the world's armed states as related to their own quarrel and as calling for some degree of intervention. As soon as one superpower found a contestant to favor, the other reflexively joined the fray.

Vietnam is the classic example of how to misinterpret a local conflict by treating it as an aspect of the End Game. American intervention was based on the assumption that North Vietnamese pressure on South Vietnam was part of a unified Sino-Soviet effort to dominate Southeast Asia. The "domino" theory held that if South Vietnam were lost, Laos, Cambodia, Thailand, and Malaysia would follow it into the Sino-Soviet empire. South Vietnam was lost, of course, but with the ironic result that Communist Vietnam then turned its efforts to the invasion of Communist Cambodia and a border war with Communist China.

In 1987, the two superpowers—still fully engaged in the End Game—were jointly nourishing combat operations in Afghanistan, the Persian Gulf, Lebanon, Ethiopia, Angola, Namibia, Morocco, Cambodia, Somalia, Chad, the Philippines, Nicaragua, El Salvador, Sri Lanka, and Burma, among other places.

The deadly quarrels jointly stimulated by the U.S. and the U.S.S.R. over the years fell into a number of familiar patterns.

• A superpower sends its own troops into another country to support a regime it considers friendly, or to overthrow a regime it considers friendly to the other. Hungary, Czechoslovakia, Afghanistan, Cuba, and the Dominican Republic come to mind. The other avoids direct confrontation but may lavish weapons and money on a resistance movement.

• War breaks out between two independent states, one or both of which are military clients of the superpowers. If the sides are already chosen, each superpower pours in assistance, and one—but not both—may become directly involved, as in the wars between North and South Korea, North and South Vietnam, and the four Israeli-Arab wars.

• A superpower helps to foment a coup against a regime it considers friendly to the other. If the coup is successful, as in Guatemala, Chile, Nicaragua, Indonesia, Libya, the other sponsors a resistance movement against the new government. If the coup is unsuccessful, as in Portugal, the Philippines, Malaysia, Thailand, the initiating superpower supports the guerrilla movement, and the other side pours in military aid for the government.

• War breaks out between two independent states, neither clearly aligned with the superpowers. Examples that come to mind are the three India-Pakistan wars and the long war between Iran and Iraq. The superpowers may offer arms to both sides in the effort to secure them as clients.

• Tribal, religious, or regional quarrels erupt into civil war in a third world country—the Congo, Nigeria, Angola, Kenya, Mozambique, Ethiopia, Sudan, Morocco, Borneo, Guyana, Yemen, Sri Lanka. The U.S.S.R. supports the faction that labels itself revolutionary. The U.S. offers guns, money, and training to the other side.

There are a few cases that do not fit into these patterns, like the war between Libya and Chad, in which France was the anti-Soviet intervenor, or the Falklands War, in which the Soviet Union could find no foothold. There were even two early episodes in which the superpowers joined forces to put an end to hostilities—the Franco-British invasion of Suez in 1956 and the second India-Pakistan war in 1965—but such actions were not repeated until the remark-

able year of 1988, when a tacit suspension of the End Game with
respect to regional conflicts led to the Soviet withdrawal from
Afghanistan, the suspension of U.S. support for the Nicaraguan
rebels, a cease-fire in the Persian Gulf, progress toward negotiated
settlements in Angola, Namibia, Chad, Kampuchea, Mozambique, and the Western Sahara, and some abatement of hostilities
in Burma and Ethiopia. Only the future can tell if this remarkable
outbreak of peace presaged an eventual end to the End Game and
a new peacekeeping role for the superpowers.[12]

Chapter 3

Social Science and the Nuclear Predicament

There is nothing as practical as a good theory.
Kurt Lewin

Social science theories can be used to interpret the current nuclear predicament, which is that national governments can neither safely abandon the institution of war nor devise a rational strategy for any war between states that possess nuclear weapons. Most of the war games currently played by the superpowers and their allies are essentially irrational, since nobody can win unless implausible assumptions are adopted for the purposes of play. Social science is useful both for illuminating the contradictions in contemporary war games and as a foundation for the peace games that ought to be played instead.

The theories presented in this chapter may help us to distinguish between lines of action that offer some hope of preventing nuclear war, and other lines of action that are based on misperceptions of reality. The theories include: a classification of conflicts that distinguishes different kinds of war; a theory of coalitions in triads that explains why balances of power are unstable and universal coalitions are short-lived; Allison's models of national action that account for the apparent irrationality of governments on the brink of war; Bueno de Mesquita's war trap equations, which specify the conditions under which governments choose between peace and war; the prisoner's dilemma—a paradigm that applies with singular accuracy to the strategy of mutual assured destruction; a theory of military bureaucracy; and a theory of the reciprocal influence of war and public opinion.

Every useful peace game must be grounded on an accurate perception of human motives and behavior, which is what social science theories aim to provide. The nuclear predicament was created, in the first place, when social scientists used conflict models and game theory to devise strategies of bilateral nuclear deterrence. To replace that structure by something better calls for an intellectual effort of matching scale.

A Classification of Conflicts

For our present purposes, we recognize three basic types of conflict—chronic, prescribed, terminal—and note that they have very different consequences.[1]

A chronic conflict develops in a real or imagined situation where the gains of one group are losses for another. Chronic conflicts are neither planned nor scheduled. They appear spontaneously. The weapons and tactics of each side are regarded as illegitimate by the other. It is seldom possible to fix the moment when the conflict begins, or when it ends, and often impossible to identify winners and losers. In any set of interacting organizations, up to and including nation-states, there is sure to be a chronic conflict between the two leading members of the set as they contend for dominance. Chronic conflict is generally unpleasant for the participants and troubling for the spectators.

Prescribed conflicts are recurrent events regulated by rules of engagement that are respected by the parties. The episodes of conflict occur at scheduled times and places under prescribed conditions. The weapons and tactics that may be used are specified in advance, together with very detailed procedures for regulating the contest, determining the winner, and distributing the prizes. Prescribed conflict is intensely gratifying for both the participants and the spectators.

In a terminal conflict, the object of at least one party is to end the other's existence. There is no agreement, and no possibility of agreement, about the rules of engagement, since mutual trust is impossible. Terminal conflict readily escalates to levels of cruelty that would be unthinkable in other circumstances. The people on each side come to perceive the people on the other side as inhuman, because they inflict or endure treatment that falls outside of the normal range of human behavior. Terminal conflict is painful for the participants and shocking for the spectators.

All three types of conflict are common in the transactions of nation-states. Chronic conflict is the normal relationship of the two leading powers in an international system at any given moment: Persia and Babylon, Athens and Sparta, Rome and Carthage, the Emperor and the Pope, Venice and Byzantium, Russia and Austria, France and Germany, the United States and the Soviet Union. Such rivalry is unavoidable, and in the past it has always led to a war or to a series of wars in which dominance was the essential issue.

When the contending powers belong to what Raymond Aron calls a homogeneous system—in which all the states are organized in the same way, accept similar political values, and define their national interests by the same criteria—most wars will be prescribed conflicts; they will be large-scale games that offer adventure, glory, and social promotion to the participants, and vicarious excitement to the spectators, along with the pain and suffering of those who get hurt. The records of ancient civilizations, Egypt, Sumer, Assyria, Persia, Greece, Rome, India, China, Japan, Aztec, Inca, are mostly about prescribed wars and martial glory. The histories of modern states are much the same. Thermopylae and Marathon, Agincourt and Crécy, Austerlitz and Jena, Valley Forge and Gettysburg, are names that still have power to move us.

An almost insatiable appetite for prescribed conflict—what Norbert Elias calls the Quest for Excitement—has been characteristic of mass societies, ancient and modern. Games that have some resemblance to war attract us as easily as they did the Romans. An event like the Superbowl arouses genuine passion in millions of spectators who have no direct stake in the outcome. It should not be surprising that war itself remains appealing to the people of modern societies. The outbreak of nearly every international war of modern times has been marked by a surge of popular enthusiasm on both sides, and most warring nations find it easy to mobilize popular support for a war effort. A victorious state continues to congratulate itself for centuries thereafter. "This day" says Shakespeare's Henry V on the eve of the battle of Agincourt,

> . . . is called the feast of Crispian:
> He that outlives this day and comes safe home,

Will stand a tip-toe when this day is named . . .
. . . .
And Crispin Crispian shall ne'er go by,
From this day to the ending of the world,
But we in it shall be remembered;
We few, we happy few, we band of brothers;
For he to-day that sheds his blood with me
Shall be my brother, be he ne'er so vile,
This day shall gentle his condition:
And gentlemen in England now abed
Shall think themselves accursed they were not here,
And hold their manhoods cheap whiles any speaks
That fought with us upon Saint Crispin's day. (IV, iii)

No speech in praise of peace can hold a candle to it.

The fear of permanent peace that is based on the love of war was described by William James in a famous 1912 essay on "The Moral Equivalent of War."

. . . it all seems to lead back to two unwillingnesses of the imagination, one aesthetic, and the other moral; unwillingness, first, to envisage a future in which army-life, with its many elements of charm, shall be forever impossible, and in which the destinies of peoples shall nevermore be decided quickly, thrillingly, and tragically, by force, but only gradually and insipidly by "evolution"; and secondly, unwillingness to see the supreme theatre of human strenuousness closed, and the splendid military aptitudes of men doomed to keep always in a state of latency and never show themselves in action. These insistent unwillingnesses, no less than other aesthetic and ethical insistencies, have, it seems to me, to be listened to and respected. One cannot meet them effectively by mere counter-insistency on war's expensiveness and horror. The horror makes the thrill; and when the question is of getting the extremest and supremest out of human nature, talk of expense sounds ignominious.[2]

James proposed to preserve the martial type of character by conscripting young men and women into a kind of civilian conservation corps, organized on a military basis for the struggle against nature. It is not a convincing solution; the problem remains.

Terminal conflict, on the other hand, is not a school of martial virtue but of reciprocal degradation. Cromwell's Irish massacres do not figure largely in British schoolbooks. The Nazi Holocaust is not celebrated in Germany. There are no monuments to the "violencia" that ravaged Colombia a generation ago. Spectators are unwelcome at terminal conflicts. Nuclear war, by the nature of the effects produced by nuclear explosions, must be terminal conflict, a massacre of helpless victims by technicians who exhibit no virtue or courage. Even if the massacre is reciprocal, it lacks the hallmark of prescribed conflict—the investment of supreme effort for a temporary advantage.

The craving for prescribed war is perhaps stronger today than it was when William James wrote his essay, and there are five times as many independent nations and twenty times as many armies now equipped to indulge it. Prescribed war has flourished in the nuclear age as never before, provoked and stimulated by the End Game. The genesis of many wars was tucked into a clause of the Atlantic Charter of 1941, when Roosevelt and Churchill declared that "They respect the right of all peoples to choose the form of government under which they live; and they wish to see sovereign rights and self-government restored to those who have been forcibly deprived of them." This sentiment came to command universal assent after 1945. It encouraged the formation of dozens of new states, armed and quarrelsome. And it assured that the choice of a form of government would be a matter of armed contention in most of them.

The new states had no sooner opened for business than they set out to acquire rifles, machine guns, mortars, mines, howitzers, gunboats, missiles, tanks, fighter planes, to the limit of their credit and credibility. The superpowers and their allies helped with gifts, loans, and liberal terms of purchase. In the contemporary lexicon, arms are invariably acquired for defense, but since one side's attack is the other's defense, that is never an impediment to military adventures. In those parts of Latin America and Africa where the terrain made it difficult to reach foreign enemies, guerrilla movements, mutinous army units, rebel tribes, and "bandits" (armed by a friendly superpower) obligingly appeared to provide the new national armies with exercise and experience.

These new states are not presently disposed to give up the right to make war. It seems incontrovertible that any extensive pacification would require a reorganization of the existing international system that either reduced the number of independent states or set limits on their military forces. It is not difficult to imagine a reduction in the number of states. The consolidation of small states into larger ones is the way nations are formed. Every large state in the world was built by combining smaller states and depriving them of the right to make war. The recent trend has run strongly in the other direction—toward fragmentation rather than consolidation—but there are indications that it may be reversing, as we will see in a later chapter.

Limitations on the military forces of the smaller states are not unimaginable either. Most do not have an independent capacity to manufacture even machine guns; only a handful can produce tanks or fighter planes without outside assistance. A joint embargo by NATO and the Warsaw Pact on the shipment of arms to outsiders would drastically reduce the war-making potential of the rest of the world.

In the contemporary world system, conventional (or prescribed) war and nuclear (or terminal) war are inextricably connected. The unfought nuclear war between the superpowers has provoked and sustained conventional wars all over the globe, while every conventional war, in turn, has the potential to light the fuse for a nuclear war. Even before the invention of nuclear weapons, it had become very difficult to confine the major wars of Europe and Asia to the prescribed level. The sheer scale of twentieth-century conflicts, the destructiveness of modern weapons, and the fear of revolution and counterrevolution have long since ruined the game of war for advanced industrial states, despite the occasional occurrence of a nostalgic episode like the Falklands affair. The abandonment altogether of the game of war seems too great a deprivation for great nations to endure, but it is not easy to keep the game playable.

Coalitions in Triads

The geometry of coalitions is a fascinating subject, and it has a great deal to tell us about the past and future of the End Game. A coalition is a combination of two or more social actors who adopt a common strategy in a situation of continuous, prescribed, or terminal conflict. A social actor, in theory, may be as small as an individual and as large as a state. The geometry of coalitions is affected very little by the scale of the action.

Sociological theory about coalitions in triads—that is, systems that have three social actors contending for advantage—explains why balances of power are inherently unstable. Triads have a tendency to split into coalitions of two against one. The most important property of triads is their ability to transform strength into weakness and weakness into strength when the two weaker members of a triad form a coalition against the stronger member. The probability of such a coalition can be estimated with fair accuracy if the relative power of the three actors is known.

Imagine a triad in which party A is slightly stronger than either B or C, who are precisely equal. The formation of a B-C coalition is highly probable. After it is formed, A will be dominated by B and C. Its strength has been transformed into weakness.

Imagine another triad in which A is the weakest of the three parties. B and C are equal. A coalition of B-C would offer no advantage to B or C. Each will try to form a coalition with A in order to dominate the triad. A's weakness has been transformed into strength.

Triads are linked when they have one or two members in common. The selection of coalition partners in linked triads generally follows two spontaneous, self-enforcing rules: Rule 1. An adversary in one triad may not be chosen as a coalition partner in a linked triad. Rule 2. A party invited to join incompatible coalitions in linked triads should choose a winning coalition in the dominant triad.

Although it is not instantly obvious, Rule 1 leads to a set of familiar, political axioms: My friend's enemy is my enemy. My enemy's friend is my enemy. My enemy's enemy is my friend.

There is an apparent exception to Rules 1 and 2 that may be stated as follows: When a triad, acting as a unit, is involved in a conflict of larger scale, coalitions within the triad may be temporarily suspended. As an Arab saying has it, "I against my brother. I and my brother against my cousins. I, my brother, and my cousins against the next village. All of us against the foreigner."

Many, if not most, conflicts fall into the familiar triadic pattern of a pair of adversaries and an audience which each of the adversaries seeks to attract into a winning coalition. If this effort splits the audience, the triad becomes a tetrad—a system with four members. Systems with more than three members—tetrads, pentads, and so forth—are most conveniently analyzed as clusters of linked triads, subject to the self-enforcing rules of coalition formation in linked triads.

The End Game began as a continuous conflict between the two superpowers that emerged from the Second World War. The primary audience was the rest of Europe. Cultivated by the superpowers, the audience split into two parties, the one affiliated with NATO and the other with the Warsaw Pact nations, and the situation took the form of a tetrad. Although the two coalitions in this tetrad have persisted for a long time, neither seems destined to last forever. From the Soviet standpoint, only two of its European allies are politically reliable, Bulgaria and East Germany, and there is some question about East Germany. Poland, Czechoslovakia, Hungary, and Rumania are held restively in line by the threat of force. Yugoslavia and Albania have achieved independence. No Soviet ally is trusted with nuclear weapons.

The NATO states have much better rapport with their senior partner, although France remains half in and half out of the alliance, and the quarrel between Greece and Turkey limits their reliability. The strong Communist parties that once had reasonable expectations of taking France and Italy into the other camp have dwindled significantly. There are large antinuclear movements in all of the NATO countries, but they are not markedly pro-Soviet.

What makes the Western coalition unstable is the anomalous situation of the junior partners. The nations of the European Economic Community, taken together, had a greater population in 1986 (374 million) than either the United States (241 million) or the Soviet Union (275 million), and a gross annual product ($3.5 trillion) much larger than that of the Soviet Union ($1.9 trillion) and approaching that of the United States ($4.2 trillion).

There was a moment in the 1950s when European unification seemed imminent. As preached by Jean Monnet and his followers, the common market would be followed by a common army and eventually by a common parliament. The common market throve, but the common army was vetoed by General de Gaulle, and the common parliament came into being but did not form a government. This failure was generally attributed to national pride and jealousy, more particularly to the French apprehension that Germany might dominate a West European Union and the reluctance of the smaller countries to submerge their identities. But there was also an unmistakable connection with the End Game. The NATO alliance was formed at a time when the countries of Western Europe, devastated by war, seemed virtually defenseless in the face of Soviet military power, and were threatened internally by pro-Soviet factions. The prospect of facing a Soviet Union that had grown to include all of Europe was intolerable to the United States, which took vigorous steps to avert that danger, including the North Atlantic Treaty Organization, the continued presence of American forces in Germany to block a Soviet invasion, the Marshall Plan to speed the economic recovery of the Western European countries, massive military assistance to them, financial support for friendly political parties, prompt ripostes to Soviet feints, and the promise of nuclear retaliation if Western Europe were invaded.

The program was conspicuously successful. Prewar levels of production in Western Europe were reached and surpassed almost overnight. Centrist parties, committed to parliamentary government, came to power in every country. After the Berlin airlift, there were no more Soviet feints on the central front. But what began as a response to a perceived emergency remained as a way of life—the End Game. Forty-four years after the Second World War there is still an American army of occupation in Germany. The cost of the American contribution to the central front in Europe, as of 1988, was estimated to be about half of the total Pentagon budget, and about two-thirds of the total military expenditures of the NATO countries.

Some American conservatives see this as a free-rider situation, whereby the United States, by paying most of the bill, deprives the European states of any incentive to provide for their own defense, and encourages them to put their resources into domestic welfare.[3] We have, they say, spent ourselves into debt to promote the prosperity of the Europeans. One expert on Soviet affairs speculates that

Although the Soviets want to encourage tension between Western Europe and the United States, they may not want to see the United States withdraw or greatly reduce its land forces in Europe. Such a shock might make West European leaders decide they have no choice but to unite politically.[4]

American policy-makers have parallel concerns. The formation of a West European Union might turn the End Game into a competition for the favor of that new superpower.

In the perspective of the End Game, the 300,000 American troops in Europe and their numerous dependents are not there because of any military necessity, but because their presence makes credible the American promise to respond to a Soviet attack on the central front with nuclear weapons if the attack cannot be repelled by conventional means and to escalate to an intercontinental nuclear exchange if the battlefield weapons do not serve the purpose. In effect, the Americans stationed in Germany are hostages. One problem in this line of reasoning is that the expected cost in lives of an intercontinental nuclear exchange has risen to a level that makes the promise doubtful anyway. Another problem is that the threat of a Soviet invasion derives what little credibility it still retains from the relative military weakness of Western Europe, which is attributable to the American guarantee. This odd configuration has lasted a long time, but at the present writing, with customs barriers and border restrictions scheduled to disappear from Western Europe in 1992, and with France and West Germany beginning to combine some units of their armed forces, the consolidation of Western Europe into a unified power may be only a matter of time.

Another unstable triad consists of China, the United States, and the Soviet Union. It has an interesting history.

The doctrine of Marxism-Leninism holds that war is an aspect of the class struggle and therefore cannot occur between classless, socialist societies. The doctrine was unquestioned for the first forty years of the Soviet regime, at first because there were no other Communist states, and then because the new Communist regimes established after 1945 in Europe and Asia were for a while subservient to Moscow. Conservatives in the United States held to the same doctrine with equal fervor, taking it for granted that all Communist states would remain permanently allied and pursue common objectives. That was the basis of the Truman Doctrine and the policy of containment that led into the End Game. Many Americans still adhere to this article of Marxist-Leninist faith, against all the evidence, while on the other side, the doctrine has been continually reinterpreted to show that this or that Communist regime was heretical.

But in recent decades, events have made it obvious that Communist regimes are as susceptible to mutual hostility as capitalist regimes, and about as likely to go to war with each other as with their ideological enemies. At the time of the Korean War, the coalition of the Soviet Union and the People's Republic of China against the United States appeared to be permanent, but it dissolved in 1960, apparently over a Russian demand to control the Chinese nuclear weapons they had helped to develop. Soviet advisers were expelled from China, and the two countries began a lasting feud, with occasional exchanges of fire along their 5,000-mile border.

Nature seems to abhor a coalition-free triad, and although the United States refused through the 1960s to recognize Mao's government and continued to sponsor a Chinese government in exile, the advantages of a Sino-American coalition were so evident that Nixon and Kissinger were able to bring it about. It is a timid coalition, with reservations on both sides, but endures nevertheless. China has a larger army than the Soviet Union, appreciable nuclear forces, and a largely rural population that makes it less vulnerable to nuclear attack than any other major power. A Soviet invasion of Western Europe, the raison d'être of the End Game, is unlikely—quite aside from nuclear deterrence—as long as it invites a Chinese invasion of Siberia.

The Chinese connection, cultivated by the last five administrations in Washington was weakened by Beijing's repression of the pro-democracy movement in the spring of 1989 and there are signs of rapprochement between Moscow and Beijing. Even a partial renewal of the Sino-Soviet coalition under present conditions would greatly weaken the international position of the United States.

There is another way that the geometry of triads destabilizes the End Game. When an armed conflict—international war, civil war, tribal war, rebellion—breaks out anywhere in the world, both parties apply to the superpowers for support. In many episodes, the choice of a sponsor has been dictated by ideological identification, as in Nicaragua, or by a mixture of ideological and strategic considerations, as in the American support of Israel, or by strategic considerations alone, as in the Soviet support of Iraq against Iran. Sometimes, as in Angola, the choice of sponsors has been more or less fortuitous.

If the conversion of the original conflict to triadic form were the end of the story, the coalition containing the outside sponsor would quickly prevail and the conflict would be settled on its terms. But under the ground rules of the End Game, the appearance of the Soviet Union as a party to a conflict anywhere in the world has impelled the United States to join the other side, converting the triad into a tetrad with two opposing coalitions. The Soviet Union has followed a symmetrical policy. Coalitions in tetrads are somewhat more stable than coalitions in triads, and the effect of the double intervention is to put the conflict on a more permanent footing, since neither superpower is inclined to accept defeat or compromise until its clients are wiped out.

Sooner or later, one of these regional conflicts is likely to go nuclear, testing to the limit the geometry of coalitions.

Government Behavior in Crises

Perhaps the finest analysis of how modern governments actually behave in international conflicts is Graham T. Allison's 1971 study of the Cuban missile crisis, *Essence of Decision.* Allison sets forth his argument in three succinct propositions:

1. Professional analysts of foreign affairs (as well as ordinary laymen) think about problems of foreign and military policy in terms of largely implicit conceptual models that have significant consequences for the content of their thought.

2. Most analysts explain (and predict) the behavior of national governments in terms of one basic conceptual model, here entitled Rational Actor or "Classical" Model (Model I).

3. Two alternative conceptual models, here labeled an Organizational Process Model (Model II) and a Governmental (Bureaucratic) Politics Model (Model III), provide a base for improved explanations and predictions.[5]

The classical model assumes that the decisions of a government in an international crisis will be not only rational with respect to the pursuit of particular ends, but also effective. In other words, the model anticipates that the decisions taken by national leaders will cause appropriate orders to be issued and carried out, and that the actions taken by subordinate agencies will be consistent with their orders.

Beneath the surface of the classical model, there are additional presumptions of rationality, for example that the available options have been correctly identified and carefully compared with respect to probable costs and consequences.

Allison shows that the classical model leaves important features of the Cuban missile crisis unexplained. It cannot satisfactorily account for the Soviet decision to emplace missiles in Cuba, the way they did it, or their initial disregard of American warnings. On the American side, where the documentation is much more complete and the principal actors more familiar, the classical model fails to explain why the United States reacted so slowly, why the blockade was chosen over other available options, or how the blockade was carried out.

The organizational process model builds on an existing body of knowledge about how agencies of government operate. As Allison points out, such organizations are "blunt instruments." They know how to do certain tasks in certain ways, that is, by following standard procedures. Tasks that require them to depart from standard procedures are done slowly, poorly, or not at all. Task assignments contrary to the agency's parochial interests are actively resisted. Complex projects that require the coordination of several government agencies are rarely performed in the manner envisaged by the decision-makers, and information about the performance fed back to them is incomplete and distorted.

In the Cuban missile crisis, Soviet missiles were transported to Cuba and unloaded in great secrecy, but the missile sites were constructed on the same, easily identified pattern as those located on Soviet territory and no effort was made to camouflage the work. Analysts who used the classical model produced extraordinarily ingenious theories about why the Russians wanted the missile sites to be discovered by American overflights before the missiles became operational, but an organizational process explanation is more plausible. The shipments were handled by the security-conscious Soviet intelligence services, but on-site construction was the responsibility of the Strategic Rocket Forces, whose standard operating procedures made no provision for camouflage and concealment of a construction site.

In January 1989, some of the surviving U.S. participants in the Cuban missile crisis were invited to Moscow to meet with their Soviet counterparts for a retrospective examination of the events of 1962. Although a number of interesting new facts were revealed, such as the exact number of nuclear warheads shipped to Cuba, they did not undermine Allison's analysis. Indeed, they reinforced it by showing more confusion of purpose on the Soviet side than had been previously known.

On the U.S. side, Allison found that the ten-day delay in checking the original reports that missiles were being installed in Cuba was the time required to resolve a jurisdictional dispute betwen the Air Force and the CIA about which agency should conduct the overflights. He also discovered that the decision to blockade Cuba instead of taking the missiles out by a surgical air strike was based on misinformation provided to the president by Air Force planners. When they were asked to come up with immediate plans for a surgical air strike, an assignment that did not fit their standard planning mode, they substituted an existing plan for a massive all-points attack that had originally been designed as the first phase of a projected invasion. The decision against an air strike was clinched by an Air Force estimate that it would be only 90 percent effective in taking out the missiles—a figure based on a handbook classification of the Soviet missiles as "mobile," although in fact they were not mobile in the sense intended by the handbook. They could be moved in several days, but not under attack.

Allison's study provided many other illustrations to show that government agencies were blunt instruments in the Cuban missile crisis. A battery of Jupiter missiles in Turkey figured largely in the negotiations with Khrushchev. President Kennedy had twice ordered them removed but had been unable to get the order carried out. His decision to move the blockade line close to Cuba did not prevail over the Navy's preference for a line five hundred miles away. And not until long afterwards did it come to light that while the White House was bending every effort to avoid provocative gestures, U.S. destroyers—following a standard alert procedure—were locating Soviet submarines at sea and forcing them to surface.

The bureaucratic politics model focuses on the principal decision-makers in a conflict episode, and how their views of the situation, the options they perceive, the actions they prefer, and the actions they eventually take are affected by who they are, where they sit, and what has happened to them recently. Just as no government agency ignores its own interests when it interacts with other agencies, no individual official is likely to ignore the probable effect of offering a given piece of advice or supporting a particular decision on his own influence and credibility. Thus, President Kennedy, with the disastrous Bay of Pigs expedition close behind him, felt that he could not take any of the softer options in the missile crisis without risking impeachment. The whole affair occurred just before the congressional elections of 1962; even the Russians were aware that any American humiliation might put the Republicans in control of Congress. But Kennedy's personal sensitivity, his distrust of the military chiefs, the ethical sentiments he shared with his brother and his close advisers, held him back from acting too quickly or too aggressively. In the end, Allison suggests, it was probably a kind of mutual sympathy between Kennedy and Khrushchev, uniquely aware of the burden of responsibility they shared, that led to a peaceful settlement.

The difference between Model I, with its simplistic view of how governmental power is exercised, and Models II and III, which approach the subject empirically, is extraordinarily sharp. Many other episodes of governmental decision-making have recently been analyzed with attention to organizational processes and bureaucratic politics. For our present purposes, a particularly important example is Ian Clark's 1985 account in *Nuclear Past, Nuclear Present* of how the decision to bomb Hiroshima and Nagasaki was taken. The official version of the event, like most official versions, was a Model I account. President Truman weighed the destructiveness of the new weapon against the goals of saving the American lives that would be lost in an invasion of Japan. He issued a warning ultimatum to the Japanese government and, when they failed to respond, ordered an atomic bomb to be dropped on two Japanese cities. Japan then surrendered unconditionally, ending the war and justifying the decision.

According to Clark and others, this account is challengeable even in terms of the classical model. There were indications before Hiroshima that the Japanese were ready to surrender on certain conditions, but the American government insisted on unconditional surrender. After the bombing, a surrender was accepted that tacitly included the principal Japanese conditions—amnesty for the Emperor and the continuation of the dynasty.

But organizational process and bureaucratic politics more adequately explain why the bombings occurred. One set of actors were government agencies carrying out assigned tasks by means of established procedures: the Manhattan Project, the Department of War, the Strategic Air Force, the 509th Composite Group on Tinian, the Target Committee in Washington. As an agency, the Manhattan Project had worked night and day for three years to produce atomic weapons to be used in the war. There was no turning them aside at the moment of achievement. Suggestions for a warning demonstration of the bomb were bottled up within the Project, and that option was never presented to the president.

To the Air Force, the new weapons were simply improved aerial bombs, to be handled operationally according to routine procedures. Although a special chain of command was set up to enable the president and the secretary of war to control the operations involving atomic bombs directly, their role remained essentially passive, consisting only of the right to veto plans made at a lower level.

After Nagasaki was selected as a target, it was discovered that American prisoners of war were detained there. Clark quotes Major General Leslie Groves telling how the decision to disregard this fact was made rather casually at the operating level and then sent up for pro forma approval.

"Handy felt that the decision should be made by the Secretary of War, but later agreed with me that we should tell Spaatz to disregard the reported camps; however, we decided that I should show the Secretary the out-going cable before sending it. This would free him of the burden of making the decision. . . . At the same time he would have an opportunity, if he chose to take advantage of it, to overrule us before any harm was done. . . . I did not emphasize that he could change it if he wished."[6]

As the operation moved into its active phase, even this passive control was superseded by Air Force decisions made on the spot. The precise scheduling of the two strikes was not reported to the president in advance; there is some doubt about whether he could have stopped them had he wished to do so. The detailed operational guidelines set by the Target Committee in Washington were ignored in the Nagasaki raid. Once set in motion, the operation took on a life of its own.

The bureaucratic politics model reveals General Groves, the military administrator of the Manhattan Project, as the beneficiary of the improvised command structure that linked the Project as producer of the bombs with the service branches that delivered them to the staging areas and the targets. The policy of a "quick one-two punch" to knock Japan out of the war, which led to the hasty selection and bombing of Nagasaki in disregard of the Target Committee's guidelines, seems to have been adopted on Groves's own initiative. His lack of scruple regarding the use of the new weapon against unprotected civilians became the posture of the government, abetted by the moral ambivalence of Secretary of State Henry Stimson, which made him reluctant to exercise oversight, and by the psychological complexity of Robert Oppenheimer, who deplored what he had made but insisted that it be used. It is difficult to imagine the same events occurring with another cast of characters.

The three models, taken together, provide a theory of government behavior that is highly relevant to the possible outcomes of the End Game, and to the need for well-developed peace games to be put in place before critical choices about war and peace have to be made. Among other things, the theory tells us that

• Government action in a crisis is never as rational with respect to the identification and choice of options, the fitting of means to ends, and the estimation of probable consequences as it appears to be in official accounts produced after the event.

• The information provided to decision-makers by subordinate agencies during a crisis will be incomplete and inaccurate.

• Subordinate agencies will be unable or unwilling to carry out some of the orders they receive during a crisis, but will conceal their noncompliance.

• Subordinate agencies will take independent action during a crisis based on their own procedures and preferences, often without notice to higher authority.

• The identity of the primary decision-makers in a crisis is not always predictable.

• Decisions taken in a crisis are strongly affected by the background, the personalities, and the personal situations of the decision-makers.

• Because so many factors affect the decision-making process, actions taken by a government in a crisis may be greatly influenced by error and accident.

It should be noted in passing that most of the preceding propositions also apply to government actions unconnected with any military crisis, and to decision-making in bureaucratic organizations much smaller than governments, but of course the consequences are less momentous in those cases.

What these propositions tell us about war games is that the Model I scenarios of deterrence and limited nuclear war will never enact themselves as written. The behavior of the Soviet and American governments in another nuclear crisis will again be strongly affected by organizational process and bureaucratic politics. In a way, this is an encouraging consideration. We cannot be sure that the End Game will have the catastrophic outcome implied by the existing scenarios, because those scenarios expect the U.S. and Soviet governments to behave as rational, single-minded actors, which they seldom do. But neither can we count on those governments to behave with sufficient rationality to avert their own destruction.

The War Trap

We have scorned and rejected the classical model of government action—the single-minded decision-maker moved by rational calculation—in favor of models that explain government action as the outcome of organizational processes and bureaucratic politics.

Nevertheless, the classical model describes one type of government action fairly well. That is the final decision to go to war, almost always made by a single person.

Are these choices capricious as well as personal, or are they influenced by rational calculations? In his brilliant 1981 study of *The War Trap*, Bruce Bueno de Mesquita proposes a method of measuring the probable costs and benefits for a national state of going to war with a particular adversary at a particular time. He calls the balance of costs and benefits the "expected utility" of the contemplated war. By combining data on the interstate wars that occurred between 1816 and 1965, assembled by Singer and Small (1972), with Gochman's (1975) data on threats and interventions by the major powers during approximately the same period and extending the series backward to 1800 and forward to 1974, Bueno de Mesquita was able to calculate the expected utilities of both sides at the beginning of 251 interstate conflicts in which military hostilities occurred or were threatened.

If I understand the theory correctly, the decision to initiate a war is never solely determined by the initiator's expected utility but is always sensitive to it. As Bueno de Mesquita explains:

The choice of war or peace depends on the choices of individuals and not on compulsion by circumstances. Their choices depend on their estimation of costs and benefits and their comprehension of right and wrong. . . . We cannot provide a general framework of moral values that reveals what decision-makers believe to be right or wrong, but we may be able to capture some essential characteristics of their assessment of the expected costs and benefits.[7]

If the estimation of costs and benefits tells the decision-maker that a war would be profitable, that person is free to choose war or peace on moral grounds (i.e., for ideological, emotional, or ethical reasons). But if the calculation yields a negative expected utility, the probable costs exceeding the probable benefits, the moral factor become irrelevant.

A national leader contemplating war against a single adversary will take into account the relative war capabilities of his own nation and the adversary nation, the capabilities of third parties which might become involved, and the probabilities of their involvement. War capabilities are measured by a composite index of military, industrial, and demographic resources adjusted for distance—a complex adjustment because war capability always diminishes with distance, but less for powerful than for weak nations, and less for advanced than for simple military technologies.

The probabilities of third parties becoming involved depend upon the type of alliance relationships they have with the contending parties and with each other. Alliance relationships may be defense pacts, nonaggression pacts, or ententes, in descending order of obligation. Two other factors that are skillfully handled in this analysis are the margin of uncertainty in the decisionmaker's calculations and his orientation to risk-taking. Most of the uncertainty stems from the difficulty of predicting the actions of third parties—each state's allies, the allies of its adversary, and states that are allied to neither side but may find their interests affected by the conflict.

Much of *The War Trap* is given over to a subtle and elegant analysis of coalitions in networks of alliance relationships. I cannot do justice to it here. The point to remember is that, as usual, the geometry of coalitions transforms strength into weakness and weakness into strength. The results are often surprising, but like the elementary coalitions in triads that we examined earlier, the alliances that determine the outcome of wars always make sense within the context in which they occur.

Some counter-intuitive findings that Bueno de Mesquita derives from the expected utility theory and confirms in his sample of 251 interstate conflicts are these: (1) A military alliance between two states does not necessarily increase or decrease the military security of either of them; that depends on their relationships with third parties and the relationships among those third parties. (2) *Allies are more likely to go to war against each other than against states with which they are not allied.* (3) States often enter conflicts on what appears to be the wrong side, disregarding their differences with the party they support and their ties with the party they oppose, in order to prevent an unwanted change in some larger alignment of forces. The Crimean War—in which Britain and France intervened on the side of Turkey against Russia—was a classic example. The alliance between Nazi Germany and the Soviet Union in 1939 was another.

The formal propositions of the expected utility theory tell us that the course of a conflict between nonaligned states is highly predictable: The more powerful state is likely to initiate the war and to win it. Thus, it makes no sense for a weak nonaligned state to attack a strong nonaligned state. But if a strong state belongs to an alliance, it may be rational for a weak nonaligned state to attack it, in the expectation of attracting support from opponents of the alliance or even from members of the alliance. Another proposition of the expected utility theory says that when a state contemplates war against a pair of allied adversaries, it may be rational to attack the stronger member of the pair, as the weaker member is less likely to come to the aid of the stronger than the other way around. Finally, the theory proposes that wars occur only when the gain expected by the initiator exceeds the loss expected by the defender. When that condition is not satisfied, the parties are better off negotiating than fighting, and will move toward a negotiated settlement even if the shooting has already started.

Bueno de Mesquita uses his inventory of quantitative data on 251 interstate conflicts betwen 1800 and 1974 to test propositions derived from the expected utility theory. The empirical results are generally consistent with the theory, and interesting in themselves. In 86 percent of the wars in the sample, 76 percent of the armed interventions, and 68 percent of the cases in which hostilities were threatened, the expected utility of the initiator exceeded that of the defender. Armed conflict is usually initiated by the side that has the advantage, and that side usually wins. There was no significant difference between the nineteenth and the twentieth centuries with respect to the influence of expected utility on war decisions, nor were there regional differences. Expected utility, with its emphasis on the influence of third parties, explains the initiation of war better than a simple comparison of power, especially in the twentieth century, although it remains true that most wars are initiated by a strong state attacking a weaker one.

Belonging to an alliance did not improve the initiator's chances.

Provided their expected utilities were positive, nonaligned states attacking nonaligned opponents, nonaligned states attacking aligned opponents, aligned states attacking nonaligned opponents, and aligned states attacking members of other alliances had equally favorable chances of prevailing. About a fifth of the wars in the sample were begun by a state attacking its own ally. Military threats and armed interventions are also common between allies, and in many instances the alliance persists after the hostile incident.

Finally, Bueno de Mesquita is able to show that the costliness of wars has been strongly affected by divergence in the expected utilities of the parties. When both sides had positive expected utilities—both expected to win and to gain by winning—the cost of the war, measured by battle deaths per month per thousand of the population, was much higher than when one side was prepared to lose. The data do not permit us to see how expected utilities change in the course of a protracted war, and the theory does not imply that the decision to continue a costly war has the same rational character as the decision to initiate it.

The close fit between the expected utility theory and the military experience of the past two centuries argues against the common view of war as a form of collective insanity. The record seems to show that war often makes sense as an instrument of national policy. The governments that initiated these wars, interventions, and threats calculated that they had more to gain than to lose, and their calculations were correct more often than not. Harvey Starr's study of the distribution of payoffs and losses in coalitions that won or lost wars between 1818 and 1960 provides an abundance of evidence that wars were often profitable for the initiators.

There is one major flaw in the expected utility theory. The concept of positive expected utility implies short and cheap wars. A decision to initiate a war is almost never taken unless the initiator is confident of a quick victory. In most of the armed conflicts of the past two centuries, the initiator's confidence was justified and the quick victory was indeed secured. But the few exceptional wars outweigh the much larger number of normal wars in every way. In Napoleon's Russian campaign, the American Civil War, the Lopez War in Paraguay, both World Wars, and the

Iran-Iraq war, the expected utilities were gravely miscalculated by the initiator, and the costs for both sides mounted too high to be offset by any possible gains. The statistically deviant cases—the big wars that inflict as much damage on the winners as on the losers—have much more profound and lasting effects than the quick, successful wars that go according to plan. In international crises, reliance on expected utility leads to rational decisions in about 90 percent of the cases and to crazy decisions in about 10 percent of the cases. Given that ratio, it is not hard to understand why war-making decisions follow expected utility as closely as they do. But the crazy decisions are more consequential than the rational ones.

What light does expected utility theory shed on the End Game? Neither the United States nor the Soviet Union can plausibly calculate its expected utility in a nuclear exchange as positive, in view of the damage it must expect to sustain. Even the most enthusiastic advocates of limited nuclear war do not claim that their country would be better off after a nuclear exchange than before, only that it would be better off than the adversary. The expected utilities of both sides are negative but not necessarily equal. The advantage of having a lesser negative utility does not make it rational to go to war. Even if the favored side were about to lose that advantage, a decision for war would make no sense unless the adversary were about to acquire a positive expected utility for a nuclear exchange, which is almost inconceivable.

If the superpowers were alone in the world, the End Game might continue indefinitely, barring accidents. But each of them has allies, and those allies have other enemies and other allies, and it will happen in the near future as in the near past that a particular war against a particular adversary will have positive expected utility for Israel or India or Britain or Cuba or Vietnam. Nothing in the End Game, as played from 1948 to 1987, discouraged the allies of either superpower from choosing war whenever the choice seemed rational. But what is rational for the clients is dangerous for their patrons. Every regional war invites the intervention of both superpowers and poses some risk that they may become too deeply engaged to withdraw.

American and Soviet statesmen could hardly be more conscious of that risk than they are, or more wary of it. Over the years, they developed an elaborate repertory of political and military devices that permitted them to participate in the same regional wars and still avoid any direct exchange of fire between American and Soviet forces. These devices worked surprisingly well, but it has always been uncertain whether they would continue to work if a regional war went nuclear. The critical decisions might have to be made while the expected utilities were changing too fast to be calculated.

The Prisoner's Dilemma

Game theory, a thriving branch of investigation shared by mathematics, psychology, sociology, and political science, studies strategies and their outcomes in simple games like Parcheesi, complex games like chess, and situations that resemble games, like politics, diplomacy, and war. The strategies of nuclear deterrence owe a great deal to the work of academic game theorists. Game theory relies both on mathematical models and laboratory experiments. The typical experiment involves a small group of human subjects playing a specially designed game in a laboratory under close observation. Some experiments use animal subjects, and a growing number use computers to simulate the behavior of players. The computer has more patience than sophomores or other human subjects and can be made to repeat a game thousands of times so that the experimenter can study all the implications of a given strategy.

In *The Evolution of Cooperation* (1984) Robert Axelrod gives a fascinating account of a study he carried out to assess alternative strategies in a classic laboratory game called the Prisoner's Dilemma. That game has been used in hundreds of experiments, and analogous situations occur frequently in real life. The End Game embodies the Prisoner's Dilemma in nearly pure form.[8] In a narrative version of the dilemma, two persons are arrested and accused of jointly committing a crime. Each has the options of confessing and implicating the other or of remaining silent. If both remain silent, they will be set free. If both confess, both will be punished. If one confesses and the other remains silent, the one who confesses will be set free with a reward and the one who remains silent will be punished more severely. Confessing gives each prisoner the best outcome if the other remains silent, but if both follow this reasoning and confess, they are worse off than they would have been if both had remained silent. Each prisoner also knows that remaining silent is his worst choice unless both remain silent. Without further information, the dilemma has no rational solution.

In the numerical version of the dilemma used in Axelrod's experimental game, each of the two players receives a payoff of 3 if both decide to cooperate with each other (equivalent to remaining silent in the narrative version). If both decide not to cooperate (equivalent to confessing and implicating each other), their payoffs are reduced to 1. If one of them decides not to cooperate and the other cooperates, the defector receives a payoff of 5, and the cooperator gets the "sucker's payoff" of 0.

The experiment took the form of a tournament in which fifteen prominent game theorists were asked to propose a winning strategical rule and the proposed rules were then paired and played against each other by computer in a long series of round robin games. The tournament was then run a second time, this time with sixty-three contestants and an improved procedure. The investigator gave nicknames to the various strategical rules proposed by the contestants. Despite the abstract and impersonal character of the experiment, the rules seemed to acquire personalities during the play of the game. For example, the rule of Tit for Tat starts with a cooperative move and thereafter does what the other player did on his previous move. The rule named Random selects its moves by chance and is totally unresponsive to the other player. The rule named Downing attempts to understand the other player by calculating after each move the other player's most probable response, based on that player's prior actions. Joss is a sneaky rule. Most of the time, it cooperates after the other player cooperates and defects after the other player defects, but in 10 percent of its moves after the other player cooperates, Joss unexpectedly defects. Tit for Two Tats is a forgiving rule that does not punish a defection by the other player until there have been two in a row. The rule of All D defects on every move. It never responds to the other player's actions. Tester is a subtle rule that tries to get away with defecting but backs off if the other player retaliates. And so forth.

Tit for Tat, the simplest of all the responsive rules, was submitted each time by Anatol Rapoport, a grand master of game theory, and won both rounds of the tournament by wide margins. Curiously, no other contestant submitted it in the second round though all knew it had won the first round. Being clever, like the architects of nuclear deterrence, the game theorists in the tournament preferred more artful strategies. Tit for Tat belongs to a category that Axelrod calls nice rules, i.e., those that always cooperate on the first move. Mean rules always defect on the first move. Nice rules did very much better than mean rules in this tournament. Each of the eight top-scoring rules was nice. Most of the low-scoring rules were mean.

"What accounts for Tit for Tat's robust success," writes Axelrod, "is the combination of being nice, retaliatory, forgiving and clear. Its niceness prevents it from getting into unnecessary trouble. Its retaliation discourages the other side from persisting whenever defection is tried. Its forgiveness helps restore mutual cooperation. And its clarity makes it intelligible to the other player, thereby eliciting long-term cooperation."

Strangely enough, Tit for Tat won the tournament without ever winning against another player. It cannot do so because it lets the other player defect first, and never defects more times than the other player. So Tit for Tat either ties each of its games or loses by a trivial margin. What accounts for its overall success is that rules that are either more predatory or more exploitable lose some of their games by wide margins, which Tit for Tat never does. Another remarkable feature of Tit for Tat is that it is collectively stable. A population of players who follow that rule cannot be invaded and exploited by players following some other rule.

The rule of All D, which defects on every move, scores low when playing against any responsive rule, but its opponents do poorly also. A game between All D and Tit for Tat quickly turns into an unbroken series of hostile moves from which neither side can escape.

The rule of All C, which cooperates on every move, was not

entered in the tournament, but it is easily appraised. Against rules that are nice and responsive, it would do quite well. Against rules that are either mean or unresponsive, it would do very badly. Against All D, which is mean and unresponsive, it would suffer unending exploitation. That is sad, because All C is the Golden Rule of do unto others as you would have them do unto you. It is surely a successful rule in some games but not in the Prisoner's Dilemma.

The advantage of the nice rules over the mean rules depends on two conditions that were present in Axelrod's experiment but are absent from other variants of the game: the players expect to continue playing against the same opponents, and the value of future payoffs is not sharply discounted. If a player knows the game is about to end, he can shift to a predatory strategy without fear of reprisal. And reciprocity becomes progressively less attractive as the value of future payoffs declines in relation to immediate payoffs.

The End Game between the United States and the Soviet Union is clearly a form of the Prisoner's Dilemma. The most rewarding situation for both superpowers would be the reduction of their nuclear arsenals to levels so low that a first strike became unthinkable. But each fears that it might take the sucker's role by giving up nuclear capabilities that the other side secretly retained. The End Game rejects the high payoff of nuclear cooperation in order to be sure of the much lower payoff of nuclear deterrence. This simple but powerful theory is another way of thinking about mutual assured destruction. That strategy is a stable but not very rewarding solution to the Prisoner's Dilemma: both sides follow the rule of All D. But the cost of stable noncooperation, in which both sides limit themselves to aggressive moves, tends to increase over time as the scale of hostile preparations rises. In the language of game theory, the payoffs for mutual defection decline over time in relation to the payoffs for mutual cooperation.

The mixed strategies actually followed in the End Game fall between All D and Tit for Tat. Both the United States and the Soviet Union have made cooperative moves from time to time, and some of their cooperative moves were reciprocated. In 1958, in conjunction with the beginning of negotiations on a comprehensive nuclear test ban, the Soviet Union announced that it would unilaterally cease testing. The United States and the United Kingdom responded by suspending their own tests, and the moratorium continued until broken by the Soviet Union in the fall of 1961. By contrast, when the U.S.S.R. unilaterally ceased testing in 1986 and invited the U.S. to do the same, the invitation was indignantly refused, and the U.S.S.R. resumed its nuclear tests the following year.

The 1960s, which twice saw the superpowers on the brink of nuclear hostilities—in the Berlin blockade and in the Cuban missile crisis—were also marked by sequences of cooperation that produced the atmospheric test ban agreement (1963) and the nonproliferation treaty (1968). Both the U.S. and the U.S.S.R. adhered pretty closely to the Tit for Tat rule during that decade.

A further but more ambiguous stage of cooperation was reached with the Strategic Arms Limitation Treaty of 1972 which set up elaborate guidelines for the arms race by excluding antiballistic missiles and limiting the number of intercontinental vehicles. A bilateral agency, the Standing Consultative Commission, was set up to monitor compliance with the agreement. What made the SALT I agreement ambiguous was the absence of any provision for slowing or stopping the arms race. Instead, it established an agenda for the continued expansion of nuclear capabilities. It was a form of cooperation potentially more lethal than following the rule of All D. SALT I was succeeded by SALT II. That treaty, although never ratified by the Senate, remained informally in force until late in 1987, when the U.S. announced a ritual violation of the limits on submarine missiles in order to put an end to the agreement.

During the early 1980s, the American strategy in the End Game came pretty close to All D, being equally unresponsive to hostile and to cooperative Soviet moves. Instead of exacerbating the situation—as might have been expected—this strategy seemingly alarmed the Soviet government as never before, and elicited unprecedented offers from them to cooperate on a nuclear test ban, the reduction of missile forces, on-site inspection, and crisis management. These were initially perceived in Washington as attempts to undermine American defense preparedness, separate us from our allies, and block the development of space-based weapons, but did eventually elicit reciprocal cooperative responses.

Is Tit for Tat the best and safest rule to follow in the End Game? The question is difficult to answer. The experience of the 1960s suggests that Tit for Tat produces more agreements *and* more crises, by making it obligatory, or at least routine, for each government to respond favorably to friendly overtures but to retaliate for every hostile move. The arms race at the heart of the End Game has involved both quantitative and qualitative escalation. On the quantitative side, the U.S. developed a huge lead early in the game and had a 10-to-1 advantage in nuclear warheads at the time of the Cuban missile crisis in 1962. Perhaps in response to that event, the U.S.S.R. achieved parity in warheads by the early 1970s and a 3-to-2 advantage in the early 1980s. As of this writing, both governments are busily expanding their stocks of warheads for reasons that appear to be more symbolic than strategical, while simultaneously destroying their stocks of intermediate-range ballistic missiles by mutual agreement, and negotiating an eventual reduction of intercontinental missiles.

On the qualitative side of the arms race, the Soviet Union has generally been in the position of trying to match American initiatives. Of nine major innovations in nuclear weaponry since 1948— the atomic bomb, intercontinental bombers, the hydrogen bomb, intercontinental ballistic missiles, submarine-launched ballistic missiles, antiballistic missiles, multiple independent re-entry vehicles, cruise missiles, and space-based weapons—only intercontinental and antiballistic missiles were introduced by the Soviet Union. But in no instance has either side failed to match a major innovation by the other.

The rule actually followed in this part of the End Game is a modification of Tit for Tat whereby hostile moves invariably provoke a symmetrical hostile response, but responses to friendly moves are unpredictable, more affected by domestic considerations in each country than by payoffs in the game. We might nickname the rule Bastard. Bastard appears to be a much more dangerous rule than Tit for Tat because it guarantees a continuous sequence of hostile moves and countermoves, while friendly moves and countermoves are at best intermittent. In a game in which both sides play Bastard, it would seem that the balance of hostility and cooperation must tilt further and further toward hostility. But although that is the most probable outcome, it is not inevitable. The response to a friendly move may be unreasonably hostile, but it may also be disproportionately favorable. Bastard is a rule designed to produce surprises, and not all of them are unpleasant. Tit for Tat looks a good deal safer, but when all is said and done, no strategical rule can be either safe or satisfactory in a game where the negative payoffs so greatly exceed the positive payoffs that the best strategy would be not to play at all.

Tit for Tat on the Battlefield

In conflict situations at lower levels of organization, it often happens that decisions are made collectively by the rank-and-file. Tony Ashworth's remarkable 1980 study of trench warfare on the western front in the First World War, *Trench Warfare, 1914–1918: The Live and Let Live System*, tells how some of the Allied and German units on the western front made and enforced unofficial truces. Ashworth writes:

Essentially, the term live and let live denoted a process of reciprocal exchange among antagonists, where each diminished the other's risk of death, discomfort, or injury by a deliberate restriction of aggressive behavior, but only on condition that the other requited the restraint. . . . The quietness of a sector did not signify either a social void or vacuum between enemies but the replacement of one form of exchange with another, which trench fighters found more consistent with their needs.[9]

These truces were entirely illegitimate from the standpoint of higher commanders, who were not personally exposed to the discomforts and risks of life in the trenches. They made unending efforts to repress the live and let live system, but it persisted sporadically as long as the armies remained entrenched. Some truces involved thousands of troops and continued for weeks or months, although units rotated in and out of the front line.

Ashworth was particularly interested in how truces began and ended, and in the differences between quiet and active sectors. Some truces were arranged by direct negotiation, like the famous

Christmas truce of 1914 that involved nine British divisions. More commonly, the desire for a truce was conveyed nonverbally, by ritualized firing that followed a predictable schedule and did no damage. The explicit negotiation of truces was common early in the war, but the high commands on both sides reacted to these by punishing the offenders and by taking direct control of front-line operations. In the later stages of the war, the ritualization of combat became the predominant mode of cooperation across the lines. Enemy patrols encountered in no-man's-land were politely ignored. Machine guns were fired over the heads of opposing troops. Artillery was carefully aimed to avoid the enemy trenches and rifles were aimed to miss.

The live and let live system was both cause and effect of the sympathetic attitude toward the enemy often produced by the experience of trench warfare. Ashworth explains the phenomenon by familiar sociological principles: frequent interaction develops friendly sentiments; friendly sentiments encourage cooperative exchange; cooperative exchange reinforces friendly sentiments. The circumstances of World War I trench warfare favored this process. The enemy were close enough for almost continuous interaction; they were exposed to the same risks and hardships; many people on each side knew the language of the other; they had similar weapons, tactics, and military customs. The front-line soldier was likely to reserve his real hostility for the rear-echelon staff officers who put his life and comfort at risk by ordering aggressive actions that seemed, from his perspective—and incidentally from ours—to have no rational objectives.

Ashworth sees the relationship between the opposing forces in trench warfare as comprising two interrelated exchange processes, which he calls the mutually contingent exchange of gratifications and the mutually contingent exchange of deprivations. Both forms of exchange were conducted by the rule of Tit for Tat, but they were not symmetrical. The second process was qualified by an ethic of retributive justice. When a truce was broken by one side, either on its own initiative or because it was forced to do so by higher commands, the offended side did not respond with an emotionally neutral Tat. They were offended not only by the breaking of the truce and the betrayal of trust that it signified, but also by the injuries inflicted on their comrades in violation of previous understandings. If the opportunity offered, they would attack their erstwhile truce partners with vengeful fury.

Tit for Tat played on a battlefield is not quite the same as Tit for Tat played on a computer. On the positive side, the two versions of the game are very similar. Tit for Tit is a stable and symmetrical condition. Left to themselves, the front-line troops could have maintained their truces indefinitely. But Tat for Tat is neither symmetrical nor stable. Writings on game theory sometimes quote the biblical phrase "An eye for an eye and a tooth for a tooth" to illustrate retaliation. But that formula refers to an act of justice by an authority capable of imposing a punishment proportioned to the offense. Retaliation is altogether different. Driven by powerful emotions, the retaliator is not satisfied to inflict a hurt equal to the one received. From his perspective, the exchange is not balanced if the hurt inflicted equals the hurt received, because that leaves unpunished the malice in the original Tat. But the extra hurt he inflicts is perceived as malicious by the adversary, who then seeks vengeance in his turn. In real conflicts, the Tat for Tat sequence tends to escalate toward the commission of atrocities.

The point emphasized by Ashworth is that even in lethal combat aggressive behavior is channeled and inhibited by social processes. He brings in evidence from other wars to show that cooperation between opposing troops on the battlefield was not peculiar to trench warfare or to this particular war. It is equally important to recognize that the very processes that encouraged truces in trench warfare also provoked unusually brutal fighting at other places along the same front, where three million soldiers lost their lives.

The implications for war games are plain. Tit for Tat is not a sound strategy in war, not even in an unfought war. Although it does elicit cooperation between enemies, the certainty of escalation in Tat for Tat exchanges turns this strategical rule into a recipe for catastrophe when the weapons are nuclear.

The Dynamics of Bureaucracy

Bureaucracy is the dominant form of organization in twentieth-century societies. The serious study of bureaucracy began with Max Weber (1864–1920), who both admired and deplored it. In his view, bureaucracy is "technically superior" to other forms of organization. In the ideal bureaucracy, operations are marked by "precision, speed, unambiguity, knowledge of the files, continuity, discretion, unity, strict subordination, reduction of friction and of material and personal costs." In real life, it does not always work that way.

A bureaucracy consists of officials engaged in the manipulation of words and symbols under fixed rules. Bureaucrats occupy positions whose duties are strictly prescribed, and their authority is limited to what those duties require. Bureaucratic operations produce documents, and the documents are filed to provide material for future documents. Bureaucrats are supposed to be impartial, dispassionate, predictable, and impersonal. They are recruited for long careers and expect to advance to positions of increasing responsibility as they age. In most bureaucracies, the penalties for mistakes are greater than the rewards for achievement, and it is an especially punishable mistake for a bureaucrat to question the goals of the agency he serves.

It is often difficult to separate the bureaucratic and nonbureaucratic components of a large organization, but, loosely speaking, the bureaucracy is that part of an organization which regulates and records the useful activities performed by the other parts. Bureaucracy is the preferred method of running very large organizations because it is the only method. No one has devised any other way to coordinate the activities of thousands of people in hundreds of locations pursuing some common purpose by means of an intricate division of labor. The first modern bureaucracy was the British Admiralty of the seventeenth century, and the diary of that consummate bureaucrat, Samuel Pepys, secretary of the Admiralty from 1675 to 1679 and from 1684 to 1689, shows that many of the typical features of bureaucratic life were discernible at the outset.

Bureaucracies resemble each other, but that does not preclude very large variations in efficiency and effectiveness. A bureaucracy is a machine composed of interchangeable human parts with specialized functions, but as the parts are never perfectly specialized or fully interchangeable, the machine goes out of adjustment easily and often. Bureaucratic malfunctions take a number of familiar forms: overgrowth, goal displacement, rigidity, red tape, corruption, inhumanity.

Bureaucratic agencies normally count growth as success and contraction as failure. Growth is promotion and a corner office; contraction is a salary freeze and the unwanted transfer to a field office. Since the bureaucratic parts of an organization are responsible for allocating its resources, it follows as the night the day that the bureaucratic parts of an organization grow faster than the productive parts. The creeping growth of administrative overhead from one year to the next occurs routinely in every large organization, public or private. It can be checked by drastic pruning, but that is usually impeded by the natural resistance of bureaucrats to any kind of contraction.

The goals of bureaucratic agencies are always and everywhere the same—to aggrandize the agency by increasing its size and its resources. When a large organization contains subordinate bureaucracies of approximately equal influence, the competition among them for the means of aggrandizement may push the organization's own goals entirely aside.

In the minute division of labor that is the essence of the bureaucratic system, each official is responsible for performing a small fragment of a larger program. His or her responsibility extends no further than the correct performance of that fragment. It is literally none of his or her business to assess the contribution of the fragment to the goals of the total program. Since the bureaucratic mode of operation fosters a certain indifference to the goals of the larger organization, the consciences of bureaucrats who use their authority for private profit or pleasure are easily soothed, as are the consciences of those who commit atrocities in obedience to orders.

The bureaucratic mode of operation is not designed for quick adaptation to changing circumstances. By definition, there is no standard operating procedure for an unforeseen contingency.

The administrative component of the U.S. Department of Defense is the largest bureaucracy the world has seen so far, and it displays the normal defects of bureaucracies on a gargantuan scale. The symptoms of overgrowth, goal displacement, rigidity, red tape, corruption, and inhumanity, as they appear currently in the

Department of Defense, have been described by a number of well-informed critics and military reformers, with varying degrees of indignation.[10] Most of the writers identified as military reformers are not opposed to the End Game. They take it for granted. But they deplore the bureaucratic excesses that impair the readiness and effectiveness of U.S. forces. The overgrowth of bureaucracy in the military establishment has been fairly spectacular. The number of middle-rank officers for every 100 enlisted men increased from 1.3 in 1945 to 5.6 in 1988; the ratio of generals and admirals from .02 to .06. The great majority of this swollen officer corps were desk workers—necessarily so because they greatly outnumbered the available command positions. The Army, for example, had only 17 divisional commands for its 139 major generals. This overstaffing is absorbed in an extraordinary labyrinth of offices and directorates. Luttwak provides the following example:

Consider, for example, the role of the Air Force Systems Command, which has expanded and subdivided over the years to accommodate 10,524 officers, including no fewer than 34 generals, at last count. The Systems Command is responsible for the acquisition of all the equipment that the Air Force introduces into service. It does not manufacture aircraft, missiles or other equipment; private contractors do that. Nor does it carry out any major research or development. . . .

The central headquarters of the Systems Command at Andrews Air Force Base . . . which supervises the various divisions and offices of the Command that do the actual supervising, already forms a very large bureaucracy. Headed by a four-star full general (whose own inner-office executive group includes four full colonels), with a three-star lieutenant general serving as vice commander, the headquarters is coordinated by a chief of staff who has his own well-staffed inner office. These officers supervise the sixty-eight "directorates" that divide the functions of the headquarters among them; mostly headed by colonels who report to eleven deputy chiefs of staff (who are mostly brigadier generals). . . .

In addition to the directorates—which supervise the supervisors in the divisions outside the headquarters—there are nine supporting offices that provide services to the Andrews complex, for administration . . . public affairs, security police, and so on.

And that is only the central headquarters. The actual work of the Systems Command is distributed among four major divisions, each headed by a lieutenant general. . . . In addition, there are eight other lesser divisions and "centers." Each of the divisions has its own headquarters (very large in the case of the four major divisions), which coordinates and supervises the different functional offices and directories.[11]

One effect of this system is the reluctance of the Air Force to purchase "civilian" items, however cheap and satisfactory they may be, because that would oversimplify the procurement process. Another is the practice of having specifications more complex than the products they describe,[12] which greatly increases their cost. The most important consequence is the loss of the ability to make common sense decisions about anything connected with procurement. The Systems Command is not a special case. That is the way the Pentagon operates.

The cumulative result of bureaucratic overgrowth on this scale is that only a small fraction of the people in uniform are trained for combat; their weapons and equipment are often defective or in short supply. The procurement process is slow, cumbersome, and costly. By the time a new vehicle or weapons system is finally put into production after years of development and redevelopment, the unit cost has usually been driven so high that few units can be put into service. Thus, the vast military expenditures of the United States buy relatively small and inefficient combat forces, which must be protected from the chosen adversary by a nuclear umbrella, because, according to the accepted bureaucratic doctrine, we cannot hope to match their conventional forces.

Goal displacement in the U.S. military takes the form of a running battle among the services and among the branches of each service for the means of growth. Each service has its own version of national strategy, designed to maximize its share of the defense budget. Each service fiercely defends its operational territory and invades the territory of its neighbors whenever an opportunity occurs. The rivalry among the services continually distracts them from their assigned tasks. The Army, the Navy and the Air Force used different radio frequencies in the Grenada intervention, and in one famous incident an infantry officer requested air support by making a long-distance credit card call to Fort Bragg, for lack of any local channel.

The significance of this competition for the End Game is that each of the major services insists on having its own nuclear deterrent, as indeed they do. In the development of the strategic triad of land, sea, and air missiles, the nuclear balance among the services has weighed as heavily as the nuclear balance between the superpowers. The case for the MX missile, for example, relies in part on the security threat created by the increased accuracy of Soviet ICBMs, but as much or more on the Air Force's need to protect itself against the competitive threat represented by the accuracy of the Navy's Trident II SLBMs (Submarine-Launched Ballistic Missiles).

The already difficult problem of reducing the arsenal of nuclear weapons is compounded by the equally difficult problem of allocating reductions among the rival services, which, in any given case, are certain to disagree about what constitutes an equitable allocation. Each service has a powerful constituency in and out of Congress, and their mutual suspicions are aroused by every proposed reduction of forces in much the same way as the mutual suspicions of the superpowers.

All bureaucracies are rigid. The defense bureaucracy, being larger and more complex than any other, is exceptionally rigid. In consequence, there is no way that it can adjust smoothly to a changing situation or react swiftly to an unforeseen problem. The chains of command are too long, the labyrinth of procedures is too intricate, the overlapping authorities are too strong to ignore and too numerous to coordinate.

If, as many believe, the national interest will be best served by disengaging from the End Game, the defense bureaucracy must be reckoned as one of the major obstacles. It is hard to show that the interests of the defense bureaucracy would be served by such a settlement and difficult to imagine it adopting any vision of national purpose that requires the sacrifice of its own interests. Bureaucracies are incapable of selflessness. They have no procedures for it.

The reform of a military bureaucracy that has overgrown and gone to seed is normally accomplished after the loss of a few battles in the early stages of a long war, or after a quick defeat in a short war. That was the story of the British Admiralty in the Napoleonic Wars, the British army in the Crimean War, the Union's War Department after First Manassas, the French army after 1871, most of Europe's general staffs in 1915 and 1916, and the British and Soviet war ministries between 1939 and 1943. But the post-Vietnam reorganization of the Pentagon was only superficial. The reform of a military bureaucracy that has not recently failed the test of battle is a rare event, although the size of a military establishment is often reduced during a long peace.

It is a peculiarity of the End Game that it does not allow the military bureaucracies involved in it either to be tested in battle or shrunken by peace. In the absence of these normal checks, they have grown to monstrous proportions and acquired formidable capacities to defend the status quo against many of the changes that common sense and the national interest seem to call for.

War and Public Opinion

Immanuel Kant, in his essay on perpetual peace, wrote that republics were more peaceful than other states, because citizens were less willing than princes to go to war. Woodrow Wilson, planning the League of Nations, conceived international public opinion to be the mainstay of a peacekeeping system. But in Wilson's time, as in Kant's, public opinion was difficult to ascertain. What passed for the reaction of a nation to public events was in most cases only the mood of influential circles in the capital. Since the 1940s, however, the sampling of public opinion by interview surveys has made it possible to discover how a given event is perceived by an entire population and what sentiments it arouses among them. The fluctuations of public opinion can be charted from week to week, and the inevitable differences of opinion connected with gender, age, region, race, religion, party, education, occupation, and other attributes can be measured with fair precision. For recent decades, the reactions of the American public to wars, threats of war, and other military episodes are known in great detail, and similar information is available for other modernized countries. Once identified, the pattern is so clear that we seem to recognize it retrospectively in earlier situations about which we know much less.

In peacetime, the majority of the public resists involvement in future or ongoing wars, sometimes very strongly. But as soon as hostilities begin, these sentiments are replaced by more bellicose ones. A government embarking on war can generally count on almost unanimous popular support at the outset. As the war proceeds, the level of support declines, particularly after defeats or heavy casualties. Since public opinion can be swung in favor of war by commencing hostilities, it is seldom an effective brake on a government that is preparing to resort to force. A large section of the public continues to back the war until victory is won, or until their government begins to negotiate a settlement, or until their government collapses.

An excellent, detailed account of how the American public reacted to the military involvement of the United States in Korea from 1950 to 1953 and in Vietnam from 1961 to 1973 is found in John E. Mueller's *War, Presidents and Public Opinion* (1973). When a survey question about the Korean War was worded without ideological bias, "Do you think the United States made a mistake in going into the war in Korea, or not?" (American Institute of Public Opinion, asked with minor variations from August 1950 to July 1953), the prowar responses declined from 66 percent at the outset to a low of 36 percent in October 1952, when the truce talks were recessed indefinitely after more than a year of inconclusive negotiations. But it rose again to 50 percent early in the following year. When the question was worded to include a war aim, "Do you think the United States was right or wrong in sending American troops to stop the Communist invasion of South Korea?" (National Opinion Research Center, asked without variation from September 1950 to June 1952), the trend was parallel but the percentage of support was higher, beginning at 81 percent and never declining below 50 percent. Mueller makes the important point that support for the war did not come solely from those who approved the war as an appropriate action in the existing political situation but also from those who supported the war because, right or wrong, it was "ours."

For the Vietnam War, a question without ideological reference was repeated often enough to be tracked over the entire course of the war: "In view of the developments since we entered the fighting in Vietnam, do you think the U.S. made a mistake sending troops to fight in Vietnam?" (American Institute of Public Opinion, asked without variation from August 1965 to May 1971). The level of support began at 60 percent in 1965; declined below 50 percent in 1967, when the first peace overtures were made by the U.S.; and fell below 40 percent in August 1968 after North Vietnam agreed to preliminary peace talks, at which level it remained until the end of the war.

Mueller found a close statistical relationship between the public support for both of these wars and the number of American casualties, which he summarized by saying that every time American casualties increased by a factor of 10, support for the war dropped by about 15 percentage points.

Both the Korea and Vietnam Wars were distant wars. The American Revolution, the War of 1812, the Civil War, and the Indian wars were the only nearby wars in U.S. history. It often happens, of course, that a nearby war for one side is a distant war for the other side. The reason for introducing this distinction here is that nearby wars seems to command an even higher level of initial support than distant wars and to maintain it longer. A high level of public support at the beginning of a nearby war can be taken for granted, although the mood may vary from exuberance to somber solidarity. It seems to make no difference what the state of public opinion may have been just before. The shift to nearly unanimous support occurs overnight.

The best-documented and most discussed shift of public opinion at the beginning of a war occurred in August 1914. In Britain, France, Germany, Austria, and Russia, the unexpected outbreak of war was followed by a storm of popular enthusiasm which swept away the pacifist principles of the socialists and the transnational commitments of the intellectuals in the twinkling of an eye. "I discovered to my amazement," wrote Bertrand Russell in 1914, "that average men and women were delighted by the prospect of war. I had fondly imagined, what most pacifists contended, that wars were forced upon a reluctant population by despotic and Machiavellian governments."[13]

Earlier in the same year, the French Socialist party had voted for a general strike in case of war. As late as July 30, the executive committee of the International was meeting in Brussels to formulate a peace strategy. As late as August 1, a representative of the German Socialists assured the French Socialists that his party would never vote for war credits, but just three days later they did so in a body, while at the same hour the antimilitarist French Socialists were doing the same thing in Paris.

Roland Stromberg, in *Redemption by War: The Intellectuals*

and 1914 (1982) points out that the socialist opposition to war had never been unequivocal. The Marxists, taking their lead from Marx and Engels themselves, could never quite decide whether international war was a capitalist aberration to be resisted or a necessary part of the historic unfolding that would lead from capitalism to socialism. The Marxist view of nationhood was similarly ambiguous, and remains so to this day. But even when these qualifications are recognized, the conversion of European socialists from pacifist internationalism to patriotic jingoism in less than a week remains astonishing.

Socialism was only part of a larger pattern of European ideas ranging from relativity to relativism, from cubism to psychoanalysis, from symbolism to sociology, that was profoundly transnational and antiauthoritarian. With insignificant exceptions, the bearers of this culture abandoned their former principles in 1914 to fall in behind the colors.[14] The roster of writers enlisted by the War Propaganda Bureau in London included nearly every major literary figure in Britain: Galsworthy, Barrie, Chesterton, Hardy, Gilbert Murray, Kipling, Conan Doyle, Zangwill, Trevelyan, H. G. Wells, Buchan, Toynbee, Masefield, and scores of others. Nor was this enthusiasm confined to England or to writers; it was the same in all the warring countries and in all the fields of intellectual effort. Scriabin, Berg, and Stravinsky welcomed the war, as did Freud, Gandhi, Kropotkin, and Henry James. In France, Emile Durkheim thought the war would revive the sense of community, and in Germany, Max Weber wrote that "No matter what the outcome will be, this war is great and wonderful."[15]

The themes of support for the war were rich and varied: the purification of a sick society in the crucible of war, redemption through suffering and sacrifice, the nation as an endangered community, war as the ultimate adventure, the promise of erotic liberation, the rediscovery of antique virtues, the realization that the Germans had been barbarians all along. Stromberg concludes that "It is, then, difficult to invoke public opinion of any sort as a cause of the coming of the war. But it is quite possible to see it as by far the most important cause of the war's long continuance. . . . What really calls for an explanation is not why the war began but why it went on for more than four awful years, consuming millions of lives. And the reason for this is clearly the incredible support public opinion gave to the war."[16]

At the outbreak of the Second World War, the European public was shocked and somber rather than exuberant, but public opinion in France, Britain, and Germany supported the war with the same virtual unanimity as in 1914. Much has been written about the mutual suspicions that developed between France and England during the inactive phase of the war on the western front from September 1939 to April 1940, but the elaborate soundings of public opinion made by the French government through its administrative channels indicated that opposition to the war was confined to 10 or 15 percent of the population.[17] For Britain, careful opinion polls, conducted by the British Institute of Public Opinion beginning in the last week of September 1939, yielded these figures in response to the question "Should we continue to fight as long as Hitlerism exists?": 89 percent of the sample said Yes, and only 7 percent said No.[18] Although the level of support declined somewhat in reaction to the disasters of 1940, the great majority of the British population never wavered in supporting the war and in approving the government's management of it.

Indeed, there is no instance in the last two centuries of a nearby war that failed to evoke massive public support at the outset. Distant wars have less predictable effects on public opinion, but most national publics respond to any commencement of hostilities with a surge of support. Every military action launched by the United States since public opinion polling began has raised the popularity of the president as measured in the polls. In 1987, more than 70 percent of the public supported the Reagan administration's sending of naval forces to the Persian Gulf to protect reflagged Kuwaiti tankers against hypothetical attacks by Iran, although very few understood the rationale of the operation. This sweeping and reflexive approval covers only those military adventures involving U.S. forces. It is not evoked by the military adventures of allies, like the Israelis in Lebanon, or of foreign troops supported by the U.S., like the Nicaraguan contras. The reactions of the American public do not seem to be more or less bellicose than those of other national publics in similar circumstances. The most adventurous of recent wars, the Falklands War between

Britain and Argentina, was overwhelmingly supported by public opinion in both countries.

The subgroups of a national population always differ in their attitudes toward a war. In general, it may be anticipated that men will be more pro-war than women, and young people will be more pro-war than old people. Other subgroup differences are specific to particular wars. For both the Korean and the Vietnam conflicts, Mueller's study, cited above, shows that support increased with education, with occupational level, and with income, and was almost unaffected by religion. Democrats were somewhat more supportive of the Korean effort than Republicans, and somewhat more supportive of the Vietnam War until it was taken over by the Nixon administration, whereupon they became less supportive of it than Republicans. Relative to white respondents, blacks reacted to both wars as doves. The subgroup differences become increasingly salient as a war winds down, but it should be noted that majorities of *all* of the subgroups supported both the Korean and Vietnam wars at the outset.

So much for domestic public opinion. It is much more likely to incite hostilities than to restrain them. But what about international public opinion, the foundation on which the League of Nations was built? Today it is often called "world opinion"; in the eighteenth century it was the "opinion of mankind."

There are two distinct kinds of international public opinion about war: the opinions of national publics about wars in which their own nations are not directly involved, and the opinions of that special public which consists of governments and their representatives. The reflexive reaction of public opinion to the outbreak of hostilities between third parties is often isolationist; the first impulse is to avoid involvement. Wilson in 1916 and Roosevelt in 1940 were reelected over more hawkish opponents; both claimed credit for averting U.S. involvement in the ongoing European war. So far as I can determine, there have been no instances in modern times of a chauvinistic population pushing a reluctant government toward active hostilities. The pattern is *invariably* the opposite: public support develops in proportion as a government moves from neutrality to partiality to active participation in an ongoing war.

In the case of the End Game, it is not easy to disentangle opposition to Communism from hostility to Communist states in the web of American public opinion, but both sentiments are instantly responsive to alterations of government policy, as may be seen, for example, in the rapid shifts of public opinion that followed the Nixon-Kissinger opening to China, and Gorbachev's visit to Washington in December 1987.

The other kind of international public opinion—the moral sentiments of sovereign states and their representatives—is a perpetual disappointment to the well-meaning. In a system where force is the ultimate arbiter, the moral sentiments expressed by governments are generally—and correctly—perceived to be only peripherally related to their actions. The contemporary etiquette of international relations requires that the naked self-interest that drives the foreign policy of every government be always covered by a cloak of high principle. The custom is a graceful one but hardly affects the outcomes of either war games or peace games.

The War System

The social science theories just reviewed—about types of conflict, the formation of international coalitions, models of government action, the expected utilities of war, the implications of various strategies, the dynamics of military bureaucracy, and the connections between public opinion and war—can be drawn upon to develop a highly simplified model of what Charles Sumner long ago called "the war system of the commonwealth of nations,"[19] the framework within which war games are played and actual wars are fought. Peace games too must start from the existing war system. It can only be circumvented if it is fully understood.

The model of the war system may be summarized as follows: Each government in the system has two constant goals: to dominate other governments and to avoid domination by others. The payoffs for achieving a dominant position include the acquisition of disputed territories and populations, concessions and resources for one's traders, immunities and privileges for one's citizens, foreign bases for one's armed forces, converts for one's ideological missionaries. But national prestige (i.e., the place accorded to a nation in the rank order of international domination) is often in itself and for its own sake a sufficient motive for diplomatic and military actions.

The fear of being dominated is a more powerful and more consistent motive for most governments than the ambition to dominate. Most of the governments in today's war system are relatively weak. They can resist the domination of more powerful neighbors only by putting themselves under the protection of one of the superpowers, or by playing the superpowers off against each other, or by joining a bloc that pursues one or the other of these strategies. The relatively weak governments that attempt to dominate one or two of their neighbors—Syria, Israel, Libya, Iran, India, Nicaragua, Indonesia, Vietnam—must be continually attentive to the relationships with the superpowers that permit them to pursue their local ambitions.

It happens frequently that a weak government sees a clear opportunity to dominate a weaker neighbor, or to shake off the domination of a stronger neighbor, by going to war. There is nothing in the war system to prevent it from doing so, and the selected adversary, having no choice but to fight or yield, is likely to fight. It is often the case that a weak government is challenged to war, not by a neighboring government, but by a rebel movement within its own borders. Such movements can usually find outside backers. The goal of the rebel movement is to displace the government. The government, unless it is extremely weak, will not refuse the invitation to war. Many of the numerous wars involving weak governments that have been fought since 1945 would presumably have occurred without outside intervention. They represent the routine functioning of the war system in which interstate—and often intrastate—domination is achieved by superior military strength, and in which military strength is eventually measured in battle.

From the viewpoint of the ambitious leaders of a relatively weak government—an Iran or a Vietnam—nothing is wrong with the war system. It offers rich opportunities for national aggrandizement, ideological triumph, and personal glory. The defects of the war system are more apparent at the level of the superpowers and their major allies. The governments of strong states, like all others, seek to dominate and to avoid being dominated, but their chances of achieving either objective are severely limited by the excessive cost of any war involving highly industrialized nations and by the geometry of coalitions, which constantly creates and upsets balances of power among the leading contenders for domination of the entire war system. Wars among strong governments are often protracted and indecisive. Each of the three greatest wars of that type—1798–1815, 1914–1918, 1939–1945—saw a gigantic coalition formed to resist a government that seemed within reach of achieving universal domination. The efforts were successful, but at enormous cost to both victors and vanquished, and in each instance the strongest of the victors presented new threats of domination to their recent allies.

In the present century, the costliness of the war system for strong governments has continued to rise while the benefits they derive from it have continued to decline. For various reasons, the military forces of advanced industrial nations are no longer very effective against guerrilla forces fighting on their home territory, as in Vietnam or Afghanistan. When the military forces of advanced industrial nations are directed against each other, victory may be as disastrous as defeat.

The defects of the war system for advanced industrial nations were apparent long before the introduction of nuclear weapons increased the costs by several orders of magnitude and decreased the benefits correspondingly. There was a nearly universal consensus in 1918 that the war system should be abolished, but for reasons we will explore presently, it was reinforced instead. One of the commonest reactions to the unveiling of the atomic bomb at Hiroshima was the opinion that technology had done what statesmanship had been unable to do, and removed the war system at one stroke. When that hope proved to be premature, a similar claim was made for deterrence; it was—and is—alleged to make war between nuclear-armed states impossible. "Safety," said Churchill in a speech to the House of Commons in 1955, "will be the sturdy child of terror and survival the twin brother of annihilation." But everything that is known about governments as actors suggests the contrary. For a government, the fear of foreign domination is a stronger motive than the fear of devastation. In matters of war-making, the masses of a modern state do not oppose their own interests to their government's; they follow where they are led. There is no permanently satisfactory resolution of the Prisoner's Dilemma even for a totally rational actor, and governments are not totally rational actors. Their decisions are reached at many levels as the outcome of unpredictable cross-purposes. Bureaucracies, moreover, can do only the tasks they are constructed to do. The military bureaucracies are part of the war system; they will neither disband voluntarily nor undergo spiritual change. The war system, in sum, is most unlikely to abolish itself without powerful intervention, and, failing that intervention, it is most unlikely that the outbreak of nuclear war will be permanently postponed by any calculation of its costs and benefits.

Chapter 4

Changing the Rules of War

What? Will you never cease prating of laws to us
that have swords by our sides?
Pompey

The oldest and best-tried peace game is a change in the rules of war. Changes of this kind are generally intended to assure that wars do not become terminal and threaten the warring parties with extinction. More particularly, the objects are to limit the costs of future wars, to assure the safety of protected classes of persons and property, to make it possible for belligerents to communicate, to prohibit morally repugnant behavior, and to limit combat to appropriate times and places.

Might it be feasible to change the current rules of war so as to remove or greatly reduce the risk of nuclear exchanges? This is a less ambitious project than the abolition of war as an institution but perhaps more practicable and certainly more urgent. In the worst case, a large-scale nuclear exchange could exterminate mankind. In the best case, it would be a monumental folly. In anything but the worst case, the first priority of postwar authorities would be to prevent the repetition of what had just occurred by preventing the further use of nuclear explosives as weapons.

The human race evolved in an environment in which the strong force that binds the atom was never locally released. Since we are too fragile biologically to live with the strong force, we must be sociologically insulated from it in order to survive. The problem of preventing the use of nuclear explosives as weapons did not appear in the world until 1945, but it may fairly be considered as a variant form of the perennial problem of how to keep the violence of hostile collectivities within reasonable limits. To that perennial problem there are only a finite number of solutions, of which the easiest to visualize are changes in the rules of war.

International law—the body of customs, conventions, and treaty obligations that include the rules of war—is said to differ from domestic law in being unenforceable. Nonetheless, international law is obeyed by most governments most of the time, so that its effects are not negligible. The Hittites and Sumerians had rules about the initiation and conduct of war more than three thousand years ago, as did the ancient Hindus, Hebrews, and Chinese. The Greeks and Romans expanded the sphere of regulation. With occasional bloodthirsty lapses, they were scrupulous about the safety of prisoners, the immunity of priests and temples, and the observance of truces and safe-conducts.

Christianity was originally a cult of peace, and during its early centuries Christians were not permitted to become soldiers. When Christianity became a state religion, the Church fathers were confronted with the problem of how to reconcile the extreme pacifism of the Gospel—"If thine enemy smite thee on the cheek, turn the other cheek to him that he may smite that also"—with the military obligations of subjects and citizens. In the sixth century, St. Augustine formulated the concept of the just war, which has enabled Christians to shed each other's blood in good conscience ever since, as all wars appear just to the attackers and even more so to the defenders.

To be considered just, a war had to meet a number of tests. Was it necessary, unavoidable, and intended to restore peace? Was it waged without treachery or excessive cruelty?[1] From these questions arose the fundamental division of international law into *jus ad bellum* and *jus in bello,* rules about going to war and rules about the conduct of hostilities. A thousand years after St. Augustine, this division was codified in an influential treatise *On the Law of War and Peace* by the Dutch lawyer Hugo Grotius (1583–1645), a scholarly but cruel book that gave a color of legitimacy to the atrocities of the Thirty Years War. Among the harsh principles promulgated by Grotius were these:

• The right to inflict injury extends even over infants and women.

• The right to inflict injury extends even over those who have surrendered unconditionally.

• Even enemy property that is sacred may be destroyed and pillaged.

• All persons captured in a war become slaves, their descendants become slaves also, and "There is no suffering which may not be inflicted upon such slaves, no action which they may not be ordered, or forced by torture, to do, in any way whatsoever" (VII, iii).

Grotius's rules of war were considerably harsher than the customary practices of European warfare, although, to be fair, he did suggest that they be tempered by moderation. What made his work so influential was the subordination of all private rights to the will of the sovereign engaged in public war, a thesis immensely agreeable to the expanding national governments of the seventeenth century.

Grotius was not the first or the last author to treat the rules of war as a literary exercise. He was preceded by Belli, Ayalá, Vittoria, and Suarez and followed by Pufendorf, Zouche, Vatel, Moser, and Kant, among others. They drew on a mélange of sources: customary practice, natural law, historical examples, the Gospels, the Old Testament, the Greek poets, the Roman jurists, the Church fathers, and the medieval scholastics. They were writers, not legislators, but bit by bit their ideas began to crop up in the regulations established by European states for their military and naval forces, in diplomatic correspondence, in manifestos and remonstrances, and finally, toward the end of the eighteenth century, in bilateral agreements like the 1785 "treaty of amity and commerce" between the new republic of the United States and the kingdom of Prussia. It provided that in case of war between the contracting powers, "all women and children, scholars of every faculty, cultivators of the earth, artisans, manufacturers and fishermen unarmed and inhabiting unfortified towns, villages or places . . . shall not be molested in their persons, nor shall their houses or goods be otherwise destroyed, nor their fields wasted by the armed force of the enemy . . . but if anything is necessary to be taken from them for the use of such armed force, the same shall be paid for at a reasonable price." Prisoners of war were not to be "confined in dungeons, prison-ships, nor prisons, nor be put into irons, nor bound, nor otherwise restrained in the use of their limbs" but "lodged in barracks as roomy and good as are provided by the party in whose power they are for their own troops."[2] This is 150 years after Grotius, and infinitely more humane. With respect to the immunities of noncombatants, it is infinitely more humane than the practices and policies of modern governments, including our own.

Nineteenth-century writers on the rules of war rejected religion and natural law as sources, and held the rules to be founded on the consent of sovereign states, expressed either by public acts or by treaty. This doctrine suggested that enforceable rules of war could be created by international agreement, and a great effort along that line began in the middle of the nineteenth century. The earliest of these multilateral treaties about the rules of war was the Declaration of Paris, signed by Great Britain, Austria, France, Prussia, Russia, Sardinia, and Turkey in 1856, with an open invitation to all other powers to join. It was admirably brief, less than two pages long; the legal principles it proposed were almost universally adopted. Privateering was prohibited; the neutral flag was held to protect enemy goods, except contraband of war; neutral goods under an enemy flag were not to be subject to capture; blockades would not be legitimate unless backed by a sufficient force to close the blockaded ports.

The next rule-making treaty was the Red Cross Convention of 1864, signed at Geneva. The original parties were Switzerland, Belgium, Denmark, Spain, France, Italy, the Netherlands, Portugal, and four of the German states. It provided for the neutrality of hospitals, ambulances, and medical personnel, including civilians who aid or shelter the wounded; for the care and eventual return of wounded prisoners; and for the use of the red cross insignia to identify protected persons and installations. Other rule-making treaties followed thick and fast. In 1868, the Declaration of St. Petersburg outlawed explosive bullets. The unratified Declaration of Brussels of 1874 proposed standards of conduct for occupying armies that had never before been approached. The occupying power was to respect both public and private property; pillage and plunder were forbidden; guerrillas were to be recognized as soldiers; prisoners of war were to be treated with humanity, not confined unless absolutely necessary, and allowed to keep their personal effects. The legacy of the Brussels Declaration to modern practice is the rule that a prisoner of war is not required to disclose more than his name, rank, and serial number when interrogated.

The Hague Conventions of 1899 were the first multilateral treaties signed by non-European powers. Along with the major European states, the signatories included the United States, China, Persia, Siam, and Japan. One of these treaties provided for the peaceful settlement of disputes by the mediation of friendly powers, by commissions of inquiry, and eventually by arbitration; it established a permanent Court of Arbitration for that purpose. Two other treaties signed at the Hague the same year placed limitations on the use of force for the collection of debts, and stipulated that hostilities would not be opened among the parties without a formal declaration of war. Another treaty on the laws and customs of war established meticulous criteria to identify combatants, noncombatants, and prisoners of war, declaring that "prisoners of war shall be treated as regards food, quarters, and clothing, on the same footing as the troops of the Government which has captured them" (VII). Other clauses of the same treaty covered the punishment of spies, permissible and nonpermissible ruses, truces, capitulations, and military occupations. During the Second World War, while millions of civilians were sent to extermination camps by the German Reich, most of its prisoner-of-war camps were managed in conformity to the Hague rules. The provisions of these 1899 treaties have been generally accepted as binding by belligerent states in the present century; they were intended to regulate wars among the high contracting parties and do not apply to civil, revolutionary, and guerrilla wars.

Additional Hague conventions followed in rapid succession during the next few years. Section II, Chapter 1, of the fourth Hague treaty of 1907—"Means of Injuring the Enemy, Sieges, and Bombardments"—turned out to be difficult to enforce. Indeed, the failure of Section II accounts for the widespread opinion that the Hague conventions were ineffectual. The intention behind Section II was expressed in a single sentence: "The right of belligerents to adopt means of injuring the enemy is not unlimited" (II, I, xxii). Accordingly, it attempted to prohibit the use of poisoned weapons or other weapons calculated to cause unnecessary suffering, the bombardment of undefended places, and any form of pillage.

No fewer than ten other treaties were signed at the Hague in 1907 by representatives of all the states then having significant military forces. They covered the rights and duties of neutral powers and persons, the status of enemy merchant ships at the outbreak of hostilities, the conversion of merchant ships into warships, the laying of submarine mines, naval bombardments, the adaptation of the Red Cross rules to naval war, restrictions on the right of capture in naval war, the establishment of an international prize court, the rights and duties of neutrals in naval war, and—last and briefest—an agreement to prohibit, for a period extending to the close of the Third Peace Conference (which was never held), "the discharge of projectiles and explosives from balloons or by other new methods of a similar nature" (XIV).

Meanwhile, at Geneva the previous year, a more comprehensive Red Cross Convention "for the amelioration of the condition of the wounded and sick in armies in the field" had been signed, with an even longer list of signatories, including Korea and most of the Latin American states. It has been the most successful of all the efforts to enact rules of war by multilateral treaty. The guiding principle was stated in the opening sentence: "Officers, soldiers, and other persons officially attached to armies, who are sick or wounded, shall be respected and cared for, without distinction of nationality, by the belligerent in whose power they are" (I, i). Throughout the twentieth century, the rules set forth in the 1906 treaty have been generally obeyed in international wars, and often in internecine wars.

The last treaty in this extraordinary series was the Declaration of London in 1909, an agreement among the naval powers which elaborated the rules of naval war with respect to blockades, contraband, and the procedures to be followed by warships when intercepting enemy and neutral merchant vessels.

It is sometimes said that the First World War put a stop to such niceties and showed that the effort to establish international law by treaty had been futile. There were indeed conspicuous violations of the Hague treaties, notably the breach of Hague 1907 V, Article II, "Belligerents are forbidden to allow troops or trains of ammunition or provisions to pass through the territory of a neutral power," by the German invasion of Belgium in 1914; the violation of Hague 1899 IV, 3, prohibiting poison gas, by both the Allies and the Central Powers; the British blockade that barred access to neutral coasts and ports in contravention of London 1909 XVIII; and the systematic violation by German U-boats of Article L of the same treaty whereby all persons on board a neutral vessel were to be placed in safety before the vessel was destroyed.

On the other hand, the rules of war set down in the prewar treaties were meticulously obeyed in thousands of other instances, and the violations stood out by contrast and did not go unpunished. The resentment aroused by the disregard of Belgian neutrality and the sinking of neutral vessels helped to bring the United States into the war, although it must be conceded that American public opinion did not distinguish sharply between the sinking of a ship called the *Gullflight*, which was plainly illegal under the treaties, and the sinking of the *Lusitania*, whose legality was at least debatable.

Four years after the war, the effort to construct international law by treaty was resumed at another Hague conference that prepared a new Declaration for air warfare. It was less confident and more equivocal than the prewar declarations, as the following excerpt shows:

In the immediate neighborhood of the operations of land forces, the bombardment of cities, towns, villages, dwellings or buildings is legitimate provided that there exists a reasonable presumption that the military concentration is sufficiently important to justify such bombardment, having regard to the danger thus caused to the civilian population. (XXIV, 4)

This Declaration was never ratified, but it foreshadowed the eventual abandonment of virtually all restraints on aerial bombing.

A treaty on Submarines and Noxious Gas, signed by the United States, Britain, France, Italy, and Japan in 1922, finally provided the long-missing rules for the stopping and searching of merchant vessels by submarines. Germany, as a defeated and demilitarized power, was not invited to sign. Without distinguishing between enemy and neutral vessels, it said that merchant vessels must not be attacked unless they refused to submit to visit and search, and must not be destroyed unless the crew and passengers were first placed in safety. It stated emphatically that belligerent submarines were not exempt from these rules "under any circumstances."

The Geneva Protocol of 1925 did include Germany, along with Estonia, Abyssinia, Salvador, and other remote states. It reiterated the prohibition of asphyxiating and poisonous gases as weapons, and extended the prohibition to bacteriological agents—a short and sweet treaty. The Red Cross Convention of 1929, signed by nearly all governments, added some ribbons and flourishes concerning the handling of enemy dead, and the display of the Red Cross emblem to the existing rules that protected sick and wounded soldiers. Signed on the same day, the 1929 Geneva Convention on Treatment of Prisoners of War extended the protection afforded to prisoners of war by Hague IV, going into great detail on such matters as: "Within a period of not more than one week after his arrival at the camp, and likewise in case of sickness, every prisoner shall be enabled to write his family a postal card informing it of his capture and of the state of his health. The said postal cards shall be forwarded as rapidly as possible and may not be delayed in any manner" (IV, xxxvi). The Convention not only provided for the payment of cash allowances to prisoners, according to rank, but specified the exact amounts, in Swiss francs (VIII, lx).

The last bit of lawmaking by treaty before the outbreak of the Second World War was an agreement about the rules of submarine warfare, signed at London in 1936 by the United States, France, Britain, Japan, and five British dominions. It stipulated that

a warship, whether surface vessel or submarine, may not sink or render incapable of navigation a merchant vessel without first having placed passengers, crew and ship's papers in a place of safety. For this purpose, the ship's boats are not regarded as a place of safety unless the safety of passengers and crew is assured, in the existing sea and weather conditions, by the proximity of land, or the presence of another vessel which is in a position to take them on board. (II)

After the war, the lawmaking effort resumed, with two revised Red Cross conventions, a revised convention on the treatment of prisoners of war, and a new convention on the protection of civilian persons in time of war, all signed at Geneva in 1949 by a long list of powers including the United States, the Soviet Union, the Holy See, and Monaco, but not the two Germanies. The language was more legalistic than in the prewar treaties, and it became the practice for governments to ratify multilateral treaties with niggling reservations.

The four Geneva conventions of 1949 marked the culmination of the long effort to establish a body of enforceable rules of war by multilateral treaty. Treaty-making did not cease at that point, but changed its style. The scene shifted to the United Nations, where committees of experts prepared an unending series of resolutions on genocide, nuclear weapons, human rights, mass communications, and other topics. These documents were more often intended to score propaganda points than to enact enforceable rules. Thus, the 1970 UN Resolution on War Criminals *"Condemns* the war crimes and crimes against humanity at present being committed as a result of aggressive wars, and the policies of racism, *apartheid* and colonialism and calls upon the States concerned to bring to trial persons guilty of such crimes." The most important multilateral agreement negotiated during this period was the 1968 Treaty on Non-Proliferation of Nuclear Weapons, which was envisaged as a form of arms control rather than an enactment of war rules.

We have reviewed the long effort to enact enforceable rules of war in order to ask whether this type of peace game has been successful enough in the past to offer hope for the future. Very little research has been done on the history of compliance with the rules of war established by international agreement, but common knowledge suggests that compliance has not been negligible. Indeed, some rules of war are better obeyed than most rules of municipal law.

Some of the rules enacted by multilateral treaty from 1856 on reflected customary practice. Others proposed the reform of customary practice or covered new contingencies. They may be grouped as follows:

• Rules for the protection and good treatment of certain categories of persons: neutrals, prisoners of war, sick and wounded enemy combatants, enemy civilians, journalists.

• Rules for the protection of property: neutral state and private property, personal property of combatants, enemy state property, enemy private property, cultural and historical monuments, undefended places.

• Rules for the interaction of hostile forces: (1) communications: declarations of hostilities, insignia, espionage, ruses and stratagems, warnings, ultimatums, truces, capitulations. (2) rights and duties of warships and merchant ships: belligerent ships in neutral ports, neutral ships in belligerent ports; warships and neutral merchant ships; warships and enemy merchant ships.

• Rule prohibiting certain classes of weapons: explosive and soft-jacketed bullets, asphyxiating gas, other chemical weapons, bacterial weapons, etc.

None of these rules became dead letters. Even those most frequently violated, such as provisions for the protection of cultural and historical monuments, have often been obeyed by belligerent forces at considerable cost to themselves. The best-enforced rules have been those providing for the interaction of armed forces. All of them are generally respected by modern governments, except for the requirement that hostilities be formally declared, which went out of style after 1945. With the exception of Germany in World War I, the major powers have been scrupulous about the rights of neutrals.

The prohibition of chemical and biological weapons was effective for many years but has recently begun to erode with the extensive use of gas by Iraq in the Gulf War, the building of production facilities by Libya and Syria, the step-up in U.S. production and research, and the breakdown of international consensus at the January 1989 Paris conference on a new comprehensive ban. At that conference Arab and third world delegates took the position that it is unfair to ask them to renounce chemical weapons while others (especially Israel) keep nuclear ones.

The background of the current effort to negotiate a comprehensive treaty ban on chemical and biological weapons (CBW) is confusing. The Reagan administration repeatedly called for CBW disarmament while reviving and greatly expanding U.S. CBW programs that had been dormant since the 1960s. The rationale, of course, was that the Soviet Union might be doing the same thing. As relations between Washington and Moscow warmed during Reagan's second term, the U.S.S.R. announced that it had halted chemical weapons production in 1987 and agreed to the long-standing U.S. demand for on-site inspection. But in the meantime, the U.S. buildup had acquired too much momentum to be checked[3] and the issue of inspection became unresolvable as it widened to include the 140 governments represented at the Paris conference.

These developments are the more regrettable because the earlier treaties, while less comprehensive, were scrupulously obeyed by nearly all belligerents after 1918. Of course, on the central front of the End Game, both sides have full stocks of chemical weapons and protective equipment. And with less fanfare, the United States and the Soviet Union are prepared to attack each other's military forces and civilian populations with CBW weapons of fearsome potential. The 1925 Geneva Protocol and the 1972 Biological Weapons Convention are understood to permit retaliatory use. They promise no first use rather than total abstention and are subject to many of the same problems as nuclear deterrence, especially the need to maintain parity by continued research and development, and the difficulty of knowing when parity has been achieved.

The bans on chemical and biological weapons have endured in limited form for other reasons than the prevention of needless suffering. Chemical and biological weapons are difficult to control. The attackers are exposed to nearly as much risk as the defenders, and protective measures disrupt the routine operations of a military force. If the decision is left to field commanders, agreements to abstain from the first use of these inconvenient weapons are self-enforcing. The possibility that nuclear explosives might eventually be added to the list of weapons whose use in war is prohibited by international agreement should not be lightly dismissed. Like poison gas, nuclear weapons make it almost impossible to fight a decent and well-ordered battle.

The least-respected rules of war have been those concerning the protection of enemy civilians and private property. Modern regular forces are never given formal permission to rape and pillage—a customary indulgence in earlier times—but some of them have practiced rape and pillage on a grand scale, as in the reciprocal occupations of the Germans and Russians during the Second World War, and in the colonial wars in North Africa and Southeast Asia. Throughout the world the people of occupied territories are subjected to compulsory relocation, unpaid requisitions, destruction of livestock and crops, forced labor, hostage-taking, judicial torture, and other barbarities.

The two rules of war that were repealed in effect during the Second World War were the immunity of undefended places from military attack and the requirement that the crews of merchant ships be placed in safety before the ships are sunk. The German violation of both these rules in 1940, by the destructive bombing of Rotterdam and Coventry and by their U-boat tactics, outraged public opinion in the Allied nations, which then adopted both procedures and practiced them on a vast scale in the bombing of such German cities as Cologne, Hamburg, and Dresden and in the Pacific theater, where Japanese merchant ships were sunk by American submarines without any concern for their crews. In the European theater, scores of undefended places were hit by British and American strategic bombing. In the final days of the Pacific war, nearly all of the Japanese cities were heavily damaged, including two undefended places called Hiroshima and Nagasaki.

On the record so far, changes in the rules of war do offer some promise of limiting the nuclear threat, since the rules have been conspicuously effective in shaping the conduct of armed forces toward each other. Soldiers have long recognized that it is to their collective advantage to have war played as a game under set rules, and to their individual advantage to treat prisoners of war and wounded enemies with consideration, in order to be sure of like treatment when fortunes are reversed. Indeed, it is not inconceivable that a rule prohibiting the use of nuclear weapons on the battlefield might eventually be enforceable. Soldiering is a profession, not a form of suicide. Despite the best efforts of staff and command schools, nobody has so far been able to visualize plausible battlefield tactics under nuclear fire.

A ban on the use of nuclear weapons in war, analogous to the earlier bans on chemical and bacterial weapons, would probably work in much the same way. It would be, in effect, an agreement on no first use and would depend as much on mutual deterrence as on good faith. By making the first use of nuclear weapons technically illegal, such an agreement would compel military strategists to plan for entirely nonnuclear wars and thereby reduce the probability that a conflict would go nuclear before other options had been explored. But such a rule would not accomplish very much unless the use of nuclear weapons against undefended places were prohibited also. The recent record is not encouraging with respect to the protection of civilians and their property from hostile armed forces, and even, on occasion, from friendly armed forces. They are tempting targets precisely because of their inability to resist. The element of reciprocity that underlies the courtesies of the battlefield is missing.

Moreover, many of the rules written for the protection of noncombatants were nullified by ambiguities, such as the proviso that "collateral damage" might be lawfully inflicted on civilian targets in the course of legitimate operations against military targets. Although the doctrine of strategic bombing developed by the German, British, and American air commands during World War II justified direct action against civilian populations as the way to break the enemy's will to resist,[4] it was customary to explain any particular raid as directed against military targets that happened to be located in urban areas. Since factories, refineries, power stations, railroad yards, warehouses, and government offices all qualify as military targets, very few urban places are entitled to immunity under this doctrine. Moscow alone is said to contain 150 military targets.

The contradiction between the contemporary view of what constitutes a legitimate target and the immunity claimed for undefended places remains unresolved. With respect to nuclear missiles, all cities are defenseless for the time being. A formula for changing the current scenarios of nuclear war might be found in a multilateral treaty among the nuclear states prohibiting the emplacement of nuclear missiles, control centers, or detection facilities within fifty miles of any urban area, and likewise prohibiting the targeting or firing of nuclear weapons against an urban area. If the movement toward restraining war by international agreement is ever to regain momentum, it will have to challenge the habit of mind that, since 1940, has regarded the casual massacre of an unarmed population by warplanes or missiles as a legitimate military action. In short, the moral basis of the rules of war would have to be restored and broadened.

Not many observers of contemporary world politics expect the rules of war to be humanized in the near future by moral progress. But around 1900, the leaders of opinion in Europe and America were confident that war itself would soon disappear from the annals of civilized nations along with other barbaric customs inherited from the past. Their belief in moral progress rested on substantial evidence. During the nineteenth century, slavery and the slave trade, human sacrifice, judicial torture, female infanticide, blood feuds, burning at the stake and breaking on the wheel, flogging and keel hauling, piracy, serfdom, child labor, imprisonment for debt, the castration of boy sopranos in Rome, the plundering of wrecks on the New England coast, and a host of other traditional brutalities had been effectively abolished.

War, too, had lost much of its former cruelty. The rules of war now prohibited the killing of enemy wounded, the enslavement of prisoners, the pillage of captured towns, the seizure of private property, impressment of recruits, and other indignities that had been visited on the less powerful players in the game of war since time immemorial. Indeed, war itself seemed to be going out of style. The wars and military excursions of the European powers between 1815 and 1900 were brief, decisive, and professional. The only large-scale wars of that period took place on the periphery of the international system—the American Civil War, the Lopez War in Paraguay, and the Taiping Rebellion in China—and each was exceptional in some way.

It was generally understood after the Hague Conference of 1899 that war would be gradually legislated out of existence. In the interim, war would be closely controlled to prevent excesses. There was nothing absurd about this program at the time. It assumed the continuation of an international system operated by half a dozen European powers (France, Britain, Germany, Austria-Hungary, Russia, perhaps Italy) and a score of peripheral powers including the smaller European nations, the United States, Turkey, and Japan. With insignificant exceptions, the remainder of the world was controlled directly or indirectly by these powers, which had a common set of military and diplomatic institutions. Turkey and Japan participated in the system by virtue of having adopted the same institutions during the nineteenth century. Nonpowers like China, India, and the Latin American states were incapable of resisting the armed forces of even a minor power. Acting in concert, the powers seemed easily capable of enforcing a decision to restrain, and eventually to abolish, international war.

The Concert of Europe had continued to perform the double task for which it was originally formed: to prevent the domination of Europe by a single power, and to prevent social revolutions modeled after 1789. The revolutions of 1830 and 1848, although they aroused much excitement, did not shake the foundations of the European order. The Paris Commune was quickly suppressed. The partition of Africa and Asia by the colonial powers was accomplished with few serious quarrels among them. Writing around 1910, that most astute observer Max Weber concluded that capitalist imperialism would persist for the predictable future.[5]

The moral progress registered in the Hague treaties, and the actual changes in the conduct of war reflected by those treaties, were regarded around the turn of the century as part of an irresistible trend toward the improvement of the human condition. In every one of the powers, even despotic states like Russia and backward states like Spain, the nineteenth century witnessed the extension of political rights to hitherto excluded groups, the disappearance of traditional forms of rough usage, the amelioration of working conditions, the softening of penalties for crime, the extension of state welfare programs, and the proliferation of educational, health, and social services. The powers claimed to have a civilizing mission in the foreign territories they controlled, and although there was a large element of hypocrisy in that claim, they did export many of the social improvements introduced at home to their colonies and protectorates. Radicals of that era believed as firmly in the inevitability of moral progress as conservatives did. Secure in their belief that capitalism was the sole cause of modern war, and confident that the replacement of capitalism by socialism was imminent, they took the disappearance of war for granted.

No one who studied social trends around 1900 seems to have foreseen that international war, instead of fading away, would rage unchecked in the new century and that it would make the idea of moral progress almost untenable. Even with the advantage of hindsight, it is hard to show that the interruption of moral progress in the early part of the twentieth century was inevitable. The First World War was not the result of any apparent necessity. It began with a series of accidents, garbled messages, and mislaid orders. The fighting was expected to be brief and decisive.

When a stalemate developed on the western front in the summer of 1914, with both armies impregnably entrenched, the high commands resorted to the strategy of mass infantry attacks against heavily defended lines, and the human cost soon mounted beyond any relation to the limited objectives for which the war had begun. The only reason to continue was the investment already made, a motive that became less and less rational as the losses mounted. According to U.S. War Department estimates, 65 million men were mobilized, of whom more than 8 million were dead by the end of the war and 29 million were wounded, prisoners, or missing. The casualty rates were far above those of previous European wars: 52 percent for the Allies, 67 percent for the Central Powers. The number of civilian casualties attributable to military action was also much larger than in any previous war.

The economic costs were correspondingly high but would be made up within a few years. The intangible costs were incalculable and have not yet been recouped. The spectacle of Europeans killing each other by the millions for no discernible purpose began to dispel the conviction of European superiority that had gripped the inhabitants of the other continents ever since the soldiers of Cortez, emerging from the jungle, were mistaken for Aztec gods. The confidence of Europeans in their own gods and rulers was so gravely undermined by the miseries of the war and its aftermath that they scarcely resisted the bizarre fanatics who seized control of some of the European states between the wars.

It is not farfetched to consider the wars of 1914–1918 and 1939–1945 as a single thirty years war, having two active phases separated by an uneasy truce.[6] The victors of the first round were unable to reestablish the Concert of Europe or to put effective peacekeeping arrangements in its place. The losers of the first round substituted new and more ruthless tyrants for the tyrants who had failed them and began to prepare seriously for the second round, while the victors were fatuously congratulating themselves for having abolished war. The second round was centered, like the first, in Europe, and the battles on the eastern and western fronts were refought over the same ground. But the peripheral powers, especially the United States and Japan, and the peripheral theaters, especially the Pacific, South Asia, and North Africa, were much more important in the second round. The settlement, too, was a partial reenactment. Once again, the victors were unable to put effective peacekeeping arrangements in place. But this time it was the victors rather than the losers who began to prepare seriously for another war.

The first phase having begun by accident, its objectives remained hazy to the end. Although the slogan of "making the world safe for democracy" was popular in the United States, it was not—except for a brief moment in 1919—widely accepted elsewhere; nor was it wholly appropriate for a war that originally pitted tsarist Russia against imperial Germany, and that included Japan and British India on the Allied side.

The second phase was quite different. Four of the major participants—Germany, the Soviet Union, Italy, Japan—had overt designs of foreign conquest. The war aims of Britain and France were straightforward—to block the German scheme of world domination ("Heute gehört uns Deutschland, morgen die ganze Welt"). The United States came to share this aim, but was more directly concerned with the Japanese plan to dominate the western Pacific (the Greater East Asia Co-Prosperity Sphere.) Meanwhile the Germans conceived themselves to be fighting against the long-standing Soviet plan to communize Europe and dominate the world. Thus, in the second phase the war became ideological, a struggle against absolute evil, a holy war. Holy wars are crueler than ordinary wars because the stakes are so high and because the extirpation of evil seems to require that the enemy be not only defeated but destroyed.

The first phase had been marked by serious moral lapses—violations of neutral rights, unrestricted submarine warfare, the needless shelling of cathedrals, the use of poison gas, and the occasional refusal of quarter. But these acts were recognized as moral infractions; the perpetrators pleaded tactical necessity or the right of reprisal. The second phase witnessed the wholesale abandonment of moral principles. Both sides sank ships without warning on a grand scale, refused quarter to surrendered enemies, bombed residential districts without mercy, pillaged their allies as well as their enemies, and demolished cultural treasures without scruple. The civilian populations of enemy territories occupied by the Germans and Russians were maltreated in every possible way, and even in friendly territories the armies of both sides were careless about civilian rights and civilian lives.

The deterioration of moral standards during the second phase was progressive. What seemed outrageous in 1940, like the bombing of Rotterdam after an ultimatum, became so commonplace by 1944 that not a single public figure in Britain or the United States objected audibly to the firebombing of Dresden or Tokyo. The massacre of children and the destruction of temples had become normal acts of war, and no longer called for excuse or explanation. It came to the point, eventually, that moral scruples were not invoked even to protect one's own people. Thus, the information that there were American prisoners of war in Nagasaki was not allowed to interfere with the designation of that place as a target for the second atomic bomb.[7] The full revelation at the close of the war of how the German government had organized the pitiless killing of millions of Jews and hundreds of thousands of other victims further discredited the idea of moral progress, and there has been no serious attempt to revive it since. In the light of twentieth-century events, the idea seems grotesque. Nevertheless, it must not be dismissed without reflection.

In sociological terms, moral acts are intentional acts that conform to the norms of a social group to which the actor belongs, or with which he identifies. Morality is an aspect of group membership. "The mores," in W. G. Sumner's famous phrase, "can make anything right and anything wrong." The ethnographic literature is full of wonderful examples. Among the Bedouin of Cyrenaica, according to E. L. Peters, if a man kills his father, the crime, being unthinkable, shows that the killer cannot possibly be the victim's son, and the killer's mother is punished for adultery. But underneath the fascinating peculiarities of tribal ethics, there seem to be a number of universal attitudes and behaviors: group loyalty, faithful performance of kin and community roles, observance of sexual prohibitions, promise-keeping, fear of gods and rulers, courage, generosity, protection of the weak, respect for tabus, fairness in fighting and exchange, congruence of public and private actions. At an even more basic level, the common elements in moral action are the voluntary performance of socially integrative actions, and voluntary abstention from disruptive actions.

The moral progress of the nineteenth century with respect to war meant, on the one hand, enlarging the sphere of moral action to include outsiders, enemies, and neutrals, and on the other hand, declaring states to have moral obligations to each other by virtue of belonging to a giant social group. "If the national spirit is truly human and social," wrote a pioneer American sociologist, "it should be capable of a moral development and of participating in a moral order similar to that which prevails in personal relations."[8] The idea of a social group that includes all of mankind is a very old one; what was new in the nineteenth century was an awareness that the ties connecting distant peoples were being multiplied by the diffusion of European culture and technology.

That process is still under way. While it may seem foolish to inquire about the possible resumption of moral progress after so much bestiality, the question cannot be evaded in any serious attempt to imagine peace. Social systems, large or small, are founded on moral consensus. Other elements—self-interest, habit, forceful constraint—help to integrate social systems, but the moral element is indispensable. The enactment of rules of war capable of protecting humanity from nuclear weapons implies the prior development of a moral consensus about what should and should not be done with nuclear technology. If the resumption of moral progress were impossible, there would be no way out of the present dilemma.[9] But there are several reasons to think it is not impossible:

• Most of the ideological fervor has gone out of the End Game. The goal of a world revolution achieved by the violent overthrow of capitalism is no longer realistic and the fear of one has diminished accordingly. The American Century is turning into the Japanese Century. The satellite populations of Eastern Europe are indifferent Marxists, and the Socialist statesmen of Western Europe are not readily distinguishable from their conservative colleagues.

• Social equalization, a worldwide trend that had already been running for several hundred years when Alexis de Tocqueville took note of it 150 years ago, continues without abatement. As political, economic, and social inequalities between men and women, rich and poor, elite and masses, white and black, native and foreign, diminish in the developed countries, the members of these categories are brought more and more into the sphere of a common morality, as both agents and subjects.

• In matters unconnected with the rules of war, there has been discernible moral progress in recent years. The relief of famine, epidemics, and natural disasters like earthquakes has become accepted as a moral obligation that transcends national boundaries. The definition of individual rights has been perceptibly broadened in the Soviet Union and in Eastern Europe, as well as in the United States and in Western Europe. Important projects of cultural preservation have been accomplished with international support. The protection of refugees and displaced children is a recognized international obligation. The matter of endangered species and habitats has become a global issue. In the United States and Western Europe, extreme moral sensitivity with respect to such matters as animal rights and discrimination against homosexuals seems, in some obscure way, to be connected to a lack of moral sensitivity about the End Game. In any case, moral judgments and responses have not gone out of style anywhere.

• The political slogans of the world reflect a moral consensus—more honored in the breach than in the observance, but still a consensus. Almost without exception, tyrannical regimes claim to be democratic, and bellicose powers proclaim their devotion to peace. The glorification of war, once a central political theme, has disappeared from the lexicon of advanced societies. Straws in the wind, of course. But enough to cast doubt on the proposition that evil must inevitably triumph over good in the next round.

The most concrete expression of these moral impulses within the context of the End Game has been the effort of the superpowers in the past two decades to restrain the nuclear arms race by mutual agreement. Unlike the other rules of war, arms control is a relatively new concept. The disarming of the vanquished by the victors is as old as warfare, but the first serious attempts by governments engaged in an arms race to negotiate limits on their armaments occurred just before the turn of the century. It was Tsar Nicholas II who set the ball rolling when he called the first Hague Conference in 1899 to negotiate the general disarmament of the European powers. Finding that difficult, the Conference turned to other matters, and the project of disarmament was not seriously renewed until it appeared as one of Wilson's Fourteen Points, which called for the reduction of armaments "to the lowest point consistent with national safety." This Point was eventually embodied in Article 8 of the Covenant of the League of Nations, which read in part:

1. The Members of the League recognize that the maintenance of peace requires the reduction of national armaments to the lowest points consistent with national safety and the enforcement by common action of international obligations.

2. The Council, taking account of the geographical situation and circumstances of each State, shall formulate plans for such reduction for the consideration and action of the several Governments.

3. Such plans shall be subject to reconsideration and revision at least every ten years.

4. After these plans shall have been adopted by the several Governments, the limits of armaments therein fixed shall not be exceeded without the concurrence of the Council.

Thus, the reduction of armaments was linked to "the enforcement by common action of international obligations," which in this context was understood to mean common military action. For fifteen years, from the appointment of the Permanent Armaments Commission in 1919 to the adjournment of the World Disarmament Conference in 1934, the founding states of the League sought but did not find a formula for connecting disarmament and security. France, with the largest army, refused to disarm without firm guarantees of military support from Britain and the United States in case of a renewed conflict with Germany. The British and American governments, strongly supported by public opinion in each country, were opposed to any arrangement that might automatically involve them in hostilities. Britain would not go further than the Locarno agreement of 1925, which guaranteed only one of France's borders against only "flagrant" aggression, and the United States was never willing to go that far.

Meanwhile, the Germans had returned to the game. Clemenceau's reply to the German delegation's objections to the peace terms presented to them in June 1919 included the following fateful remarks:

The Allied and Associated Powers wish to make it clear that their requirements in regard to German armaments were not made solely with the object of rendering it impossible for Germany to resume her policy of military aggression. They are also the first steps towards the general reduction and limitation of armaments which they seek to bring about.[10]

The failure of the Allies to carry out the general reduction and limitation of armaments projected at Versailles was naturally used by the Germans to justify their step-by-step repudiation of the military clauses of the Versailles treaty and the vast rearmament program they undertook after Hitler's accession to power in 1933.

We need not here go into the details of the interminable reports, arguments, and empty compromises that marked the League's long struggle with disarmament and culminated in the World Disarmament Conference at Geneva in 1932. Fifty-nine governments were represented. All sorts of interesting propositions were put before the conference. France proposed to internationalize all aircraft. Britain and America demanded the abolition of submarines. The Soviet delegate, Maxim Litvinov, pressed for total disarmament. No one was very serious, and nothing came of it all.

Article 8 of the League Covenant envisaged the Council as an autonomous body, which, having reviewed the distribution of military capabilities in the world, would prepare and carry out a plan to reduce them. But, as might have been anticipated from the constitutional structure of the League, the Council was never more than a forum for traditional diplomatic negotiations, and not even the most important forum. The disarmament agreements of that era were reached elsewhere.

In 1921, some of the Republican senators who had blocked American membership in the League came forward with a "liberal and constructive" proposal for a 50 percent reduction in the naval appropriations of the allies. The idea, at least in part, was to undercut the League, and the Harding administration was persuaded in August 1921 to invite Great Britain, France, Italy, and the United States to what became the Washington Naval Conference, "to discuss limitation of armaments and other problems which have arisen in the Pacific area." That Conference unexpectedly produced results. It fixed ratios of 5/5/3/1.67/1.67 for the capital ships of Great Britain, the United States, Japan, France, and Italy; agreed on a ten-year holiday in the construction of capital ships; set limits on the size of battleships and the caliber of their guns; and restricted the development of new naval bases. As in the SALT I agreement fifty years later, the parties did not agree to end their arms race, but did agree to conduct it according to strict rules. As with SALT I, the rules of the race were no sooner defined than attention turned to circumventing them. After the Washington Conference settled the relative strength of the powers in battleships, naval competition shifted to the unrestricted construction of cruisers, destroyers, and submarines. The net effect, as with SALT I, was a rapid buildup of offensive capabilities.

The naval conferences continued. At Geneva in 1927, the principal controversy was between the United States, which wanted to extend the capital ship ratios to cruisers, and Britain, which was unwilling to do so. When no agreement was reached, the cruiser race intensified. At the London Naval Conference of 1930, the holiday in the construction of battleships was extended for another five years, and the tonnage of cruisers was restricted to prevent them from becoming as large as battleships. But the rules of the game were beginning to unravel. France and Italy refused to accept the same ratios as before, and the new treaty had an "escalator clause" that generously allowed any signatory to exceed the agreed limits if its security appeared to be threatened by an outside power—a delicate reference to the German naval buildup already under way.

The last of the naval disarmament conferences, in 1935, broke up in disarray after France, Italy, and Japan objected en bloc to the existing ratios. The representatives of Japan and Italy walked out, and the three remaining powers adjourned after adopting an escape clause that allowed them to release themselves from any of their prior agreements. That marked the end of naval disarmament for the time being, and all the parties set about building as much naval tonnage as they could afford. In 1935, with the Japanese preparing to challenge the United States in the Pacific, it made no sense for them to accept inferiority in the ratio of 5/3. Italy was close to war with Britain in the Mediterranean; 5/1.67 no longer seemed attractive. The French, watching the Germans lay down pocket battleships of ingenious design, had good reason to build new capital ships.

At San Francisco in 1944, they began all over again, with Article 26 of the United Nations Charter:

In order to promote the establishment and maintenance of international peace and security with the least diversion for armaments of the world's human and economic resources, the Security Council shall be responsible for formulating, with the assistance of the Military Staff Committee referred to in Article 47, plans to be submitted to the Members of the United Nations for the establishment of a system for the regulation of armaments.

The initial effort to put Article 26 into effect began auspiciously in December 1945 when the American, British, and Soviet foreign ministers met in Moscow and drafted a resolution—unanimously passed at the first session of the United Nations Assembly—that called for a commission to make proposals "for the elimination from national armaments of atomic weapons and all other major weapons adaptable to mass destruction." It was to that commission that Bernard Baruch, the U.S. representative, presented an offer six months later. The Baruch (more properly the Acheson-Lilienthal) Plan proposed the creation of an International Atomic Development Authority, which would have managerial control of atomic weapons activity, the power to inspect and license all other atomic activities, and the duty of fostering the beneficial uses of atomic energy. The Authority would control uranium and thorium in the ground and all stockpiles of those materials, would have rights of access and inspection everywhere, and jurisdiction over atomic offenders.

To the American public, it seemed a fair and generous offer. To the Soviet government, it was a Machiavellian plot to perpetuate the American monopoly of atomic weapons through a proxy. The Soviet suspicions focused on two clauses of the Plan: the United States would surrender its atomic monopoly to the Authority on a schedule of its own choosing, and the Authority's inspectors would have unlimited access to Soviet installations. The differences between the U.S. and the Soviet Union on other issues having deepened during 1946, the Truman administration was not disposed to compromise. By the spring of 1947, the Baruch Plan was dead and buried.

Another attempt to negotiate disarmament under UN auspices was made in 1961, when the McCloy-Zorin report submitted to the Sixteenth General Assembly[11] expressed the agreement of the United States and the Soviet Union on a set of agreed principles for the guidance of disarmament negotiations. The McCloy-Zorin principles called for a "programme of general and complete disarmament" with the following modest provisions:

1. Disbanding of armed forces; dismantling of military establishments, including bases; cessation of the production of armaments as well as their liquidation or conversion to peaceful use.

2. Elimination of all stockpiles of nuclear, chemical, bacteriological, and other weapons of mass destruction and cessation of the production of such weapons.

3. Elimination of all means of delivery of weapons of mass destruction.

4. Abolishment of the organization and institutions designed to organize the military effort of States, cessation of military training, and closing of all military training institutions.

5. Discontinuance of military expenditures.

Whether the authors of this document were at all serious about it is impossible to determine. On the same day their report was submitted, they exchanged angry notes over the issue of verification, described by McCloy as a "key element in the United States position" and by Zorin as "legalized espionage." The rhetorical exercise ended there, along with the effort to implement Article 26, although further ritual gestures have been made from time to time. For example, at the close of the Helsinki conference on Security and Cooperation in 1975, the high contracting parties, including the Soviet Union and the United States, as well as Malta, Monaco, and San Marino, proclaimed themselves to be committed to "the ultimate achievement of general and complete disarmament under strict and effective international control." The ritual phrase "general and complete disarmament," often abbreviated to GCD, is chanted rather than spoken, and has no reference to the real world.

Like the naval agreements of the 1920s and the 1930s, the nuclear arms control agreements of the 1970s and 1980s have been negotiated outside of the world organization, and are designed to regulate the ongoing arms race, not to end it. Indeed, the parallels are inescapable. The SALT I agreement of 1972 fixed for five years the number of intercontinental ballistic missiles each superpower might deploy but did not set limits on submarine-launched, bomber-launched, or short-range missiles. Just as under the Washington Naval Treaty of 1921, there was a massive realignment of effort on both sides to take maximum advantage of the loopholes in SALT I. The SALT II agreement of 1978, unratified but generally observed until 1987, fixed the number of delivery vehicles for long-range missiles. The immediate result was MIRVing, (the development of Multiple Independent Reentry Vehicles) to increase the number of warheads, and the accelerated development of intermediate-range missiles on mobile launchers. The 1987 U.S.–Soviet agreement to scrap intermediate-range nuclear missiles immediately accelerated the development of enhanced capabilities for short-range missiles, although the promise of subsequent reductions in intercontinental missiles and the provisions for on-site verification did encourage hopes for a new era in arms control.

The regulation of an arms race by treaty has obvious advantages for both parties. It allows them to halt the construction of obsolescent weapons in order to concentrate on more advanced weapons. It requires them to exchange information about their existing arsenals, which they would otherwise have tried to keep secret, and the improved information facilitates strategical planning on both sides. Under an arms control agreement, the difficult task of planning for all possible contingencies is replaced by the simpler and more elegant task of achieving strategical superiority under fixed rules.

The major defects of such agreements are that they preclude any slowing of an arms race, and that they self-destruct as soon as one party manages to do what all of them are trying to do and achieves strategical superiority under the rules, or is thought to be doing so. When that happens, the disadvantaged party repudiates the rules. There seems to be no way of disabling the mechanism. The ultimate objective of the parties to an arms race—to achieve military dominance—is not abandoned when they agree to accept parity for the time being. In any event, parity is too unstable a condition to endure indefinitely.

The question whether arms control agreements like the naval treaties of the interwar period or the more recent ABM and SALT agreements reduce the probability of war is difficult, perhaps impossible, to answer.[12] At the outset, they seem to have a pacifying effect, but the inevitable violation of the rules by one side or the other creates dangers that otherwise might not have arisen.

The only arms control agreements that seem to point toward an ultimate resolution of the nuclear predicaments are the Non-Proliferation Treaty of 1968 and the Intermediate Nuclear Forces Treaty of 1987. The NPT distinguishes between nuclear weapon states—those that manufactured or exploded nuclear devices before 1967—and all others. At the time it was drafted, the NPT was a joint effort of the superpowers to discourage the development of nuclear weapons by other states, in return for a joint promise by the U.S. and the U.S.S.R. to reduce their nuclear arsenals. The promise was not kept and the proliferation of nuclear weapons proceeded apace; those states wishing to develop them merely refused to ratify the treaty. Perhaps the most important consequence of the NPT was that it gave the Soviet Union a legal basis for preventing the acquisition of nuclear capabilities by its Warsaw Pact satellites, and gave the United States a similar but less effective means of discouraging nuclear ambitions in Latin America. In the bleak world of arms control, where there are not many good intentions to begin with, and the failure of good intentions is taken for granted, the non-proliferation regime is often counted as a success, although the number of states with nuclear capabilities has tripled since the treaty was adopted.

The NPT contains the germ of a promising idea—that the superpowers might jointly use their otherwise futile nuclear strength to impose nuclear restraint on all other states. Through the International Atomic Energy Agency, they are able to inhibit the transfer of nuclear weapons materials and technology from nuclear to nonnuclear states. The Agency's controls are not foolproof and are frequently evaded, but they have so far been sufficient to prevent the development of a black market in which rogue states and terrorist gangs could buy nuclear weapons.

In the real world, the maintenance of order is inseparable from armed force and will remain so for the foreseeable future. If an international authority ever comes to exercise strict and effective control over armaments, it will have to be quite heavily armed to maintain order and discourage rebellion. Since nuclear technology is not likely to be forgotten, that future authority will have to protect itself against the possibility of a rebellion equipped with nuclear weapons. General and complete disarmament is a chimera without substance, but the disarmament of small states by large states is the classic form of peacekeeping, and the non-proliferation regime is a faltering step in that direction.

The innovative feature of the INF Treaty of 1987 was that it called for the removal of an entire class of nuclear missiles from their deployed positions, their physical destruction in the presence of inspectors from the other side, and the inactivation of manufacturing facilities, also subject to on-site verification. The agreement had more political than strategic significance, and the missiles taken out of play represented fewer than 3 percent of existing nuclear warheads, but the actual accomplishment of a disarmament measure, after decades of meaningless resolutions on the subject, may have been an historic turning point.

Chapter 5

The Peace Game Called the Grand Design

The Abbé de St. Pierre has sent me a fine book about how to restore peace in Europe and preserve it forever. All that it would take to make it work would be the consent of Europe and other such trifles.
Frederick the Great

One way of preventing international wars might be to organize a league of sovereign powers who agreed in advance that disputes arising among them would be settled peacefully. The idea is not very new. It has been around for nearly seven hundred years. In 1306 a lawyer named Pierre Dubois proposed to Philip the Fair of France that he undertake the formation of a peacekeeping council of Christian princes. The council would arbitrate quarrels among its members, and impose settlements by force if necessary.

Dubois's objections to the wars of his time were not humanitarian but political. After two centuries of intermittent triumph and defeat, the Crusaders had just been driven out of their last strongholds in the eastern Mediterranean. The effort to reunite the divided halves of the Christian world, while initially successful, eventually failed because the Crusaders were more eager to fight each other than to maintain a common front against the Saracens. It seemed plain to Dubois that the thirteenth-century wars of the Christian princes had been highly unprofitable, wasting their wealth and undermining their authority. And it did not escape him that the proposed council would strengthen his king's hand against the pope and the emperor.

A better-known fourteenth-century figure saw the same problem and suggested another solution. In the unfinished *Convivio*, written in the same year of 1306, and the slightly later treatise *De*

Monarchia, the great Dante Alighieri argued that war should be suppressed by a new Roman emperor. He affirmed that God had ordained humanity for temporal felicity, under the authority of the emperor, and for eternal felicity, under the authority of the pope. Dante attributed the wars of his time to the weakness of the temporal authority.

The next notable work in this tradition, the universal peace plan of King George of Bohemia, was drafted in 1461 by a roving French promotor named Antonius Marini, who had found his way to the court of the elected Hussite king in Prague. The project was essentially the same as that of Dubois—a league of Christian princes who would arbitrate their disputes in order to maintain a common front against the infidels. The hidden agenda was the same also—to undermine the pope and the emperor. A draft treaty to establish the league was circulated for the approval of European princes and was actually signed by the kings of Poland and Hungary, but the project fell through when Louis XI of France balked at the exclusion of the pope and the emperor from the proposed league.

The draft treaty, long unavailable, was published in Prague on its five hundredth anniversary in 1964. The organization was to include a council of princes, an assembly of permanent delegates who moved to a different capital every five years, a permanent court of justice, and even a secretariat. Membership was to be open to all Christian princes. The assembly was charged to establish a new body of international law: "new laws drawn from the heart of nature must be introduced and new evils must be opposed by new remedies." The assembly would vote by regional groups, to avoid disparities in representation. The league would be supported by a specified percentage of the taxes collected by its members, with specified increases in wartime. Disputes between a member and an outside power were to be settled by mediation, "even if the attacked companion does not so request." The army would be centrally administered and paid in the coinage of the league.

The project of a league of Christian princes remained alive throughout the war-torn sixteenth century. In 1513, the monarchs of Europe were invited to a congress in Burgundy for the purpose of founding a league. In 1518, Cardinal Wolsey secured the actual ratification by England, France, Spain, and Rome of a treaty whose signatories promised to keep the peace among themselves and a common front against the Turks. It was a much weaker league than King George's, with no central organization and no army, and it fell apart very soon.

The project reappeared at the end of the sixteenth century as the Grand Design of Henri IV of France. The only first-hand account of the Grand Design is found in the memoirs of Henri's chief minister, Maximilien de Béthune, duc de Sully, who credited Elizabeth of England with originating the plan, and claimed to have met with her at Dover in 1601 to discuss the details. Modern scholars lean to the opinion that Sully invented the whole episode after the two principals were dead, but, like much else about the Grand Design, that finding is debatable.

The ulterior motive was to reduce the power of the Hapsburgs by depriving them of all their European possessions except Spain. After various redistributions of territory, Europe would consist of fifteen powers: the hereditary monarchies of France, Spain, England, Denmark, and Sweden; the emperor and the pope; the elected kings of Poland, Hungary, and Bohemia; and the republics of Venice, Italy, Switzerland, and Flanders. There would be a supreme general council, and a number of regional councils, controlling a common European army more than 300,000 strong. An interesting feature of the scheme was that religious wars would be discouraged by encouraging the Protestant subjects of Catholic sovereigns, and the Catholic subjects of Protestant sovereigns, to emigrate.

Those who credit Sully with the sole authorship of the Grand Design suspect that he may have borrowed some of its details from the *Nouveau Cynée* of Eméric Crucé, an author about whom nothing whatever is known except for his one book, published at Paris in 1623. Crucé had lots of ideas, all mixed up together—a canal from the Caspian Sea to the Mediterranean, bribing the Barbary pirates to take up agriculture, abolishing the study of theology (too difficult) and jurisprudence (lawsuits should be settled by common sense). He made short work of the problem of establishing a league of princes. "To come to an agreement, one needs only a good idea that will touch the hearts of rulers." A council of ambassadors would sit permanently at Venice and settle out of hand any international disputes that happened to arise. The only serious problem was how to determine the precedence of the ambassadors, and Crucé gave more attention to that question than to anything else. His preferred order of precedence put the pope first and the Turkish emperor—of all people—second, followed by the German emperor, the kings of France, Spain, and Persia, the procope of Tartary, the king of China, the duke of Muscovy, the kings of Great Britain, Poland, Denmark, Sweden, Japan, and Morocco, and the Great Mogul. This was to be a global, not a European, league.

Many other proposals along the same lines appeared during the seventeenth century. One of the best known was the work of William Penn, the founder of Pennsylvania. In 1693, he published "An Essay Towards the Present and Future Peace of Europe by the Establishment of an European Diet, Parliament, or Estates." There was not much new in Penn's version of the league of princes, but it had an air of reasonableness. For example, the problem of precedence was neatly resolved by having the European Diet meet in a round room with many doors. This league would not have an army of its own but would use the armed forces of its members against a recalcitrant state. Penn modestly ascribed the whole project to Henri IV. "So that to conclude, I have very little to answer for in all this affair; because if it succeed I have so little to deserve. For the great King's [Henri IV] example tells us it is fit to be done, and Sir William Temple's history [of the United Provinces] shows by a surpassing instance that it may be done; and Europe, by her incomparable miseries, makes it now necessary to be done." One new element in Penn's tract is the analogy he draws between the social compact whereby individuals yield their unchecked autonomy to government in return for peace and protection, and the proposed compact whereby princes would do the same. Some twenty years later, there appeared at Utrecht the first edition of the Abbé de St. Pierre's Project of Perpetual Peace.[1] Charles Irenée Castel de St. Pierre (1658–1743) was the first European to make social invention a lifelong career. In addition to this project, he devised ingenious plans for improving poor relief, elementary education, criminal justice, and the care of orphans, as well as schemes for progressive taxation, the regulation of highway traffic, the use of public lands, and military reform.

The years of St. Pierre's youth were marked by a series of destructive wars begun by Louis XIV for personal or dynastic advantage, and continued by his adversaries for no better reasons: the War of Devolution, the Dutch Wars, the War of the League of Augsburg, the long War of the Spanish Succession. These wars caused great misery and destruction without achieving anything to speak of. It was a period in which every oscillation in the balance of power was likely to provoke a war. St. Pierre did not underestimate the difficulty of reforming the system, but it seemed to him to be so unprofitable for the participating sovereigns that they might be induced to try a rational alternative.

St. Pierre took the old idea of a peacekeeping league of princes and gave it what still appears to be an improved constitution. Modern thought on the subject has not advanced much beyond him. He envisaged a permanent league of western European powers (the Italian city republics, the pope, the kings of France, Spain, England, Austria, Holland, Sweden, and Poland). They would combine voluntarily, but as soon as the majority had joined, the others would be coerced to do so. The league would be indissoluble and heavily armed. Members would be taxed according to their resources, but would send equal contingents to the common army. The league would have ambassadors at the court of each member, and officials in every sizable province to detect warlike preparations and other breaches of the peace. Its own courts would adjudicate commercial disputes. Its council would have the power to enact laws, levy taxes, regulate markets, and set trade standards. Disputes between members would be settled by arbitration, and the settlement would be imposed by force if necessary.

St. Pierre's league differed from those that had been proposed earlier in two important ways: (1) the league would guarantee the boundaries and the form of government of each member state; and (2) the authority of the league would be exercised over individuals as well as governments.

St. Pierre was the first of the peace writers to understand that international war is inextricably connected to civil war and to revolution. Governments maintain armed forces not only to protect themselves against foreign enemies but also—and often principally—to uphold their domestic authority. The earlier versions of the Grand Design (and some later ones too) proposed to limit sovereignty without giving sovereigns anything in return. St. Pierre believed that a plan for reducing the war-making power of sovereigns might be accepted if it protected them from both foreign and domestic enemies better than they could protect themselves. He also understood that if the laws of a league applied only to member states, they would be enforceable only by military action, whereas if they applied to individual officials, they could be enforced by judicial process, and that only the latter arrangement was potentially stable.

Thus, after four hundred years of intellectual fumbling, the idea of a league of princes to keep the peace became—on paper—a feasible project. That is to say, if it were ever formed, it might well endure and accomplish its purposes. But there was no reason to hope that it *would* be formed. That dilemma haunted St. Pierre's principal commentator, Jean-Jacques Rousseau. They met in 1741, when Rousseau was twenty-nine and St. Pierre eighty-three, and impressed each other favorably. After the Abbé's death, Rousseau applied to the St. Pierre family for the job of editing his papers. He spent most of two years writing commentaries on the Project of Perpetual Peace and some other pieces. The family did not get their money's worth—if indeed any money changed hands. The bulk of the papers remained unedited, and Rousseau's commentaries were not published until many years later, in 1782, when he too was dead.

Yet that posthumous work was extremely influential. St. Pierre was, to put it gently, a mediocre writer. Rousseau was one of the best. Under his hand, the three thick volumes of the Project were distilled into twenty-three eloquent pages,[2] including an historical introduction that covers war and peace in the ancient world, the role of Christianity in the emergence of modern Europe, the factors that made Europe a single society, and those that insured perpetual discord within that society.

In his *Critique of Perpetual Peace*, Rousseau wrestles with a contradiction. The advantages of the Project for princes, for their subjects, for all of Europe, are incontestable. If the European republic could be established for a single day, it might last forever. But the same princes who would defend it with all their power if it existed would fight desperately to keep it away. The real purposes of kings and their ministers, says Rousseau, are always the same: to increase their power inside and outside their realms. The true interest of princes lies in the success of their political, military, and fiscal projects. The happiness and prosperity of their subjects concern them only as means to their own aggrandizement. But the aim of the Project is to limit the power of princes, not only abroad but at home. Princes cannot be guaranteed against the revolts of their subjects, Rousseau observes, unless the subjects are at the same time protected from the tyranny of their princes.

While a prince is likely to reject perpetual peace for the sake of his own interests, his ministers are certain to do it. Their interests are equally opposed to those of the people and those of the prince. They count on war to gratify their ambitions, increase their fortunes, promote their favorites, and forward their intrigues.

St. Pierre, writes Rousseau, was very good at visualizing new institutions but reasoned like a child about getting them accepted. Anticipating the sociological theory of Vilfredo Pareto, Rousseau observed that "St. Pierre seemed not to know that princes, like all other men, are led to action only by their passions, and that they use reason only to justify the stupidities their passions make them perform."[3]

Toward the end of the eighteenth century, the Grand Design took a long step forward, and another long step backward. The forward step was the appearance in 1787 of Numbers 15 to 20 of the Federalist papers, in which Alexander Hamilton and James Madison defended with great eloquence and erudition the theory of federation embodied in the new Constitution of the United States. The backward step was the publication in 1792 of Immanuel Kant's influential essay *Zum Ewigen Frieden* (On Perpetual Peace), which muddled the problem so authoritatively that the effect lingers to this day. In both these essays the league of princes so long and patiently proposed to the rulers of Europe has become a league of nations, preferably republican.

Madison collaborated with Hamilton on numbers 18, 19, and

20 of the Federalist papers. Number 18 reviews in detail the experience of "the confederacies of antiquity," the Amphictyonic council and the Achaean league. Number 19 examines the early Germanic empire, the kingdom of Poland, and the union of the Swiss cantons; Number 20, the United Provinces of the Netherlands. The object was to illustrate by example the argument of the preceding papers—that for a federation to be durable and effective, its authority must extend beyond the member states to individual citizens. As Hamilton put it in Number 16:

Even in those confederacies which have been composed of members smaller than many of our countries, the principle of legislation for sovereign States, supported by military coercion, has never been found effectual. It has rarely attempted to be employed, but against the weaker members; and in most instances attempts to coerce the refractory and disobedient have been the signals of bloody wars in which one half of the confederacy has displayed its banners against the other half.

. . . a federal government capable of regulating the common concerns and preserving the general tranquillity . . . must carry its agency to the persons of the citizens. It must stand in need of no intermediate legislation; but must itself be empowered to employ the arm of the ordinary magistrate to exercise its own resolutions.

Their arguments prevailed in the constitutional convention, and the new constitution that came into effect in 1789 established a federal government whose authorities spoke directly to individual citizens. It also embodied the other critical element of the Abbé de St. Pierre's Project—a guarantee of the boundaries and governments of member states:

Article 4, Section 3, Clause 1: New states may be admitted by the Congress into this Union, but no new state shall be formed or erected within the jurisdiction of any other state, nor any state be formed by the junction of two or more states, without the consent of the legislatures concerned as well as of the Congress.

Article 4, Section 4. The United States shall guarantee to every state in the Union a republican form of government, and shall protect each of them against invasion; and on application of the legislature, or of the executive (when the legislature cannot be convened), against domestic violence.

Can the United States of America itself be considered a successful league of nations? Does it demonstrate the validity of the St.

Pierrian formula? These are not easy questions. When the U.S. Constitution was drafted, the thirteen American colonies had been independent for only a few years, and had been united under a common government, although a weak one, for all of that time. Although they were separate and sovereign in theory, there were no divisions among them comparable to the deeply rooted differences of culture and polity among the European nations. They had emerged from the Revolution with nearly uniform political forms and nearly uniform property laws, with the significant exception of slavery. The boundaries between states were mutually acceptable. Their quarrels were trivial, and they spoke a common language.

Despite all these advantages, the American league did not establish perpetual peace. The founders skirted the issue of perpetuity and failed to stipulate, as St. Pierre would have done, that the decision to join was irrevocable. And they were not able to resolve peacefully their one important difference—that some states were attached to the peculiar institution of Negro slavery and other states opposed it. Within three generations, these unresolved issues split the league and provoked a great war.

Against the view of the United States as a successful league of nations, it may also be argued that the independence and sovereignty of the member states has been gradually eroded, and that federal authority has steadily expanded, so that today the several states are hardly more than administrative districts and their sovereignty is a legal fiction. Whether that development constitutes success or failure depends on the value assigned to local autonomy. As regards perpetual peace, the American league eventually achieved that object. War between states is now unthinkable; the state patriotism of Hoosiers or Texans is mostly in fun.

Rousseau would certainly have regarded the merging of small sovereignties into big ones as an improvement, inasmuch as he blamed the miseries of the European social system on its political fragmentation. But Kant showed the world how to avoid the choice between local and cosmopolitan, particular and universal, by simply demanding both. Like several of his predecessors, Kant put his ideas in the form of a draft treaty, with explanatory remarks. The treaty contains six "preliminary" articles:

• No treaty of peace shall be regarded as valid, if made with the secret reservation of material for a future war.

• No state, great or small, having an independent existence shall be acquired by another through inheritance, exchange, purchase, or donation.

• Standing armies shall be abolished in the course of time.

• No national debt shall be contracted in connection with the external affairs of the state.

• No state shall violently interfere with the constitution and administration of another.

• No state at war with another shall countenance such modes of hostility as would make mutual confidence impossible in a subsequent state of peace.

And three "definitive" articles:

• The civil constitution of each state shall be republican.

• The law of nations shall be founded on a federation of states.

• The rights of men, as citizens of the world, shall be limited to the conditions of universal hospitality.

Each of these articles was derived from one or more ethical propositions advanced as self-evident. A treaty of peace should not be made with mental reservations, because that would be "beneath the dignity of a ruler." No state should be acquired by another, because "a state is not property." Standing armies should eventually be abolished, because "the practice of hiring men to kill or be killed seems to imply a use of them as mere machines."

From Pierre Dubois and King George of Bohemia to the Abbé de St. Pierre and Alexander Hamilton, peacekeeping had been approached as a problem in social mechanics—to design political arrangements capable of preventing wars, or certain kinds of wars. For Kant, perpetual peace was a problem in ethical philosophy— to discover the moral principles that ought to govern the conduct of national governments toward each other.

At the close of the Napoleonic era, with the idea of perpetual peace very much in the air, the victorious allies flirted with the possibility of establishing an armed and autonomous league of nations, but eventually settled for a league that relied for peacekeeping upon the high moral principles of its member states. The choice between a St. Pierrian league and a Kantian league was first made at the Congress of Vienna in 1814–1815, but it was renewed at intervals throughout the nineteenth century. After the First World War the possibility of a St. Pierrian league presented itself to another set of victorious allies at the Congress of Versailles, and was again rejected. And then it happened once again, at the San Francisco Conference of 1945, when a third set of victorious allies preferred the Kantian formula and created still another peacekeeping league without adequate peacekeeping machinery. These enormous peace games were important enough to review in detail.

The league of nations that reorganized Europe at the end of the Napoleonic wars had no executive and no judiciary. It acted through international congresses held at frequent intervals— Chaumont in 1814, Vienna in 1814–1815, Aix-la-Chapelle in 1818, Frankfurt in 1819, Troppau and Laibach in 1820–1821, Verona in 1822—before it dissolved over the issues raised by the revolt of the Spanish colonies in Latin America and the promulgation of the Monroe Doctrine.

The chronology of this league, sometimes called the Confederation of Europe, is complicated. The Quadruple Alliance of Russia, Austria, Prussia, and Great Britain, which accomplished the defeat of Napoleon and staged the Congress of Vienna, was formed earlier. The Holy Alliance, originally synonymous with the Confederation, outlasted it by many years, but changed its purposes from the preservation of peace to the suppression of liberalism.

The central event in the history of the Confederation was the Congress of Vienna, which met from October 1814 to June 1815. At the invitation of the emperor of Austria, Francis I, all the sovereigns of Europe—215 from Germany alone—came or sent representatives. They brought enormous retinues and attracted hordes of adventurers, lobbyists, bankers, courtesans, artists, dressmakers, and secret agents. A hundred thousand people crowded into Vienna, increasing its population by a third.

The imagination of all Europe had been struck by the idea of a congress to regulate affairs. It was seen as a constituent body which would be guided by the highest principles of equity and justice. The dispossessed princes whose territories had been obliterated by Napoleon looked forward to having their stolen rights restored; the governments of the small states that still existed hoped they would be given long coveted cities and counties. The people, as a whole, however, expected more than the mere settlement of frontier questions. They felt in an ill-defined way that means must be found to prevent the recurrence of the horrors of the last twenty years.[4]

The Congress never sat as a body except to ratify its Final Act and adjourn. But the delegates worked hard in committees and caucuses. They played hard too. There were masked balls for ten thousand guests, banquets for hundreds, gigantic picnics and hunts, all-night operas and concerts, and innumerable parties. Women had great influence. Most of the principal statesmen at the Congress were involved in a network of amorous and political intrigues, recorded for posterity by an army of Austrian spies.

Shortly before the Congress opened, Napoleon was forced to abdicate and was sent into luxurious exile on the island of Elba. Allied troops occupied Paris. Tsar Alexander I made triumphant tours of England and France. With 600,000 troops in Europe, he was clearly the dominant figure of the victorious coalition. Alexander at this time was both a passionate liberal and a triumphant despot. His plans for the reorganization of Europe had been stated ten years earlier in a long communication to William Pitt. They have an uncanny resemblance to Woodrow Wilson's Fourteen Points.

"Nothing would prevent, at the conclusion of peace, a treaty being arranged, which would become the basis of the reciprocal relations of the European states. It is no question of realizing the dream of perpetual peace, but one could attain at least to some of its results if, at the conclusion of the general war, one could establish on clear, precise principles the prescriptions of the rights of nations. Why could not one submit to it the positive rights of nations, assure the privilege of neutrality, insert the obligation of never beginning war until all the resources which the mediation of a third party could offer have been exhausted. . . . On principles such as these one could proceed to a general pacification and give birth to a league, of which the stipulations would form, so to speak, a new code of the law of nations, which sanctioned by the greater part of the nations of Europe, would without difficulty become the immutable rule of the cabinets, while those who should try to infringe it would risk bringing on themselves the forces of the new union."[5]

Alexander regarded constitutional government and national self-determination as the essential elements of this new international order. Pitt responded by laying out the major goals of British policy: first, to divest France of its conquered territories; second, to form a barrier against future French aggression; third, to fix the rights and possessions of the principal European powers. This looked enough like agreement to be embodied in a treaty of 1805 that committed Russia and Great Britain to "the establishment in Europe of a federative system, to ensure the independence of the weaker states," but the agreement was more apparent than real. Pitt, like his successors in office, wanted a much weaker federation than the tsar envisaged.

In 1814, the tsar still dreamed of a general reorganization of Europe based on constitutional government and national self-determination. Britain, Austria, and France had no such dream. They were represented at Vienna by three astute diplomats who were more than a match for Alexander, although frequently pitted against each other: Castlereagh, Metternich, and Talleyrand. Talleyrand, who had served the ancien régime, the Revolution, and the Empire, now appeared as the spokesman of the restored Bourbons, and handled matters so adroitly that France was soon admitted to equality with the four allied powers.

There was considerable confusion at the beginning of the Congress about what should be its form of organization. Even before the opening date, the ministers of Great Britain, Austria, Prussia, and Russia began to meet regularly, and this committee, which eventually included France, became the decision-making body. Sweden, Spain, and Portugal were included in this inner circle for some purposes; there was an auxiliary council of German states; and delegates from weak states served on the commissions that handled special issues. But the weak states were supplicants, not participants.

The key issues at the Congress were how far to reduce the boundaries of France; whether to restore the partitioned kingdom of Poland; how to partition the kingdom of Saxony, whose ruler had refused to join the allies against Napoleon; whether to leave Murat, one of Napoleon's marshals, on the throne of Naples; and what political structures to give to Switzerland and the Low

Countries. The fate of Poland was the principal sticking point. Alexander wanted to restore the kingdom of Poland in the name of national self-determination and to make it a constitutional monarchy with himself as king. Prussia would lose its share of Poland but would be allowed to annex a large part of Saxony. The proposed expansion of Prussia was unacceptable to Austria, and the proposed expansion of the Russian empire so alarmed Austria and Britain that they formed an alliance with France to block the designs of Russia and Prussia. Only three months after the opening of the Congress, the four-against-one coalition that had won the war against France gave way to a three-against-two coalition that divided the victorious allies.

We will examine the conflicting purposes that created these coalitions in more detail later. For the moment, we follow the sequence of events. While the Congress was still in session, Napoleon escaped from Elba and regained control of France, announcing as he landed that "the Congress is dissolved." But the Congress went right on, and its Final Act was signed nine days before the battle of Waterloo. The only effect of the Hundred Days on the peace terms was to stiffen the indemnities imposed on France and to settle the matter of removing Murat from Naples. Otherwise, the settlement of European affairs proceeded as if nothing had happened. Poland remained partitioned, except for a small territory around Warsaw, which became a constitutional monarchy under the tsar. Prussia took a piece of Saxony and part of the Rhineland, but in return, Austria was allowed to control northern Italy. The small German principalities were not restored; the larger ones were united in a federation dominated by Austria and Prussia. Switzerland was made into an independent republic, and the Netherlands into an independent kingdom. Bourbon monarchs were restored in France, Spain, and Naples. The civil rights of the Jews were weakly affirmed and the slave trade was feebly prohibited. The project of a European army—perceived by four of the powers as a Russian plot—was decisively abandoned.

At Aix-la-Chapelle in 1818, the powers agreed to end the occupation of France and to form a Quintuple Alliance. Alexander urged the proclamation of a single and indivisible European system. "Such a system," he suggested in a memorandum to the Russian cabinet, "would guarantee the security of Governments by putting the rights of nations under a guarantee analogous to that which protects individuals. The governments, for their parts, being relieved from the fear of revolutions, could offer to their peoples constitutions of a similar type; so that the liberties of peoples, wisely regulated, would arise without effect from this state of things once recognized and publicly avowed." He proposed that the powers meet regularly to carry out these obligations, and prepare "a plan of military concert, to be at once acted upon in case of necessity." In other words, he proposed to enact St. Pierre's Project of Perpetual Peace.

The British would have none of it. Castlereagh in a letter to his prime minister explained that the proposal "was opening up to such a Power as Russia . . . an almost irresistible claim to march through the territories of all the Confederate States to the most distant points of Europe to fulfill her guarantee."[6] His objections prevailed, and the declaration of Aix-la-Chapelle, issued at the close of that conference in November 1818, was as toothless a piece of rhetoric as the declarations issued much later at Locarno and at Dumbarton Oaks:

The object of the union is as simple as it is great and salutary. It does not tend to any new political combination—to any change in the relations sanctioned by existing treaties; calm and consistent in its proceedings, it has no other object than the maintenance of peace.[7]

The Congress of Verona in 1822 was almost a replay of the glamorous convention at Vienna. Two emperors, four kings, and numerous beautiful women, including the ex-empress of France, now duchess of Parma, graced the festivities. But the Congress was unable to reach any agreement about Spain, which had revolutions in progress both at home and in its Latin American colonies. Alexander kindly offered to send an expeditionary force to support legitimacy in Spain, but the offer was strongly resisted by Austria and Britain. Then France sought the approval of the Confederation for an invasion of Spain to maintain order, and, failing to obtain it, invaded anyway, restored the authority of the Spanish king, but was unable to obtain British acquiescence to an effort to regain the Spanish colonies. Then Alexander invited the United States to join the Holy Alliance in order to extend the principle of guaranteeing peace by armed intervention to the new world. The American response was the Monroe Doctrine, proclaimed in President Monroe's message to Congress in December 1823, which acknowledged the existence of the European Confederation at the moment that marked its disappearance:

The political system of the allied powers is essentially different . . . from that of America. . . . We owe it, therefore, to candor, and to the amicable relations existing between the United States and these powers, to declare that we should consider any attempt on their part to extend their system to any portion of this hemisphere as dangerous to our peace and safety.

As George Canning, the British foreign minister, had written earlier in the same year, "and so things are getting back to a wholesome state again. Every nation for itself and God for us all."[8]

Nearly a hundred years elapsed before the next attempt to put the Grand Design into practice, at the 1919 peace congress that followed the First World War. The congress was held in Paris, but the final treaty was signed in the Hall of Mirrors at the palace of Versailles. There were many similarities to the Congress of Vienna 105 years before. This time, thirty-two nations were included in the conclave of victorious allies, represented by heads of governments or foreign ministers. Again, the great powers excluded the small powers from the decision-making process, but allowed them to serve on the commissions that dealt with special issues.

As at Vienna, the congress had a dominant figure, who was again the ruler of the peripheral power that had turned the tide of battle. Once more, that outsider was determined to establish perpetual peace by means of a league of nations, was hailed as the savior of Europe, and came to believe he could reshape the European system to accord with his high ideals. Once more, the outsider was outmaneuvered by the experienced diplomats of the core powers, so that the congress, while nominally acceding to the project of perpetual peace, settled most of the issues before it on the old and comfortable principle that might makes right.

Of the two would-be saviors, Woodrow Wilson was less successful than Alexander I. The confederation established at Vienna and the Concert of Europe that grew out of it did give Europe a century of relative peace. The league of nations founded at Versailles collapsed within twenty years. Alexander left Vienna with his power and self-confidence only slightly diminished. Wilson went home broken and discredited.

These different outcomes reflect both personal and organizational differences between the two congresses. The leading actors at Vienna were more knowledgeable, more intelligent, and perhaps more honest. It is painful to compare Wilson's diplomatic correspondence with Alexander's, or Clemenceau's reports with Talleyrand's. At Versailles, only Lloyd George was acquainted with the history of the Grand Design and sensitive to its implications. But unlike Castlereagh and Wellington, Lloyd George changed his policies from day to day. Moreover, there were fewer minds engaged at Versailles. Alexander had three brilliant negotiators at his side: Nesselrode, Capo d'Istria, and Pozzo di Borgo. Castlereagh alternated with Wellington and Clancarty. Wilson had only the fatuous Colonel House, and Clemenceau played a lone hand.

The most significant feature of the 1919 peace conference was the exclusion of the defeated enemies, Germany, Austria, and Turkey, and of the defected ally, Russia. The exclusion of the Central Powers occurred by accident rather than design, when what was intended to be a preparatory meeting of the victorious allies became by imperceptible degrees the final peace conference. The inclusion of Russia, whose new Bolshevik regime was viewed with loathing, was scarcely considered. But Bolshevism was much on the delegates' minds, and their fear that the Germans might follow the same path if pushed too hard was what restrained them from dismembering Germany, just as in 1814 France had not been carved up because of apprehensions that the revolution might be rekindled, or the defeated adversary driven into alliance with Russia.

Like their predecessors at Vienna, the 1919 conferees spent most of their time redrawing boundaries and shuffling populations. Once again, Poland presented the most difficult problem, but this time the boundaries of Poland were redrawn at the expense of Germany and Russia instead of to their profit. The Austro-Hungarian empire was broken into new, small nations. The Ottoman empire was dissolved and its territories parceled out to France, England, and Italy. Lithuania, Latvia, and Estonia obtained independence. The German colonies and overseas concessions were distributed to France, the British dominions, and Japan. Alsace-Lorraine was returned to France, with draconian provisions for the confiscation of German property. The mining districts of Eupen and Malmédy were given to Belgium, and the Saar was internationalized, although the Rhineland was not separated from Germany as the French proposed.

The treatment of Germany in 1919 posed the same issues as the treatment of France in 1814. While each great war was still in progress, the allies had proclaimed that their quarrel was only with the enemy emperor and his bellicose government, not with the enemy people. The defeated powers in each case relied on these assurances, fulfilled at Vienna but brutally denied at Versailles, where no distinction was recognized between the Kaiser's government and the German people. Although forcible disarmament and reparations figured in both settlements, the Versailles provisions were far more punitive. At Vienna, the victorious allies supported the fragile monarchical government of the restored Bourbons in the name of legitimacy; the vengeful victors of Versailles wasted no sympathy on the struggling republican government of Germany.[9]

Wilson gave such a high priority to inclusion of the Covenant of the League of Nations in the peace treaty that he was prepared to compromise on any other issue in order to have his way on that one. He counted on the League to rectify the injustices to which he reluctantly consented when, for example, large numbers of Germans were transferred to Poland and Czechoslovakia, the Ottoman territories were parceled out to new masters without regard to the wishes of their inhabitants, and the Japanese were allowed a free hand in China over the vehement objections of the Chinese. Curiously enough, Wilson was rather casual about the details of the League's peacekeeping machinery, seeming to believe that the mere fact of the organization's existence would put international relations on a new footing.

The Covenant of the League of Nations, as first drafted in February 1919 by an Anglo-French team, provided for an assembly representing all member states, an Executive Council in which the United States, Britain, France, Italy, and Japan would hold permanent seats, to which other states directly affected by a matter under discussion would be added as temporary members, together with a Secretariat headed by a Chancellor. The expenses of the League would be borne by member states in the same proportion as the expenses of the International Postal Union.

The League would "respect and preserve *as against external aggression* the territorial integrity and existing political independence of member states." The Executive Council would prepare plans for the reduction of armaments, the abolition of compulsory military service, and the abolition of secrecy in military affairs. The member states would agree to submit intractable disputes among themselves either to arbitration or to an inquiry by the Executive Council and to abide *voluntarily* to the recommendations of the arbiter or the Council. A Permanent Court of International Justice would be empowered to judge any matter that the parties recognized as "suitable for submission." This version of the Grand Design was Kantian, not St. Pierrian. The internal stability of member states would not be guaranteed, the authority of the League would not extend to individuals, and international public opinion was to be the only means of coercing a defiant state.

The final version of the Covenant, as it appeared in the Treaty of Versailles, was weaker than the draft version in some respects but stronger in others. It provided that members might withdraw on two years' notice, that decisions of both the Assembly and the Council—except on procedural matters—must be unanimous, and it contained a clause affirming the validity of the Monroe Doctrine. Some rudimentary teeth were added in the form of Article 16, which provided for economic sanctions against a state initiating war and referred in carefully ambiguous terms to the possibility of joint military action against an aggressor. The final draft was further amplified by references to the numerous good causes to which the League would offer moral support: fair wages and working conditions, the abolition of the white slave trade and of the international drug traffic, freedom of communication, and international public health.

At one point in the negotiations, the French pressed very hard to give the League its own armed forces, proposing, among other amendments in the same sense, the following: "It [the Executive Council of the League] will establish an international control of troops and armaments, and the High Contracting Parties agree to submit themselves to it in all good faith. It will fix the conditions under which the permanent existence and organization of an international force may be assured." The French plan was strongly opposed by Wilson, who said at one point, "To propose to realize unity of command in time of peace, would be to put forward a proposal that no nation would accept. The Constitution of the United States forbids the President to send beyond its frontiers the national forces."[10] The reference was apparently to the constitutional provision that Congress has the right to declare war. But it was clear, in the context of the discussion, that Wilson opposed the idea of a permanent international army on principle, believing like the British that it would convert the League into an instrument for the domination of Europe by France.

The Treaty of Versailles, as every schoolboy knows, was finally rejected by the U.S. Senate on March 19, 1920, by a vote of 49 to 35, seven votes short of the required two-thirds majority. It would have passed easily had Wilson been willing to accept some compromises in the language of the Covenant stipulating the prerogatives of Congress with respect to American participation. Both in the United States and in Europe, the subsequent failures of the League as a peacekeeping organization were commonly blamed on the abstention of the United States, but, given the extraordinary defects with which the League was endowed by its creators, it is difficult to imagine how it could ever have functioned well. Lacking any coercive powers, hobbled by the rule of unanimity, it was charged with maintaining the integrity of national boundaries that had just been redrawn in disregard of the principle of self-determination and without the consent of Germany and Russia, the two powers most directly concerned.

Nevertheless, when the League of Nations came into operation in 1920, it was widely believed that the war system of the commonwealth of nations had been, or at least would soon be, abolished. The forty-one original members included all the European states except Germany, Russia, Austria, Hungary, Turkey, Ireland, Bulgaria, Estonia, Latvia, Lithuania, Luxembourg, Albania; nearly all the Latin American states; the larger British possessions—Canada, Australia, New Zealand, India, South Africa; and a few independent Asian states—Japan, China, Persia, Siam. The missing European states eventually joined—Germany in 1926, Turkey in 1932, the Soviet Union in 1934. The non-European contingent was eventually augmented by Afghanistan, Iraq, Egypt, and Ethiopia. Costa Rica and Brazil were the first members to resign, in 1925 and 1926. Japan and Germany withdrew in 1933, Italy in 1937, Hungary in 1939. Many of the Latin American countries departed during the 1930s. The Soviet Union was expelled at the last meeting of the League in 1939. The organization officially disbanded in 1946 and turned its continuing activities over to the United Nations.

The Council of the League had originally four permanent members—France, Britain, Italy, and Japan. Germany and the Soviet Union were added when they joined the League. The number of temporary members ranged from four to nine at various times, but they were never permitted to outvote the major powers. The Council functioned as an interim committee of the Assembly, exercising influence rather than authority.

The achievements of the League were, for the most part, in activities peripheral to peacekeeping: the admirable refugee programs initiated by Fridtjof Nansen in 1922, the economic rescue of Austria, the settlement of minor frontier questions, and the moderately successful activities of the World Court and the International Labor Organization. But the League was quite helpless in the face of Japan's invasion of Manchuria in 1931, Italy's invasion of Ethiopia in 1935, the Spanish civil war in 1936, Hitler's remilitarization of the Rhineland in 1936, the German occupation and annexation of Austria in 1938, the dismemberment of Czechoslovakia in 1939, and the Italian annexation of Albania in the same year. When Germany invaded Poland in September 1939 to begin World War II, the League was not invoked at all. It did, however, accept an appeal from Finland in 1939 for help against the invading Russians, and the expulsion of the Soviet Union was the League's last gesture.

For a moment in 1924, it appeared that the feeble peacekeeping machinery of the League might be strengthened. At the Assembly's meeting in the fall, the Czechoslovak foreign minister, Edvard Benes, encouraged by Aristide Briand and Ramsay Mac-Donald, introduced a document called the Protocol for the Pacific Settlement of International Disputes. The Protocol set aside the Covenant's distinctions between justified and unjustified wars, and proposed that any nation that refused to submit a dispute to compulsory arbitration would be labeled as an aggressor. It empowered the Council of the League, by a two-thirds vote, to impose an armistice on any conflict in progress, and to employ military sanctions against an offending power. The Protocol was approved, without dissent, by the forty-eight nations represented at that meeting, and was ratified almost immediately by France and a number of the smaller European states. But it was rejected by the British cabinet early in 1925 in response to the strong objections of the British dominions, which "shared the horror of British military circles at the thought that the British Fleet, on which they all relied, might be set in motion—or restrained—at the bidding of a Council of foreigners."[11]

In place of the Protocol, the great powers substituted the Pact of Locarno in 1925. Germany was admitted to the League and given a permanent seat on the Council; French sovereignty over Alsace-Lorraine was reasserted; and occupation forces were withdrawn from the Rhineland, which was demilitarized. The signatories were Germany, France, Britain, Belgium, and Italy. During the same year of 1925, the League actually managed to halt a small war that had broken out between Greece and Bulgaria and to impose indemnities on Greece. This episode, in which none of the great powers had any direct interest, was the only successful suppression of hostilities in the League's history. Thereafter, the drift away from actions to words was never interrupted. In 1928, the United States was brought peripherally into the League structure with the signing of the Kellogg-Briand Pact by the United States and thirteen members of the League, including Germany, France, and Britain. In that remarkable document, the high contracting parties solemnly agreed to abandon war as an instrument of national policy but made no provision for enforcing their agreement.

When Japan invaded Manchuria in 1931, the League talked and talked, appointed committees, dispatched an investigating commission, invited the participation of an American observer, and eventually proposed to appoint a conciliation commission, whereupon the Japanese, having completed their occupation of Manchuria and set up a puppet state, withdrew from the organization. Manchuria was more remote from Europe in 1931 than any place is today, and there was enough uncertainty about the situation there to permit the Japanese to deny the facts of their invasion until it was a fait accompli. The attitude of the Chinese government was ambiguous—it continued to maintain diplomatic relations with Japan—and there was a real question whether China had controlled the disputed territory. The episode decreased the credibility of the League, without destroying it.

But the next major crisis marked the end of the League as a political force. The infringement of the League Covenant by Italy in its attack on Abyssinia in 1935 was as flagrant as it could be—a massive, unprovoked military assault on another League member with the declared object of putting an end to its national existence. Moreover, Italy was peculiarly vulnerable to the economic sanctions provided in the Covenant, being dependent on imports, especially of oil, to keep its war machine going, and on the Suez Canal to reach the theater of operations. Following the initial border incident in 1934, the League went into action with a flurry of negotiations, which dragged on for many months while Mussolini, in plain sight of the world, prepared the massive military operation against Abyssinia planned for the fall of 1935. A committee of the Council offered Italy numerous concessions in East Africa, but the offer was promptly rejected. During the summer, an unexpected surge of British opinion in favor of the League stiffened the attitude of the British government, and in the fall meetings of the League Assembly, the British and French foreign ministers took strong public positions in favor of sanctions, while privately exploring the possibility of further concessions to Italy. After the Italian invasion was launched in October, all the members of the League Council except Italy voted for the application of Article 16 of the Covenant, which obliged all member-states to apply sanctions against the aggressor. The decision was endorsed by the Assembly a few days later, although not unanimously.

Under Article 16, the obligation to impose sanctions was automatic. A coordinating committee, representing the entire membership of the League, was set up to orchestrate the program, which involved five parts: (1) an embargo on the shipment of arms and ammunition to Italy; (2) the withholding of loans and credits; (3) an embargo on imports from Italy; (4) a ban on the export of certain key products to Italy; and (5) mutual arrangements among the sanctioning states to equalize their economic sacrifices. Measure number 4 was crucial. The original list of key products did not include oil or iron and steel. When it was proposed to add these items, which were essential to the Italian war effort, the British and French balked. The proposal was referred for study to one committee after another and in the end was never adopted. As the discussions dragged on for month after month, the French government became more and more apprehensive about the possibility that strong action against Mussolini would drive him into alliance with Hitler, and the British government more and more nervous about exposing its Mediterranean fleet to possible Italian attack. The outcome of these fears was the Hoare-Laval proposal worked out in December, which would have given Italy about half of Abyssinia in return for a cease-fire. It was leaked to the French press and raised storms of disapproval in England and France that forced both Hoare and Laval into retirement. Nevertheless, the publication of the Hoare-Laval plan broke the back of the sanctions movement:

Whereas, the day before the plan was out in the open, the smaller countries in the League—states like Czechoslovakia, Rumania, Yugoslavia— could feel that, after all, there might be some safety for them under the League umbrella, which Britain and France were bravely holding over their heads, the news that these two erstwhile League champions had been plotting for months to carve up the victim's body and reward its attacker with substantial parts of it dealt the campaign for collective action a mortal blow.[12]

Mussolini was allowed to complete the conquest and annexation of Abyssinia without further impediment. When another major crisis, the civil war in Spain, erupted later in 1936, it was handled—with equal maladroitness—by an ad hoc international committee entirely outside the framework of the League.

The League's capacity for action was gone, but it still retained

the power to evoke eloquence, as in Haile Selassie's farewell state-
ment to the Assembly:

Denied all succor, the Ethiopian people mounts its Calvary alone. . . .
Since 1935, Ethiopia has observed with sorrow how, one after another,
the signatures affixed to the Covenant have been denied. A number of
Powers, themselves threatened with aggression and realizing their own
weakness, have abandoned Ethiopia. . . . They have torn up the treaties
which ensured their independence—Non-aggression Treaties, the Covenant of the League of Nations, the Pact of Paris. . . . Of the two evils, they
choose that, which in their fear of the aggressor, seems the less. May God
forgive them!

Not even two years elapsed between the effective demise of the
League at the end of 1939 and the first steps toward the creation
of a successor organization. The Atlantic Charter, issued by Roosevelt and Churchill in August 1941, well before American entry
into the war, referred indirectly to a future international organization. It spoke of creating a "wider and permanent system of general
security" that would "afford to all nations the means of dwelling
in safety within their own boundaries." The lack of specificity
was intentional:

Churchill asked the President if the charter could explicitly endorse some
kind of "effective international organization." Roosevelt demurred; he
said that he himself would not favor the creation of a new assembly of
the League of Nations, at least until after a period of time during which
a British-American police force maintained security. Churchill warned
that a vague plank would arouse opposition from strong internationalists.
Roosevelt agreed, but he felt that he had to be politically realistic. Churchill gave in, with the understanding that he could add some language that
would strengthen the plank without invoking the dread words "international organization" or invoking the ghost of Woodrow Wilson.[13]

But that ghost would not stay down. The following year, the
Declaration of the United Nations was signed by the twenty-
six nations at war with the Axis. In 1943, the U.S. Congress
overwhelmingly approved the Fulbright-Connelly Resolution
committing the United States to join an international organization for the maintenance of peace. Also in 1943, Churchill proposed a new international organization "which would embody the
spirit, but not be subject to the weakness of the former League of
Nations." It would be composed of a Council of Europe and a

Council of Asia. The Council of Europe would be an effective government, with armed forces of its own and courts exercising compulsory jurisdiction. It would be composed of the great powers and of a number of confederations—Scandinavian, Balkan, Danubian—uniting the smaller powers. The Council of Asia would be organized along similar lines. Later in the same year, he added a third Council to the scheme, for the Western Hemisphere.[14]

Roosevelt briefly adopted a similar position, but by July 1944, when the U.S. transmitted its "Tentative Proposals for an International Organization" to Britain, China, and the Soviet Union, there was substantial agreement on restoring the League in a somewhat improved form, the principal improvements being the greater use of armed force to maintain the peace and a more dominant role for the major powers. The details were worked out by the representatives of the United States, Britain, the Soviet Union, and China at the Dumbarton Oaks Conference of 1944. The new organization, like the League, would have an assembly, a council, a secretariat, and an international court. The council would be its executive organ, and would have one sequence of procedures for arranging the peaceful settlement of international disputes and another sequence of procedures for coping with threats to peace or breaches of the peace, escalating from measures not involving force, such as sanctions, to armed action against an aggressor. But it would have no permanent armed forces of its own. Contingents would be requested from member states as needed.

There was no disagreement about giving a veto to each of the permanent members of the council, but there was considerable dissension about how their vetoes would be exercised in disputes to which they themselves were parties. The United States and Great Britain wanted to make a distinction between the mere consideration of such matters and actions to resolve them. The Soviet Union held out for an absolute veto. This issue was left undecided along with a number of others: the exact composition of the council, the role of regional bodies, the criteria for membership, and whether the new organization would have any responsibility for the promotion of human rights. The stickiest point was Stalin's demand for separate membership for each of the sixteen Soviet republics.

Meanwhile, other components of the new international order were developing independently: the United Nations Relief and Rehabilitation Administration in 1943, the Food and Agriculture Organization a little later. The Bretton Woods Conference in July 1943 led to the formation of the International Monetary Fund and the World Bank, and later in the same year the new International Civil Aviation Organization appeared.

In April 1945, the representatives of fifty nations gathered at San Francisco to form the new peacekeeping league. The war was not over, but an Allied victory was taken for granted. Roosevelt had just died and Truman was in the White House. Such serious strains had developed in U.S. relations with Russia that there was talk of canceling the United Nations conference. The most divisive issue was the same one that had troubled the Congress of Vienna in 1815—Russia's insistence on having a subservient Polish government. Another key issue—which had confronted both the Holy Alliance and the League of Nations—was how to reconcile the Monroe Doctrine, freshly reinforced by the Act of Chapultepec, with the idea of a universal peacekeeping organization.

The San Francisco conference began with a prolonged wrangle about procedures and then proceeded to the issue of regional security agreements, an issue that began with the Monroe Doctrine but came to include the Soviet claim to a free hand in Eastern Europe and the British claim to naval control of the Mediterranean. The resulting compromise was embodied in Article 51 of the UN Charter: "Nothing in the present Charter shall impair the inherent right of individual or collective self defense, if an armed attack occurs against a Member of the United Nations, until the Security Council had taken the measures necessary to maintain international peace and security." The key word was *collective,* and on that narrow foundation NATO, the Warsaw Pact, and half a dozen other regional blocs were eventually built. The shift from universal security arrangements to a balance of regional blocs was the decisive step taken at San Francisco. Whereas the plans for perpetual peace drawn at Vienna and Versailles were each tried out to some extent before they were replaced by a balance of power between hostile alliances, the San Francisco plan was strangled in the cradle.

The next crisis at San Francisco—and the most serious—concerned the precise nature of the veto power to be enjoyed by the

Big Five (at that time the United States, Britain, France, the Soviet Union, and China) as permanent members of the Security Council. There were two overlapping issues in the veto crisis. The precise wording of the veto clause pitted the Soviet Union against its Western allies. The larger implications of the veto question placed the smaller powers in opposition to the Big Five. None of the permanent members were disposed to give up the veto they were to enjoy in the Security Council, and the Western powers had already accepted the Russian position that the veto must apply to Council actions involving the peaceful settlement of disputes as well as those involving the use of force. But the Russians wanted to be able to veto the *discussion* of an issue, and to this the U.S. government was adamantly opposed. After a secret appeal from Truman to Stalin, the Russian delegation yielded the point. But a small-power demand that the veto be inapplicable to peaceful settlements was strongly rebuffed:

Stettinius, applying his own pressure, called several chairmen of small power delegations to his penthouse, and told them privately that unless they accepted the voting formula as presented by the sponsors there would be no United Nations. He also ordered Rockefeller to warn the Latin American leaders to vote with the United States or face an uncooperative attitude by the United States in the future.[15]

On the broader issue of Security Council supremacy, the small powers did win one important concession. The Assembly was given the right to discuss any question within the scope of the Charter and to make recommendations regarding international peace and security in any matter not under active consideration by the Security Council. The mandate system was revived under another name. There would be a Trusteeship Council to supervise the administration of unliberated colonial territories by member states. And the activities of the new organization with regard to social and economic issues were to be vastly greater than those of the League.

The Charter was completed and adopted on June 25, 1945, with the usual showers of eloquence. Halifax, who was presiding, called it "one of the great moments of history." But there was much less talk about perpetual peace on this occasion than there had been at Vienna and Versailles.

As of this writing, the United Nations Organization has been in operation for more than forty years. Its peacekeeping achievements have not been impressive, but it has played a large part in international affairs. The first decade was the most eventful. During that time, the Western bloc led by the United States enjoyed an overwhelming majority over the Eastern bloc led by the Soviet Union. In the Security Council, a gentlemen's agreement provided two seats for Latin America, one for Western Europe, one for Eastern Europe, one for the British Commonwealth, and one for Asia, besides the five permanent members, of whom the United States, Britain, and France were a majority. The UN became an instrument of Western bloc policy, and the Eastern bloc practiced active and passive resistance to the organization's initiatives. Because action by the Security Council was subject to the Soviet veto, the Western bloc turned increasingly to the Assembly, and in the Uniting for Peace resolution of 1950 secured the adoption of a procedure whereby the Assembly could intervene in a dispute and call for the use of force when the Security Council was deadlocked—an important constitutional change:

... the shift in authority to the Assembly meant that any attempt to negotiate solutions or compromise courses among the permanent members, scarcely attempted even in the Council, was now totally abandoned. ... Since, in the veto-less Assembly, majority views could be pushed through anyway, there was no need to discuss or take account of minority opinions. Thus one of the main objects of the veto—to create a need to negotiate mutually acceptable courses of action among the great powers— a need universally accepted in the successful system of the nineteenth century—was now frustrated.[16]

With one important exception, the issues of the first decade all took the form of East-West confrontations. The first matter handled by the Security Council was a complaint against the Soviet Union by Iran, concerning the slow withdrawal of a Soviet occupation force from Azerbaijan. It wound down inconclusively after a long wrangle. The second issue had to do with the presence of British and French occupation forces in Lebanon and Syria, which ended in similar fashion. In retaliation for the Iranian issue, the Soviet Union complained to the Security Council about the presence of British troops in Greece at a time when both blocs were intervening in a bitter civil war. The General Assembly, at the initiative of the United States, established a special committee on the Balkans, boycotted by the Soviet Union and Poland. Its efforts were inconclusive. The first and only issue on which the United States and the Soviet Union found common ground in the first decade was the 1947 dispute between the Netherlands and Indonesia over the arrangements for Indonesian independence. Both of the superpowers favored the rapid dismantling of the British, French, Dutch, and Portuguese overseas empires.

The organization's efforts to arrange a settlement in Palestine at the end of the British mandate in 1948, and to prevent the first Arab-Israel war, were conspicuously unsuccessful, as was its involvement in the Corfu Channel dispute between Britain and Albania, the dispute between Italy and Yugoslavia over Trieste, the 1948 Communist coup in Czechoslovakia, and the Berlin blockade. All of these crises were eventually resolved outside the UN framework.

In 1950, the Soviet Union made the tactical error of boycotting the Security Council to protest the occupancy of China's seat in that body by the Taiwan government. When North Korea invaded South Korea in June of that year, the absence of the Soviet delegate, who would have vetoed the action, permitted the Security Council to side firmly with South Korea and to call upon all members of the UN for assistance, a call to which the United States responded with a full-scale military and naval force, eventually supplemented by token forces from sixteen other UN members and contributions of supplies from as many more. For the first time, an army had taken the field under the banner of a peacekeeping organization to repel an invasion. But when that had been accomplished, the Assembly, at the urging of the United States, authorized UN forces to invade North Korea for the purpose of reuniting the divided country. This action provoked the intervention of China, and eventually, after two and a half more years of fighting, led to a compromise making the partition of Korea official.

UN efforts to mediate the recurrent war between India and Pakistan were inconclusive, and the Security Council virtually ignored Guatemala's complaint when that country was attacked in 1954 by Nicaraguan and Honduran forces encouraged by the

United States. Two years later, the U.S. and the U.S.S.R. unexpectedly found themselves agreeing to oppose the joint Anglo-French expedition to take control of the Suez Canal while Israeli forces were seizing the Sinai desert. When a Security Council resolution calling for a cease-fire was vetoed by France and Britain, it was the Assembly rather than the Council that took action, calling for the withdrawal of invading forces from Egypt and creating an international military force to supervise the withdrawal and to patrol the Israeli-Egyptian frontier. The unusual display of U.S.-Soviet solidarity secured almost immediate compliance.

But only a few weeks later, when Hungary appealed to the Security Council to negotiate the withdrawal of Soviet forces that had invaded Hungary to put down an uprising, the UN was unable to take any meaningful action. After the Hungarian crisis, most disputes involving the superpowers were settled outside the UN, although the organization was used as a forum in the Cuban missile crisis of 1962, the U.S. intervention in the Dominican Republic in 1965, the *Pueblo* case of 1968, the Soviet intervention in Czechoslovakia in 1968, the Panama Canal negotiations of 1973, the seizure of American diplomats by Iran in 1979, the Soviet invasion of Afghanistan in 1979, the Soviet downing of a Korean airliner in September 1983, the U.S. intervention in Grenada in October of the same year, and the U.S. campaign against Nicaragua by proxy from 1984 to 1987. During that long period, the sequence of a complaint by one side and a veto by the other became virtually automatic. In the 1983 Korean airliner matter, the Soviet Union vetoed a Security Council resolution that deplored the loss of life and called for an investigation by the Secretary-General. The following month, the U.S. had the matching opportunity to veto a Security Council resolution condemning the Grenada intervention as a violation of international law and calling for the withdrawal of foreign troops from the island.

The UN has always had a full peacekeeping agenda. The cases current in 1985, for example, included the various issues connected with the Soviet occupation of Afghanistan, and the support of Afghan guerrillas by Pakistan; apartheid in South Africa; Guatemalan claims on Belize; a dispute over the sovereignty of one of the Comoro islands, whose inhabitants wish to remain French against the insistence of the General Assembly; the sovereignty of the Falkland Islands; the opening of the border between Spain and Gibraltar; Venezuelan claims to part of the territory of Guyana; border incidents between India and Pakistan; the continuing wars between Iraq and Iran and between Vietnam and Cambodia; unresolved border questions between North and South Korea; the Israeli and Syrian interventions in Lebanon; a dispute between France and Madagascar over the Malagasy Islands; the reorganization of the Strategic Trust Territory of Micronesia; the continuing dispute among Israel, the PLO, and the Arab countries; the question of Namibian independence; and the Western Sahara war.

It is difficult to summarize the peacekeeping activities of the UN, because it has never developed standard procedures for processing complaints or for responding to crises. In some cases, the Security Council takes the initiative; in other cases, it is the General Assembly or the Secretary-General. Often, they work at cross-purposes. The only invariable element is that every matter brought before the UN evokes an enormous outpouring of words. The fine art of delay is often deployed to permit a forcible annexation of territory or a revolutionary change of regime to be completed before the complaint of the victim is considered. On-site investigations have been known to take ten years.

Unlike the League, the UN has raised military forces or military observation teams of its own on a dozen occasions—for service in Greece, Palestine, Kashmir, Suez and Gaza, Lebanon, Jordan, the Congo, West Irian, Yemen, Cyprus, India, Pakistan, and Syria. These expeditions, too, have had no common format. Most had such noncombatant missions as separating belligerent forces or monitoring the observation of a truce. In Korea, however, a large force nominally belonging to the UN was committed to combat, and in the Congo a UN peacekeeping force took part in a civil war. In the Middle East a number of UN forces, with varying command structures, have been put in place at different times.

Meanwhile, the organization was evolving in several interesting ways. Since even the smallest and weakest states were eligible for membership, the roster of members continued to grow as former colonial territories became independent and many subdivided. From 50 in 1945, the number of member states rose to 114 in 1965 and 159 in 1989. As early as 1965, Asian and African states held a solid majority in the General Assembly. In 1989, UN members with populations under one million had thirty votes in the General Assembly, while China, with upwards of a billion inhabitants, had one vote. As Thomas Franck remarked in a 1985 book highly critical of the organization:

In part because this system so utterly distorts reality, the Assembly produces huge paper majorities for resolutions that seem to us, at least, absurd. For example, the U.S., Britain, and France, which between them have given independence to one billion ex-colonials, are verbally battered for not forcing "freedom" on the handful of inhabitants of the Marianas, the Falklands, and the Isle of Mayotte, persons who perversely wish only to remain American, British, or French; meanwhile, not a word is said of the captive nations of Eastern Europe.[17]

There is a similar incongruity with respect to the UN budget, which is authorized by the General Assembly, most of whose members do not contribute significantly to the organization's support. The combined contribution of 60 percent of the members is less than 2 percent of the annual budget. The combined contribution of 147 members is less than that of the United States alone. Although assessments are supposed to be based on ability to pay, the formula has been repeatedly modified for the benefit of third world countries so that about half of the organization's members pay less than $100,000 a year, and even these trifling amounts are commonly in arrears.

After the early years of the UN, when American domination was taken for granted and the Soviet Union followed a policy of obstruction, the Asian and African states identified with the Non-Aligned Movement developed a consistent tilt toward the Soviet Union that gave it a working majority in the General Assembly and disproportionate influence in the Secretariat and in such auxiliary bodies as UNESCO. The UN bureaucracy, unlike the League's, shows no sign of evolving into an international civil service. Appointments are made according to geographic and ideological quotas, and are often short-term. UN officials routinely report to, and receive instructions from, the governments of their home countries.[18]

During the 1970s, the General Assembly, supported by the Secretariat, devoted much of its agenda to the condemnation of U.S. client states—Israel, Chile, South Africa—and gave short shrift to complaints against Soviet clients, like Syria, Poland, and Vietnam. A resolution passed by the General Assembly on November 10, 1975, declared that "zionism is a form of racism and racial discrimination," but after 1979, the General Assembly passed annual resolutions condemning the Soviet presence in Afghanistan.

The organization's present membership is grouped into a number of overlapping blocs: the third world or developing nations bloc includes about 120 states; the Non-Aligned Movement claims 99 UN members, the African group 50, the Islamic conference 41. The Eastern European group has 11 members, as does the European Economic Community. The United States is said to be the only member—except Israel—that belongs to no bloc. Yet it does occasionally prevail, as in the successful 1982 campaign to keep the "decolonization of Puerto Rico" off the General Assembly's agenda.

To put the matter in perspective, during most of the UN's history, the permanent confrontation between the United States and the Soviet Union has prevented the UN from performing its intended peacekeeping functions with respect to any war or threatened war involving the superpowers or their clients. It can only discuss, investigate, and delay until one side or the other achieves its military objectives and is ready for a cease-fire. This was the pattern of the several Israel-Arab wars in which the Arabs were backed by the Soviet Union and Israel by the U.S. After the outbreak of the Yom Kippur War in 1973, the Security Council took no action at all because the Soviet Union and its third world allies were unwilling to press for a cease-fire while the Egyptians were advancing, and the United States, confident of a turnaround, was unwilling to consider a cease-fire while its side was losing. Only when Israel, reinforced by a U.S. airlift, threatened to overwhelm Egypt was a joint U.S.-Soviet plan for a cease-fire imposed on the Security Council by the superpowers.

When one of the superpowers is a principal party to an armed conflict, the UN enacts an elaborate charade of involvement but scrupulously abstains from substantive action—as in the Soviet excursions into Hungary, Czechoslovakia, and Afghanistan; Soviet-Cuban activities in Africa; the American interventions in the Dominican Republic, Vietnam, Laos, Cambodia, Lebanon, and Grenada; the Iran hostage episode; the Korean airliner affair; the bombing of Libya; U.S. involvement in the affairs of El Salvador, Nicaragua, and Panama; and the downing of an Iranian airliner by an American cruiser in 1988.

The superpowers have found themselves in consistent agreement with respect to only one category of disputes: those involving Western European nations and their former colonies. In several of these cases, the UN has acted decisively against the European party, without excessive scruple about legality: for example, effective pressure against the French presence in Tunisia and the Portuguese presence in Angola in the early 1960s; tacit support for the Indian seizure of Portuguese Goa in 1961; open support for the Indonesian takeover of West Irian from the Netherlands in 1962; armed intervention in the Congo against the faction allegedly sponsored by Belgium; effective support of Guinea's independence from Spain in 1966; effective pressure for the independence of French Somaliland in 1977.

The least successful branch of the United Nations has been the International Court of Justice, which has no power either to bring defendants to its bar or enforce its judgments. Not surprisingly, it has become customary for countries accused of violating international law to deny the Court's jurisdiction and refuse to appear in the case, as Iceland did when sued by the United Kingdom over fishing rights, as France did when sued by Australia and New Zealand for conducting nuclear tests that exposed them to radioactive fallout, Iran in the case of the U.S. hostages, and the U.S. when accused of violating Nicaraguan sovereignty. More than any other UN activity, the proceedings of the International Court appear to be exercises in futility.

The office of Secretary-General, by contrast, has accrued power and influence far beyond the modest administrative role envisaged by the Charter. The Secretary-General's prerogatives began to expand during the term of Trygve Lie. His successor, Dag Hammarskjöld, extended them further. They reached their high point with U Thant, who intervened in the Cuban missile crisis on his own initiative, withdrew the UN peacekeeping force from the

Sinai without consulting either the Security Council or the General Assembly, and appealed to the American people to oppose the policy of their own government in Vietnam. His successors, Kurt Waldheim and Perez de Cuellar, have been more restrained, but the post retains its pivotal importance. Arthur Rovine said of Hammarskjöld's acquisition of discretionary power that he:

turned the United Nations away from *the impossible concept of collective security*, the discredited foundation on which its Charter still rests, and turned it forcefully towards the notion of a third party neutral intermediary that could serve as a buffer keeping hostile states apart while simultaneously insuring that great power intervention did not create a meaningful threat of world war (emphasis added).[19]

In this view, it was a happy chance that rescued the United Nations from the false hope on which it was founded, and found a constructive role for it as a "neutral intermediary." But there are flaws in that picture. The first forty years of the United Nations witnessed more protracted wars than any previous era. Collective security might have prevented some of them and stopped others. The "neutral intermediary" was seldom able to interrupt hostilities until one side or the other had achieved its military goals.

The failure of collective security was hardly chargeable to the UN. It was attributable, in part, to the End Game, which made it difficult for the superpowers to act as arbiters in conflicts between lesser states; in part to the tacit agreement of the superpowers to deny any major international role to lesser members of NATO and the Warsaw Pact. But the discrepancy between national power and representation in the General Assembly, the disorderly distribution of peacekeeping responsibilities among the branches of the organization, and the chronic unwillingness of the member states to agree on the rules of the game have all contributed to the failure.

When the Reagan-Gorbachev summits of 1986–1988 unexpectedly introduced an element of cooperation into American-Soviet relations, the United Nations began to seem more effective than at any time since its early days. Within a period of a few months in 1988, Soviet forces began to withdraw from Afghanistan, Iran and Iraq reached a cease-fire agreement, Angola announced a plan for the withdrawal of Cuban troops, and an end to the endless war in the Moroccan desert began to be negotiated. The UN played a part and derived some credit in each of these developments, although all of them were more properly attributable to the new willingness of the superpowers to act together. Almost in concert, the United States and the Soviet Union began to make up the dues they had withheld in previous years. Two new peacekeeping forces—an observer group on the Iran-Iraq border and a good offices mission in Afghanistan and Pakistan—were added to the three observer groups that had been in place for many years on the borders of Israel, on the border between India and Pakistan, and in Lebanon. When its peacekeeping forces were awarded the Nobel Peace Prize for 1988, the rehabilitation of the UN seemed complete. But its peacemaking capabilities remain as limited as before. It can take effective action only in matters on which the United States and the Soviet Union have adopted a common policy, and in those matters it has only a marginal role.

Thus, for the better part of two hundred years, the nations of the European system that became the world system have been experimenting with variants of the Grand Design, only to discover that each peacekeeping league was steered by coalition processes that could not be suppressed by good intentions alone.

There were striking similarities among the three important peace conferences. Each originated in a defensive coalition against a power that threatened to achieve a dominant position in the international system by force of arms: France in 1812, Germany in 1914 and 1941. In each case, the common threat drove powers with incompatible interests into a military partnership that began to unravel as soon as victory was in sight. In each case, the first object of the peacemakers was to render the principal enemy and its satellites incapable of renewing the threat of domination, and this object was perceived as difficult and risky, because the principal enemy—France in 1815, Germany in 1919 and 1945—exceeded its neighbors in population, resources, and military potential. The partition of the principal enemy was considered and rejected in 1815 and in 1919, for nearly identical reasons: fear of driving the defeated power into the arms of Russia and encouraging the spread of revolutionary ideas. The partition of enemy satellites—Saxony in 1815, the Austro-Hungarian and Ottoman empires in 1919—was decided without hesitation. In 1945, the partition of the prin-

cipal enemy occurred more by accident than by design, and the
satellites were left intact. In each case, the victors were determined to impose their political systems on the vanquished: legiti-
mist and constitutional monarchy in 1815 and parliamentary democracy in 1919. In 1945, the victors, with no common political
system, undertook separately, with considerable success, to impose a democratic capitalist system on West Germany and Japan,
and a state socialist system on East Germany and the Eastern
European republics.

Each peace conference had two major purposes: redrawing maps
and setting up the machinery for permanent peace. These purposes
proved in each case to be contradictory, since the redrawing of
maps sharpened the differences of interest among the victors and
set the stage for future wars. All three settlements exacted heavy
indemnities in money and goods from the vanquished nations.
The unexpected result was that, in each case, the subsequent
economic growth of the vanquished nations outpaced that of the
victors.

It appears—although there is room for argument on this point—
that, in each case, one of the victorious allies achieved a peace
settlement that reflected its own interests much more than those
of its partners, and was able to do so because it had a preponderance
of military power at the moment of settlement. In 1815, the Russian army in the center of Europe outnumbered the combined
forces of Austria, Prussia, and England. The threat of a Russian
occupation of Europe persuaded Austria and England to leave
France intact and to admit Talleyrand to their counsels. In 1919,
France had vast forces still under arms although America and
Britain had already demobilized. The eagerness of Marshal Foch
to march his army across central Europe and overthrow the Bolshe-
viks helped to persuade Wilson to subordinate the Fourteen Points
to French demands. The United States, in 1945, enjoyed global
supremacy in the air and on the seas. The expectation that the
United Nations would be an instrument of American policy accounts for most of the positions taken by the Soviet delegates at
San Francisco.

At each peace conference, the coalition of victors was strained
by national priorities rooted in geography and history. The French

preoccupation with the west bank of the Rhine evoked no sympathy from the British on any of these occasions. The ancient Russian desire to subjugate Poland aroused the same resentment among Russia's allies in 1945 as in 1815. The Monroe Doctrine—which seemed to put the Western Hemisphere outside the reach of peacekeeping organizations—was as much a stumbling block in setting up the United Nations as it had been for the League of Nations and the Holy Alliance. Differences of this kind were not amenable to principled solutions; they were resolved by bargaining and mutual concessions, mainly at the expense of third parties.

Another question that arose at all three peace conferences was how to regulate the relationship between the great powers and weaker nations. More than two hundred states sent representatives to Vienna in 1814; thirty sovereigns appeared in person. Sweden, Spain, and Portugal were counted as powers for some purposes, but all significant decisions were made by the ministers of Russia, Austria, Britain, Prussia, and eventually France, sitting as a committee. The weak states were allowed to serve on special commissions. Thirty-two nations attended the 1919 peace conference, although Germany, Austria, Turkey, and Russia were excluded. Decision-making was entrusted to the Big Five—France, Britain, the United States, Italy, and Japan—and for the most part, to the triumvirate of Clemenceau, Wilson, and Lloyd George. The weak states were invited to present their claims but had no part in negotiating them. When the representatives of fifty nations gathered at San Francisco to found the United Nations Organization, there was again a Big Five, consisting this time of the United States, the Soviet Union, Britain, France, and China, which again became a Big Three, as France, which had barely emerged from enemy occupation, was preoccupied with internal matters and the government of China was operating with an uncertain mandate. The weak states again played a minor role in the conference, except that the Latin American delegates were able to pressure the United States into keeping hemispheric security arrangements out of the UN's jurisdiction. Although the weak states had little collective influence at any of these conferences, they did not go home empty-handed. Through the good offices of great powers on whom they had claims, or whose interests happened to coincide with their own, some at each conference shared abundantly in the spoils of war. At Vienna, Versailles, and San Francisco, it was taken for granted that war and peace were determined by great-power relationships. If those relationships could be peacefully regulated, the quarrels of weak states would be settled out of hand by great powers acting in concert. Not until the 1960s did blocs of weak states begin to play important roles on the international stage, a development closely linked to the End Game, which forced the two superpowers to seek the goodwill of otherwise negligible governments.

In order to understand why these three serious efforts to realize the Grand Design failed so completely, we need to look more closely at the pressures that created the victorious alliances of 1815, 1918, and 1945, and at the geometry of coalitions in triads by which they were inexorably destroyed.[20]

A system of international relations can be conveniently analyzed as a cluster of linked triads, in each of which governments form coalitions when they calculate that a coalition will enable them to dominate other governments or to avoid domination by other governments. The interacting governments in the model are differentiated by only one attribute—military power. Their agendas contain two principal items: (1) to avoid domination by other governments; (2) to dominate other governments. The model does not assume that prospective gains and losses are equally weighted. Most national governments are rather conservative with respect to external relationships. They weigh prospective losses more heavily than prospective gains, and give higher priority to avoiding domination than to achieving it. And they seem to attach more importance to the recovery of prior losses than to the conservation of prior gains.

It may be objected that governments have ideological interests of which this model takes no account, like the British cabinet's insistence on the abolition of the slave trade at the Congress of Vienna, Wilson's Fourteen Points, the doctrines of Marxism-Leninism, the Four Freedoms of Roosevelt and Churchill. But I think it can be shown that ideological goals are likely to be compromised when they clearly interfere with the primary goals of dominating or avoiding domination.

Revolutionary movements become parties in the linked triads of an international system as soon as they develop significant military capabilities. Their goals resemble those of established governments, except for being focused on a single adversary, which they aim to overthrow.

The payoffs of dominance in an international system include the acquisition of territory, wealth, and population; national prestige and ideological and political influence; and advantageous terms of trade. The negative payoffs of being dominated are just the opposite.

Peacetime coalitions—alliances—are formal agreements by the coalition partners to pool their military power in future wars against designated adversaries. Such promises are contingent and are often broken when the distribution of power changes. Wartime coalitions usually give the strongest partner some degree of control over the military forces of the weaker partners. The pooling of military power under a unified command makes it much more difficult for a weaker partner to withdraw from a coalition. If the pooling is for the duration of a campaign, the coalition will begin to dissolve before the campaign is over, as the weaker partners maneuver to avoid permanent domination by the stronger. If the pooling is permanent, as in the case of the Continental Army that won the American Revolution, the formation of coalitions among the component governments will be greatly inhibited and the merger may become permanent.

Both in war and in peace, the struggle to dominate and to avoid domination inevitably takes precedence over the maintenance of peace. The problem is perennial. As Marriott wrote in 1918:

Four times in four centuries, have the Nation-States of Europe been compelled to combine against the threatened domination of one of their number. . . . The dispersion of the Spanish Armada not only preserved the independence of England and of the United Netherlands, but it dealt a death-blow to the ambitions of Philip the Second, and asserted the nascent principle of European equilibrium. A century later, the peaceful transference of the English crown from James the Second to the Dutch stadtholder, the consequent formation of a grand alliance under William's presidency, and the genius, military and diplomatic, of John Churchill, Duke of Marlborough, delivered Europe from the threatened thraldom of Louis XIV. Another century passed, and the sea-power of England, backed by her long purse and assisted by a soldier second only, if he was second, in ability to Marlborough, frustrated, in similar fashion, the ambition of Napoleon Buonaparte. Against the fourth attempt to enthrall Europe—and not Europe only—we are still in arms.[21]

This anglocentric view of history is consistent with English policy throughout those four centuries. Its constant aim was to thwart the rise of a dominant power or coalition on the European continent.

In the three grand alliances that were victorious in 1815, 1918, and 1945, divisive coalitions developed among the victorious allies in each case. After the fall of Paris in March 1814 and the abdication of Napoleon, Britain and Austria perceived the danger of a coalition between Russia, the most powerful allied state, and a defeated but still formidable France.

. . . there arose before the eyes of the other Allies the nightmare vision, which was not soon to fade, of another Franco-Russian Alliance more fateful than that of Tilsit, in which the visionary autocrat of All the Russias would figure as the patron of the Jacobinism of France and all Europe.[22]

The nightmare vision appeared so threatening to Britain and Austria that they admitted France to the inner circle of the Congress of Vienna before the end of 1814 and made a secret alliance with her soon after, thus dividing the powers into two opposed coalitions, Russia-Prussia and Britain-France-Austria, which were approximately equal in military power. This division was never overcome during the brief life of the first European Confederation, and accounted for its disappearance. But the danger that one state might dominate Europe was averted for nearly a hundred years.

The nightmare vision of the victorious allies in 1918 was an alliance between Bolshevik Russia and a resurgent Germany, which might attempt to dominate Europe. The preventive measures they took against that threat led eventually to its realization.

The nightmare vision of the victorious allies in 1945 was split: the United States and the Soviet Union each feared that the other sought a universal imperium. The Soviet takeover of Eastern Europe and the U.S. unveiling of the atom bomb confirmed their respective apprehensions and set the stage for the End Game.

It will be recalled that most of the literary versions of the Grand

Design—beginning with Pierre Dubois in 1306—were transparently intended to enable a favored prince to dominate Europe within the framework of an international league. When real leagues began to be founded, they followed the same pattern. The Holy Alliance was transparently intended to perpetuate the domination of Europe by Russia—a purpose clearly perceived and promptly blocked by Britain. The League of Nations was intended, at least by Clemenceau, to perpetuate the domination of Europe by France—a purpose dimly perceived but promptly blocked by the United States. The United Nations Organization was intended to confirm the global dominance of the United States—a purpose immediately perceived and eventually blocked by the Soviet Union.

The reaction of the strongest state threatened by domination was the same in the first two of these episodes—to rehabilitate the defeated enemy as a counterweight to the overambitious ally. In the more recent episode, the constitutional peculiarities of the United Nations permitted the Soviet Union to form coalitions with a sufficient number of weak states to isolate the United States within the organization. In each case, the government that hoped to dominate the peacekeeping league proposed the permanent pooling of military forces under the league's command, but the governments threatened by domination rejected the proposal out of hand. From the Congress of Vienna to the Congress of Verona, it was the Tsar who urged the creation of an international army, which Britain and Austria resisted. In 1919, France wanted the League of Nations to have an army of its own; the project was firmly rejected by Wilson and Lloyd George. In 1945, the UN Charter, while stopping short of an international army, did provide for the ad hoc pooling of military forces. The Soviet insistence on the veto at San Francisco was stimulated by that danger. Two years later, the United States proposed, in the Baruch plan, to place all atomic weapons under international control, or as the Soviets perceived it, to create an international military force more powerful than any national army, which would subject them to the dominations of their erstwhile ally.

The model shows clearly why the Grand Design repeatedly failed, or rather, why it has never been tried. The key feature of the project, in St. Pierre's definitive version, is a strong, permanent military force controlled by a peacekeeping league of sovereign governments. The adoption of that arrangement was blocked by adverse coalitions on several occasions when it seemed imminent because it threatened to be more advantageous for some than for others. But it is possible to imagine conditions under which this old and battered peace game might be more successfully played.

Chapter 6

Options for Peace Games Today

> This is probably not the best of possible worlds
> but it is the only one we have. Reason may not
> assure the world of a better future, or even of any
> future at all, but unreason will inevitably assure
> that it has none.
> **Wilbert Moore**

The hawkish view of the End Game, embodied in NATO doctrine, includes certain fixed assumptions.

• The Soviet Union still has a plan for world domination, derived from the revolutionary ideology of Marxism-Leninism. The invasion and conquest of Western Europe is part of the plan.

• In case of invasion, NATO's conventional forces would be no match for the Warsaw Pact forces.

The dovish view of the End Game, held by some unofficial experts, is quite different.

• The strategy of the Soviet Union has become essentially defensive. It has no compelling reason to invade Western Europe, and would not risk the destruction of its homeland to do so.

• The conventional forces deployed by NATO on the central front are roughly equal to the Warsaw Pact forces.

In the hawkish view, the war for Europe, if it comes, can be won only with nuclear weapons. True hawks make the prospect look almost attractive:

Both sides are rapidly shrinking their missiles' explosive force in order to be able to attack military targets without causing extensive collateral damage that would invite reprisals against cities. Specifically, the megatonnage of the U.S. missile arsenal has shrunk by about half since 1970 and by about three-quarters since the late 1950s. It has become so danger-ous—and indeed useless—to attack cities in the World War II style that war once again may become professionalized, the way it was in the eighteenth century; armed forces against armed forces, with the noncom-batants on the sidelines.[1]

True doves anticipate that any exchange of battlefield nuclear weapons will escalate to the exchange of strategic weapons, and they quote climatologists who estimate that the detonation of no more than one percent of existing strategic arsenals would plunge the earth into the darkness and misery of a nuclear winter.

Both hawks and doves are attempting to predict complex, hypo-thetical events occurring at an uncertain time in the future under largely unknown conditions. There is no body of hard facts to which their dispute can be appealed. But, curiously enough, the hawks and the doves agree on an essential point: that the long-planned war on the central front is something to be avoided if possible.

There are two possible alternatives to that war: perpetual con-frontation or disengagement. The continued confrontation of the great armies on the central front implies, for the foreseeable future, the continued confrontation of the strategic missile forces with which the superpowers hold each other hostage. But perpetual confrontation is implausible, given the risks of accident and the geometry of coalitions. Which leaves disengagement as the only rational short-term goal. It is conceivable that disengagement might occur haphazardly, and that a durable peace might develop without any plan. We had better not count on it. Great political changes almost always follow a conceptual blueprint.

The concentration of troops and supplies on both sides of the central front and the arsenals of strategic missiles the superpowers have deployed against each other are both parts of the same war game. The goal of each side is to avoid eventual domination by the other. In the original scenario of the End Game, the threats were asymmetrical. The Soviet Union threatened to achieve world domination by invading and/or subverting Western Europe. The United States threatened to dominate by using its nuclear monop-oly, and later its nuclear superiority, against the Soviet Union. Each threat was plausible, but neutralized by the other. Gradually, as the Soviet Union attained nuclear parity and as the West German role in NATO expanded, the threats became symmetrical. Each side threatens to dominate both by invasion and by a first strike. Each side is deterred both by the threat of invasion and by the threat of a first strike.

Most proposals for arms reduction do not aim at disengagement. They address the absurd overbuilding of nuclear weapons. A 90 percent reduction in the nuclear arsenals of the superpowers would not constitute disengagement. The abandonment of intercontinental rockets in favor of other delivery vehicles would not be disengagement either. The burden of maintaining the arsenals and the risks of accidental firing would be attenuated by a reduction in the number of weapons. But as long as each side continued to target the hundred or so largest cities of the other side with live warheads, disengagement would remain as remote as ever. No one has so far been able to visualize any defense that would be impermeable to delivery vehicles of all kinds.

Disengagement would involve withdrawing the American and Soviet armies from the central front, and detargeting all cities. Demobilization on the central front could easily occur without detargeting, but detargeting is almost inconceivable without prior demobilization.

Just as a reduction in nuclear missiles would not constitute disengagement, the mutual reduction of conventional forces on the central front that is currently being negotiated, following Gorbachev's December 1988 announcement of a unilateral partial withdrawal of Soviet attack units from forward positions, will not constitute disengagement as long as substantial forces still face each other on the central front. According to official U.S. doctrine, a unilateral withdrawal of American forces from Germany would leave the Soviet Union dominant in Europe. The Soviet doctrine is presumably a mirror image, but with different nuances arising from the partition of Germany.

Disengagement is a political rather than a logistical problem. The United States is committed in principle to the eventual unification of Germany; so is the Soviet Union. In practice, they tacitly agree on continued partition, and their armies on the central front have the latent mission of assuring that the Germans are given no opportunity to unite. Up to the time of the Berlin crisis, unification under the aegis of the German Democratic Republic was regarded in the West as a real possibility. The addition of that new entity to the Warsaw Pact would have created a bloc possibly capable of dominating Europe and perhaps eventually able to dominate the United States.

This situation, like the central front itself, has become more symmetrical and less interesting with the passage of time. It is most unlikely that either the West German people or the United States or the other NATO powers would peacefully accept the unification of Germany under a Communist regime, and it is equally certain that any attempt to reattach East Germany to the Federal Republic would be resisted by force. Both superpowers are committed to the principle of national self-determination in general, and it is thus somewhat awkward for them to oppose it so strongly in the case of Germany. This awkwardness was temporarily resolved after the Second World War by the End Game, and, as much as anything else, this has kept the End Game going all these years. Both superpowers still insist—very softly— on the eventual reunification of Germany, but want to postpone the happy event indefinitely.

What is needed, then, is a political realignment that makes German unification irrelevant, such as the unification of Western Europe under a sovereign government. The formation of a West European Union around the existing nuclei—NATO, the European Economic Community, the European Parliament—would transform the distribution of power in the world. The new nation would have more population than either the United States or the Soviet Union, much more productive capacity than the Soviet Union, and about the same productive capacity as the United States.[2] The European Coal and Iron Community and the European Economic Community were originally proposed by Jean Monnet and his collaborators as first steps toward European nationhood, and the proposal for a European Defense Force, vetoed by Charles de Gaulle in 1954, would have brought the project to what seems to be the critical step in national mergers—the permanent pooling of armed forces under a unified command.

De Gaulle's rejection of the European Defense Force was based, as might have been expected, on the apprehension that within a West European Union founded at that time Germany might easily become the dominant state. But the geometry of coalitions does not give the same readings today. The demographic and economic advantage of Germany over France has been shrinking, the United Kingdom makes a third major power in the European Community, and Italy has become a fourth. The 1990 populations of the Federal Republic, France, the United Kingdom, and Italy are projected to be almost equal: 60, 56, 55, and 57 million respectively. Spain, with 49 million, will not be far behind. Belgium and the Netherlands, with a combined population of 25 million, more than offset the 16 million East Germans and 7 million Austrians who may some day return to the German fold.

Economically, France drew level with West Germany about 1970, as measured by per capita GNP, and they have been neck and neck ever since. Italy and the United Kingdom lag somewhat behind, but not enough to give Germany an overwhelming advantage. Nor does Germany any longer enjoy the superiority over France in military manpower that was so decisive in 1940. That superiority was traceable to the decimation of the French male cohorts of 1908 to 1918 in the First World War, reflected in the abnormally small cohorts of the next generation. Those effects have now disappeared, and both Germanies show less than zero population growth while the French population continues to increase.

The intangible factors of militarism and chauvinism are not so easily measured, but France, with its highly developed *force de frappe* is the only country in Europe where public opinion is indifferent to nuclear hazards, while Germany, for the time being, has more antinuclear and antiwar activists than any other country. These factors are beginning to count. The 1988 agreement to remove all trade barriers among the Common Market countries by 1992 is seen by many European observers as a step toward political union, just as the activation of the first joint Franco-German military units in 1989 may foretell the eventual development of a common defense force.

If a West European Union were formed, the existing pattern of coalition tendencies might prevail initially within the new nation.

It is a remarkably favorable pattern, marked by the absence of permanent coalitions among the major powers, and by flexibility in the choice of temporary coalition partners on specific issues. There are difficult economic issues, like the question of agricultural subsidies in the European Economic Community, but none that split the members into irreconcilable blocs. Religion is no longer divisive, and there is nearly as much consensus about political fundamentals in Western Europe in 1989 as there is in the United States. All things considered, there are fewer impediments to the formation of a West European Union today than at any time since 1815. Why, then, does the project remain tentative?

The answer must be sought in the simple-minded axioms of the geometry of coalitions. The United States is ambivalent about the formation of a new superpower that would be able, at least on certain issues, to form a dominant coalition with the Soviet Union. The French are still apprehensive, by reflex, about domination by Germany within a Union. The British are chronically ambivalent about the Common Market and cling to the remnants of empire and their insular independence. The Germans are acutely aware of the numerical superiority of the Latin-speaking bloc and of the anti-German sentiments that persist in some of the smaller countries.

Additionally, the governments of Western Europe have been aware that if they merged, they might eventually have to bear the full cost of defending themselves against the Soviet Union. The current annual cost of American participation in the unfought war on the central front comes to around 150 billion dollars—roughly the size of the U.S. budget deficit, and a prime cause of that deficit. The Europeans are not eager to have this handsome subsidy stopped. It has helped them to catch up with us economically without mortgaging their futures as we have.

Aside from fiscal considerations, a West European Union might want to increase its nuclear arsenal sharply to mount a more effective defense against Soviet nuclear forces. But only in France does pronuclear opinion seem strong enough to support such a buildup. Elsewhere in Europe, nuclear arms are opposed by large and active minorities, or, as in Norway and Denmark, by large majorities. The need for a nuclear buildup may be illusory, however. The existing nuclear forces of France and the United Kingdom are already capable of inflicting unacceptable damage on the Soviet Union. The argument that the West European Union would require an overkill capacity to match the overkill capacity of the Soviet Union rests on the tenuous logic of the End Game, which takes no account of ordinary human motives. It implies that the Soviets would leap at the opportunity to invade Western Europe if they knew that they might lose only 40 percent of their population while the West Europeans lost 80 percent.

The flaws in this reasoning have not escaped the notice of perspicacious Europeans. According to official NATO doctrine, Western Europe is sheltered under a U.S. nuclear umbrella, so that if Soviet ground forces began an invasion of Western Europe and if NATO ground forces were unable to hold them back, the United States would launch its strategic missiles against the Soviet Union. This first strike would assuredly invite retaliation in kind and the destruction of American cities. Some Europeans are sufficiently cynical to doubt that an American president would invite the destruction of Washington and New York in order to protect Bonn and Hamburg.[3] The presence of American troops on the central front is supposed to reassure the Europeans on this delicate point; in a sense, the troops and their dependents are hostages for the fulfillment of our treaty obligations. But even so, an American president might perversely prefer the surrender of an army to a full-scale nuclear exchange. The outcome of a Soviet nuclear attack on Western Europe is equally inconclusive. A massive Soviet strike on the central front would automatically trigger the launching of British and French missiles—but not necessarily American missiles. A selective Soviet strike elsewhere in Europe might lead almost anywhere, but the launching of a U.S. first strike would not be automatic in that case either.

In either case, the U.S. response would be determined by U.S. interests, not European interests—as is right and proper. We are not likely to accept the horrors of a general nuclear war for the sake of third parties. Nor is there any reason to suppose that the Soviets are prepared to accept those same horrors for the doubtful pleasure of occupying hostile territory in Western Europe.

The danger of Communist subversion of the Western European

regimes has waned with the passage of time. The French Communists have dwindled to relative insignificance, The Italian party, although still large, is at odds with Moscow. In Germany, the Greens have submerged the Reds. The prospect of revolution is more remote in Western Europe today than at any time since the fall of the Bastille.

By contrast, the Soviet satellites of Eastern Europe are increasingly restive, and peaceful revolutions are under way in Poland and Hungary. The willingness of the Soviet Union to disengage from the central front may be contingent on whether the United States and NATO will promise to refrain from any military contacts with East European governments. Such a guarantee would merely continue an existing rule of the End Game under new conditions.

In sum, the time is ripe for disengagement.

It could take the form of an agreed withdrawal of U.S. and Soviet forces from the central front—a possibility occasionally discussed along with less sweeping measures in the current negotiations on the reduction of conventional forces.[4] It will of course be objected that the Soviet forces, withdrawn within their own borders, would still have easy access to their abandoned positions, while the U.S. forces would be far overseas. The objection ignores the peculiarity of keeping an American army in Europe to defend a bloc of nations which collectively have more manpower, and better access to military technology, than their potential adversary.

Disengagement could also be accomplished by a unilateral withdrawal of American forces from Europe in gradual stages. One good reason for doing this is that we can no longer afford the expense. When the confrontation on the central front was established, the United States owned about 55 percent of the world's wealth and could afford almost anything. We are now down to about 20 percent and heavily in debt, while our principal military dependents, Western Europe and Japan, hold more than 30 percent of the world's wealth and are less encumbered.[5] A military withdrawal from Europe (and eventually also from Japan and South Korea) would go far toward balancing the federal budget.

One of the arguments that has so far prevailed against the withdrawal of the American armies of occupation from Germany and the Pacific is that we would be giving up our leadership of the free world. In other words, the U.S. would no longer be able to dominate France, West Germany, the United Kingdom, Italy, and Japan. But domination, in the war system, flows from power and not from administrative arrangements. It is gratifying that NATO's supreme commander is always an American general; that courtesy cannot hide the precipitous decline of American influence over the NATO allies, particularly since 1986 when the U.S. became a net debtor to them.

Would a U.S. withdrawal from the central front throw Western Europe into the arms of the Soviet Union? Under current circumstances, the question is absurd. The NATO nations are as staunchly anti-Communist and as geopolitically anti-Russian as the United States. They are more advanced technologically than the Soviet Union and can field more soldiers if they have to. The removal of American units from the central front and even the removal of the entire NATO army from the central front would have remarkably little effect on the NATO scenario for a third World War, which calls for escalation to strategic nuclear weapons after NATO forces fail to stop a Soviet drive across the central front. The scenario says more about the reluctance of the West Europeans to pay the cost of providing themselves with adequate defenses than about Soviet intentions.

The withdrawal of American forces from the central front would present the West Europeans with a choice between increasing their own commitments to the central front or negotiating disengagement on their own. Since the U.S. contribution to NATO's overhead and operating costs is much larger than the relative size of the American contingent on the central front, the additional burden would be substantial, and it is likely that the Europeans would opt for disengagement. The Soviets, relieved of the fear of an American-led intervention in Eastern Europe, would probably acquiesce.

In either event, the West European countries would be forced into closer cooperation for their common defense and for dealing with the Soviet Union and its satellites. Whether this cooperation would go as far as a common defense force is difficult to predict.[6] If it did, the West European Union would have come into existence, and the End Game would be replaced by a configuration of three superpowers, with new perspectives and new possibilities for bringing nuclear weapons under control.

Only by disengaging on the central front can the United States and the Soviet Union escape from the unfought war that neither can win but both can lose big. But the importance of the peace game called disengagement goes well beyond the nuclear predicament. The distortion of the human dimensions of war by technology did not begin with Hiroshima. Thirty years before, in the trenches of the western front, millions of men died for no discernible reason. It was plain by the end of 1915 that large-scale war was no longer the noble game that had exhilarated a hundred earlier generations of warriors; it had become an industrial process.[7] True, there were episodes of glorious adventure—the jousting of the fighter planes high above the trenches, the hunt for the *Emden,* the capture of Jerusalem—but these had little effect on the outcome.

The ineffectual peacemaking of 1919 paved the way for a string of dirty little wars and then the resumption of the Great War on a larger scale than before. This time around, the horrors of trench warfare were not repeated, but new horrors were introduced—the relentless bombing of inhabited places from the air, the assembly-line killing of noncombatants. Once again, the representatives of the victorious governments met to outlaw war as an instrument of national policy, but were unable to prevent the two hundred dirty little wars that broke out in the next few years while the superpowers prepared for a new and unimaginably dirty Great War.

The playing of peace games now seems more urgent than ever before because nuclear weapons raise the costs and pains of industrialized war by several orders of magnitude, but those costs and pains were already intolerably high when the first atomic device was built. While the technology of conflict has changed out of all recognition in the past two centuries, the sociology of conflict has not. Basic social processes are highly resistant to manipulation. It is reasonable to expect that the parts and pieces with which realistic peace games can be played are those that have been used for peacemaking in the past. There will surely be refinements of detail, but no breakthrough in social technology is likely to transform the parameters of the problem.

We are thrown back on the accumulated experience of international peacemaking, which teaches us, among other things, that public opinion is an ineffectual restraint on war, that an arms control agreement is more likely to accelerate than to retard an arms race, that nationalist sentiments generally prevail over internationalist sentiments in a crisis, that balances of power are unstable, that unarmed peacekeeping is generally ineffectual, and that armed forces seldom practice the Golden Rule. These lessons are too clear to be safely ignored. The peacemaking devices that have always failed before will surely fail the next time they are tried, and the time after that.

But the same body of experience offers more encouraging lessons. The rules of war can be effectively modified by multilateral agreements. The prohibition of atrocious weapons can be effective. Patriotism can be transferred from smaller to larger polities, and political unification is a reliable method of reducing the incidence of war. Social progress may not be continuous and cumulative but it does occur; what Tocqueville called "the gradual progress of equality" has been improving the human condition for several centuries past. Some configurations of power are quite stable; they are not particularly difficult to identify. Although governments are seldom virtuous, they are capable of rational actions.

"It is manifest," wrote old Thomas Hobbes in *Leviathan*, "that during the time men live without a common power to keep them all in awe, they are in that condition which is called *war* and such a war as is of every man against every man." In the war of every man against every other, he goes on to say, there being no common power, there is no law. Where there is no law, there is no justice or injustice.

The principal obstacle to the creation of a common power in one form or another is the enormous value that the citizens of modern states attach to their national independence, as much in microstates like Grenada as in major states like France. The desire for a nation of one's own has created more than 150 new states since 1945. Many more new states will appear if existing separatist movements are eventually successful. This fragmentation has occurred during a period when the need for political unification was perhaps more urgent than ever before—something the whole world recognized in 1945 and forgot by 1950. The End Game encouraged fragmentation by giving every microstate a military godfather, or a choice between two military godfathers, and thus endowing it with an independent capacity for mischief. The United Nations has actively promoted fragmentation by admitting scores of negligible states to full membership and giving them generously disproportionate voices and votes.

But as of this writing the End Game seems finally to be winding down and the United Nations has become a forum where the superpowers tacitly or openly cooperate to suppress regional conflicts. The world may be ready for the resumption of the long-term trend toward political unification that was interrupted in 1919. The question to ask is what forms of political unification are feasible under existing conditions?

The *merger of states* is, of course, the classic method of preventing war. As Charles Sumner put it in 1849:

It is in the order of Providence that individuals, families, tribes and nations should tend, by means of association, to a final Unity. History bears ample testimony to the potency of this attraction. Modern Europe, in its early periods, was filled with petty lordships, or communities constituting so many distinct units, acknowledging only a vague nationality, and maintaining, as we have already seen, the "liberty" to fight with each other. The great nations of our day have grown and matured into their present form by the gradual absorption of these political bodies.[8]

From the remote past, states have been merged by conquest, conveyance, and negotiation; by dynastic inheritance, adoption, and marriage; with and without popular approval; at the initiative of the stronger state or the weaker state or of third parties; on battlefields and in peace conferences. Some mergers occur by stages; others all at once.

Every sizable state in the world has been formed by successive mergers. Consider Great Britain, formed by the union of England and Scotland in 1707 after a long series of previous mergers that began when the kingdom of Wessex absorbed Kent, Surrey, Sussex, and Essex around the year 825. Or France, all of whose provinces outside the Île-de-France were once independent sovereignties. Or Spain, created by a marriage between the heirs of Castile and Aragon. Or Italy and Germany, each formed into a national state in the nineteenth century by attaching flocks of lesser states to a dominant kingdom. Or the Russian state, which appeared when the duke of Muscovy acquired Novgorod in 1471, beginning a series of mergers that continued until the annexation of the Baltic republics in 1945.

Two grand mergers appeared possible after the Second World War: first, the merging of the Soviet Union, its Eastern European satellites, and the Chinese and Mongolian People's Republics to form a Communist superstate stretching from Canton to Prague; and second, the merging of the European democracies into a single state, as envisaged by Jean Monnet. Both mergers were blocked by the reluctance of the governments and peoples concerned. In Sumner's optimistic model of the "war system of the commonwealth of nations," the merger of states into larger and larger units and the corresponding expansion of the sphere of law were evolutionary processes that occurred without human forethought. In the even more optimistic model developed at about the same time by Marx and Engels, the war system was an artifact of capitalism that would disappear when the international working class realized its destiny. In retrospect, it is plain that both models oversimplified the problem, and that prophecies based on them were usually wrong.

It is instructive to examine the characteristics of successful mergers. They appear to satisfy the following criteria.

1. *Cultural unity*. It is no accident that each of the large European states produced by successive mergers—France, Spain, Britain, Italy, Germany, Russia—corresponds fairly well to a cultural area whose identity was established long before. Italy and Germany were familiar entities a thousand years before they became national states.

2. *A dominant ethnic group*. The politics of states in which two or more ethnic or religious groups struggle for dominance—Lebanon, South Africa, Northern Ireland, for example—are generally disastrous.

3. *Convenient borders*. The merging states must be contiguous, and the borders between them must be at least as accessible as their external borders with other states.

4. *Compatible status orders.* Although the status orders of the merged states need not be identical, they must be sufficiently alike to encourage intermarriage and easy communication among their elites.

5. *Common enemies.* Every merger imposes heavy costs on one or more of the merging states, diminishing their autonomy and exposing them to new competitors. In the usual case, the only sufficient compensation is protection against their enemies.

6. *A shared mythology.* To be viable, a state must have the icons that sustain patriotism and loyalty: national heroes and heroic deeds to commemorate, sacred sites and precious relics to revere. Merging states must share or invent an heroic past.

While mergers of states do not always succeed when all of the foregoing conditions are met, they almost invariably fail when any are absent. The failures are interesting. A merger of the United States and Canada, for example, was frequently considered during the first century of American independence and occasionally during the second. All that was lacking was a common enemy, but that lack was sufficient to block the endeavor. A merger of the Central American republics seems so eminently reasonable that it has been attempted three times since 1900, but none of the new governments lasted more than a few months. These little nations are linked by language, religion, and culture, have matching status orders, and hold the heroic parts of their history in common, but their common borders are mostly inaccessible, running through roadless jungles and swamps. Scandinavia provides an even more interesting example of how the absence of a single condition may block otherwise promising mergers. The four Scandinavian nations—Sweden, Norway, Denmark, and Iceland—have been merged with one another at various time in various configurations, but no merger has endured. They are closely related by language, religion, and ethnicity, have equal claims to the heroic past of the Vikings; they have—except for Iceland—convenient borders among themselves, and natural enemies in Germany and Russia. The only missing condition is compatible status orders; theirs are dramatically incompatible: Sweden with a highly structured hierarchy headed by a landowning aristocracy, Denmark dominated by an urban merchant class, Norway and Iceland with little hereditary stratification.[9]

The cultural unity required for a successful merger should not be confused with cultural homogeneity. Some of the most unified nations of Europe, like Switzerland and Czechoslovakia, are multilingual, as are the Sovet Union, India, and scores of third world states. Homogeneity in religion is the exception rather than the rule in contemporary nations. A great many nations display some cleavage between an industrial "north" and an agrarian "south." The components of a merged state need not be alike in every way provided they are alike in some ways.

The prior configuration of power does not seem to determine the success or failure of a merger. Mergers initiated by a dominant power have not been either more or less durable than mergers formed by equals. Although mergers have occurred in all sorts of ways, they usually begin with a war and are maintained by subsequent wars. More often than not, they involve attachment of weak states to much stronger states, either by military force or under military threat. The weaker states give up their sovereignty but retain their national identities. The element of forcible subjection lingers on for centuries in the relationship between the metropolitan nation and the annexed province, as between England and Wales, Great Russia and the Ukraine, Castile and Catalonia, Prussia and Saxony. The parties to a successful merger seldom abandon their separate identities entirely. There continue to be Welshmen, Ukrainians, Catalans, Saxons, and Texans for that matter, long after the independent states that bore those names vanished. There are separatist sentiments and movements in many of the provinces that make up modern nations, but they are ordinarily satisfied by moderate concessions.

Mergers are almost sure to be attempted whenever two or more states with some kind of common identity have a common enemy, but almost certain to fail for lack of some of the other functional requirements discussed above: a dominant ethnic group, convenient borders, compatible status orders, a shared mythology. Since the first outbreak of war between Israel and its Arab neighbors in 1948, more than a dozen mergers have been attempted by the Arab states. The most serious of these, the merger of Egypt and Syria in the United Arab Republic, lacked convenient borders and began to dissolve soon after it was formed in 1958.[10] The sub-Saharan African states, without a dominant ethnic group, convenient borders, or a shared mythology, have been similarly unable to make good any of the national mergers they have proclaimed from time to time.

The centrifugal forces released by the Second World War and the End Game encouraged fragmentation nearly everywhere: the partitions of Germany, Palestine, Korea, and Vietnam; the separation of Pakistan from India and of Bangladesh from Pakistan, of Taiwan from China, and of Singapore from Malaysia; the de facto partitions of Lebanon and Yemen; and of course the achievement of independence by territories formerly controlled by Britain, France, the Netherlands, Portugal, and the United States. In newly independent colonies, fragmentation was sometimes progressive. The West Indies Federation, having achieved independence from Britain, dissolved into more than a dozen ministates, one consisting of St. Kitts, Nevis, and Anguilla. Soon thereafter, Anguilla, population 5,000, declared itself a separate state and applied for admission to the United Nations.

For the immediately foreseeable future, the centrifugal tendencies are almost certain to persist and to bar any resumption of the long-term trend toward national consolidation, without precluding certain possibly advantageous mergers, like a West European Union. Most of the states that have fought wars since 1945 are small states that came into existence after 1945. They do not seek, and would not consent to, mergers with larger and more powerful states. A peace game based on the merger of today's independent states into a single world state is unrealistic, although it may become more playable at some point in the future. In the short time frame of serious peace games, there is no rational basis for predicting the disappearance of the nation-state as an institutional pattern, and even less reason to anticipate a change in the pattern that would make nation-states peaceable without external constraint.

When the atomic bomb was unveiled in 1945, it seemed to confirm a widely held opinion that the international system was obsolete and that the safety of humanity called for a curtailment of the unlimited sovereignty of national governments. This was the position put forward by Albert Einstein. The opposing opinion—that the limitation of national sovereignty was impossible in the near term—was systematically presented in 1946 when Bernard Brodie and his Yale colleagues published their book on *The Absolute Weapon: Atomic Power and World Order*. Brodie argued that force would continue to govern the relations of sovereign nations, because the exercise of force is the basic function of sovereignty, and that atomic weapons, being more forceful than any other weapons, could not be kept out of military use. But he thought that the use of atomic weapons could be restrained by the prospect of retaliation in kind, thus introducing the concept of nuclear deterrence, which became the basis of the End Game soon afterwards.

The adoption of the Brodie position by the superpowers and the manufacture of enormous numbers of nuclear weapons for the ostensible purpose of preventing the use of nuclear weapons submerged—without refuting—the Einstein position to such an extent that, for the first time in more than two thousand years, the ideal of a moral and political order transcending the nation-state went into eclipse.

If a world order capable of preventing nuclear war is created in the reasonably near future, it will not be a world state that replaces the existing national states. A new world order must necessarily be superimposed on the existing national states whether it takes the form of a millenarian movement, a military empire, a peace-keeping federation, a nuclear consortium, or something else. Each of the foregoing possibilities suggests peace games that may, if played seriously, disclose still other possibilities.

Given the clear and present danger that the firing of the nuclear weapons now in place might exterminate the human species, it is perhaps surprising that no *millenarian movement* has appeared with a program of uniting humanity in opposition. The antinuclear movement in the United States and the Greens in Europe make only a feeble start in that direction. The word comes from the twentieth chapter of the Book of Revelation with its vision of the thousand-year rule of Christ on earth, but the millenarian tradition of Judaism was already old at the time and continued afterwards. Millenarian movements have marked the entire history of Christianity from the Cathari to modern salvationists. Islam was initially a millenarian movement and seems to be entering a new millenarian phase today. The French Revolution became a secular millenarian movement in the Year I, and movements of that type have flourished ever since—utopian socialism, positivism, scientific socialism, anarchism, fascism, technocracy, the counterculture, transcendental meditation—each promising to make fundamental changes in the human condition. Marxism in all its branches is an essentially millenarian movement, promising its followers a transformed world purified of the ills that flow from private property and the division of labor. "The public power will lose its political character," said the Communist Manifesto, "when production has been concentrated in the hands of a vast association in which the free development of each is the condition of the free development of all."

The promise of a unified world is offered by every such movement, together with the promise that when the forces of evil and unbelief have been vanquished, the perfected new order will prevail without resistance. A dialogue in a famous utopian tract, Edward Bellamy's *Looking Backward*, described it thus:

> The greater and all the better part of the Capitalists joined with the people in completing the installation of the New Order, which all had now come to see was to redound for the benefit of all alike.
> And there was no war?
> War! Of course not. Who was there to fight on the other side?[11]

The emergence of a peace system from some new social movement is a possibility that cannot be dismissed out of hand. The fear of nuclear devastation may well find expression one of these days in a new creed—religious or secular—that sweeps through the industrialized nations and loosens, at least temporarily, the terrible grip of the state on its citizens, as happened in France in May 1968. Such a movement, made universally visible by the media, might well spread like wildfire. As events in many countries have shown, even the most authoritarian governments find it difficult to prevent popular dissent in today's communication climate.

One reason for skepticism about the chance that a peace system might develop in response to a millenarian movement is that the transformations called for by millenarian creeds are, for the most part, sociologically impossible. Such creeds envisage a protracted conflict between the faithful and their enemies culminating in the triumph of the true faith and the establishment of a new order from which conflict has been banished. But conflict and cooperation are opposite sides of the same coin; a conflict-free social system is a contradiction in terms. Small communities founded on millenarian principles are not observed to be free of conflict; on the contrary, they appear to be obsessed with it,[12] while larger polities with millenarian leanings have problems as severe as those of other polities, as the history of twentieth-century Marxist states illustrates so abundantly.

Nonetheless, the imposition of a peace system by a worldwide social movement remains conceivable. The ability of popular movements to discourage or prevent the pursuit of nuclear strategies by national governments has been amply demonstrated in the Scandinavian countries, New Zealand, and West Germany. It is not difficult to imagine similar movements in other industrialized countries. Even in the United States, where the opposition to nuclear weapons has been scattered and ineffective, church authorities, trade groups, professional associations, and state legislatures often take very strong antinuclear positions, as does a substantial minority of the general public. The elements of a universal peace movement may be already in place, waiting to be galvanized into action by a nuclear accident or an international crisis.

A very different sort of peace game visualizes a *military empire* that regulates or prohibits war among subject governments. It is the easiest peace game to play beause there are so many precedents, going back as far as the Sumerians and the pharaohs. Although no military empire has ever achieved universal domination, there have been numerous imperial regimes in the past that dominated "known worlds" that were larger in terms of travel and communication time and contained more cultural diversity than today's One World. Such were the military empires of Xerxes and Alexander, Augustus and Hadrian, Attila and Charlemagne, the Great Khan and the Great Mogul.

A military empire is founded and legitimized by conquest. It does not need much political philosophy—conquest becomes its own justification—but the later stability of such a regime depends on the administrative formula by which it rules. The Roman administrative formula deserves particular attention. It successfully controlled vast territories for many centuries and survived innumerable crises. The key elements of the formula were the separation of military from civil administration and the protection of local sovereigns and institutions by the imperial authority. This recipe for preserving the fruits of conquest made a lasting impression. For a thousand years after the fall of the western branch of the Roman empire, the eastern branch at Byzantium embodied a version of the same formula. After the nominal resuscitation of the western branch by Charlemagne, it, too, lasted a thousand years.

The Constitution of the United States, as framed in 1787, had more than a casual resemblance to that of imperial Rome, particularly with respect to the division of responsibility between the federal and state governments. The resemblance was intentional, and was emphasized by the choice of Roman symbols like the republican eagle and the name of the Senate. The American polity was not, of course, established by conquest, but it grew largely by conquest, and its Constitution was perfectly adapted to the absorption of new territories.

The Napoleonic empire was as much given to Roman iconography as the American republic, but less faithful to the Roman formula. The division of responsibilities between the empire and its subordinate kingdoms was never clear. Respect for local law, local customs, and local notables was at best intermittent. The imperial army never effectively assimilated its foreign contingents, and the separation of military from civil aspects of administration was incomplete. The empire was meant to be held together by the power of shared ideas—liberty, equality, fraternity, codified law, bureaucratic rationality.[13]

The short-lived Nazi empire was the first European military empire in two thousand years that did not draw either on Roman symbolism or Roman practice.[14] Even if the Roman iconography had not been preempted by Mussolini and his fascist "legions," the Nazis would not have been tempted by it. They identified themselves in a hazy way with the Germanic tribes that resisted and ultimately despoiled Rome. They relied almost exclusively on military force to govern their conquered provinces, treated local laws, customs, and notables harshly, and were particularly contemptuous of the collaborators they were able to recruit. Even in places where the occupying Germans were initially welcome, it took only a few months of their heavy-handed rule to antagonize the population. Hitler's empire became ungovernable as fast as it was founded.

As the Third Reich crumbled, Stalin snapped up its eastern provinces, either by direct military occupation or by helping the indigenous Communists to stage a coup d'état and establish a Communist regime under the active protection of the Red Army. Lithuania, Latvia, and Estonia were annexed. The dependent governments of Poland, Rumania, Hungary, Czechoslovakia, East Germany, and Bulgaria were firmly anchored to the Soviet Union. Yugoslavia and Albania were attached at the same time; they later escaped from Soviet control. The People's Republic of China was founded in 1949 and remained subservient to Moscow for a decade thereafter. Around 1950, there were large, well-organized Communist parties, hopeful of seizing power, in France, Italy, India, Vietnam, and Indonesia, and smaller but equally ambitious Communist parties scattered through Western Europe, Latin America, and Africa. The threat of a Soviet world empire could not be taken lightly.

By 1950, the fundamental premises of American foreign policy were (1) that the Soviet goal was the establishment of a world empire and (2) that our nuclear arsenal was the only real obstacle to that goal. Stalin had described the Union of Soviet Socialist Republics as "the living prototype of the future union of peoples in a single world economic system."[15] No influential voice on either side of the Iron Curtain questioned the ability of the Kremlin to control all the Communist governments that appeared after the war and those that might come to power subsequently.

But Yugoslavia's disaffection and the split between the Soviet Union and China a few years later transformed the theory and practice of socialist internationalism. Socialist states, it developed, could resist foreign domination as vigorously as capitalist states. War among socialist states was not a contradiction in terms, as Marxist-Leninist theory held, but a normal expression of national policy. When the dust settled, the boundaries of the Soviet empire turned out to be those achieved by military occupation in 1945. Marxist-Leninist ideology helped to keep the satellite states in uneasy submission, but did not add an inch of European territory to the conquests of the Red Army. The overseas adventures of the Kremlin obeyed a similar principle. Ideology alone conquered no territory, and the advantages the Soviet Union gained by giving military support to revolutionary movements were dubious; the indigenous Communists often failed to win power, and if successful, often went their own ways.

Despite all the accumulated evidence that Communist states deal with each other in much the same fashion as non-Communist states, and resist domination as vigorously, the old belief in the monolithic character of international Communism is still strong in the right wing of American politics, relying either on ignorance of the relationships among Communist states or on the belief that a rapprochement between the Soviet Union and China may restore the solidarity of the Communist bloc at any time. The subjection of the entire world to a Communist military empire has become improbable but not inconceivable. It would require the military power of the United States and Western Europe to be neutralized and the unified market economy that stretches around the world to be wrecked, not to mention a merger between the Soviet Union and China.

These are challenging conditions, not likely to be met in the foreseeable future, except perhaps in the aftermath of a nuclear war. An iron-fisted Communist military empire is an imaginable outcome of a world war in which the Soviet Union not only prevails but retains enough military strength afterwards to impose its will on Southeast Asia, Japan, Western Europe, and the Americas, as well as China. That empire would have been established by conquest, not by ideological penetration, but it would surely represent itself as the fulfillment of socialist internationalism. It would have one great advantage over previous military empires: a monopoly of nuclear weapons would enable it to suppress rebellions with relative ease.

An American—or Western European or Japanese—world empire

is quite inconceivable for the time being. There is nothing in the ethos of the capitalist democracies to legitimize the military subjugation of one sovereign state by another, and the market economy precludes any centralized, coercive control. The occupation of Japan by the United States, and of West Germany by the Allied Powers, created competitors, not subjects. The difference appears most plainly with respect to nuclear proliferation: the Soviet Union was able to impose total nuclear abstinence on its client states; the United States was not willing or able to do the same. This is the crux of the difficulty Americans have in visualizing any solution to the nuclear predicament; any lasting solution seems to imply the creation of a supranational power and therefore seems incompatible with our attachment to national independence as a universal value.

Another set and perhaps more interesting set of peace games involve a *peacekeeping federation* to regulate or abolish international war. The project is anything but new. The long history of the Grand Design, traced in the previous chapter, includes innumerable schemes for peacekeeping federations and several major attempts to put the concept into practice. I have argued that the failures of the Holy Alliance, the League of Nations, and the United Nations to realize the goals for which they were ostensibly founded are attributable to their common lack of the minimum attributes of an effective federation, as first set forth by St. Pierre and later by Hamilton and Madison in the eighteenth century. These minimum attributes are: (1) a permanent armed force under unified command; (2) courts of law with compulsory jurisdiction reaching to the individual officials and citizens of member states; (3) the power to tax; (4) an unequivocal commitment to protect member states against armed attack and rebellion; (5) a representative assembly to make laws; (6) an executive to enforce the laws and to command the armed forces.

Successful and durable federations—the United Provinces, the Swiss Confederation, the United States of America—have all possessed these attributes, while unsuccessful federations have generally lacked them. But, needless to say, there is a vast difference between a peacekeeping federation formed by a group of states that have a common history, common enemies, and common interests and one that might attempt to unite a collection of states diverse in all these respects.

Twice in the twentieth century, in 1919 and 1945, the delegates of many nations went through the motions of founding an organization of governments to maintain international peace. In each instance, some of the delegates thought they had replaced the war system with a peace system, and even their more skeptical colleagues thought that the organization might become an effective peacekeeping federation over the course of time, though initially lacking the vital organs of such a creature.

As we have seen, none of the several European attempts to put the Grand Design into practice achieved the permanent pooling of military forces under unified command, which seems to be the key feature of an effective peacekeeping federation. But in each instance, it was seriously considered. The treaty establishing the Quadruple Alliance provided for such pooling in case of a renewed French attack, and Alexander I exhorted his reluctant allies to establish a permanent European army. The Covenant of the League of Nations was rejected by the U.S. Senate precisely because it appeared to place the American army and navy under the control of the League Council. That was not a capricious misreading of Article 16 of the Covenant, which stated that if any member of the League were to resort to war in disregard of its obligations under the Covenant, "It shall be the duty of the Council in such case to recommend to the several Governments concerned what effective military, naval or air force the Members of the League shall contribute to their armed forces to be used to protect the covenants of the League." The language wavers between the weakness of "recommend" and the forcefulness of "shall contribute," but the intention to pool forces under unified command is clear, and it took several years for the nations to discover that the Council would never be able to muster an international army.

The United Nations Charter contains a much longer provision, in Chapter VII, that comes to much the same thing. The Security Council is authorized to "take such action by air, sea, or land forces as may be necessary to maintain or restore international peace and security." Rather than recommending at the time of a crisis what forces member governments should contribute, the Council was to negotiate prior agreements governing the number and types of forces and facilities to be furnished by each member, and these forces were to be held continuously available for international use. Once again, it was widely supposed that an international armed force had been created, and once again, events disclosed that nothing of the kind had happened. Although the UN was nominally a party to the Korean War and has raised modest forces on subsequent occasions to police the enforcement of truces, the agreements called for under Chapter VII were never negotiated, and the creation of a powerful armed force under UN control has become almost unthinkable.

The hope that the United Nations may yet evolve into a peace-keeping federation by assuming new powers still flickers here and there, but dimly. To return the organization to its original purpose would require—among many other reforms—the disenfranchisement of the mini- and micro-states that hold a majority in the General Assembly and the transformation of career officials from agents of their home governments to international civil servants. Neither step would be easy. If a peacekeeping federation that includes all or most of the world's nations is ever formed, it will probably be a new organization, founded either by a constitutional convention for the world or by the initial federation of a few major states which invite other major states to join on equal terms. In either case, a formula for representation will have to be devised that allows weak states to participate, perhaps through regional blocs, without acquiring disproportionate influence.

Before we play this peace game further, we need to ask whether it is possible for one-party and military governments to participate. If it were not possible, the largest possible peacekeeping federation that could be formed today would include only about a third of existing states and an even smaller proportion of the world's population. A state that joins a peacekeeping federation with the attributes described above must as a bare minimum permits its citizens to be taxed directly for the support of the federation, and to be arrested and punished by the federation for violations of its laws. In order for a federation to exercise these minimum powers, it must be able to do certain other things: to enumerate and identify individual citizens, to command their appearance and testimony, and to seize and sequester property. If the individual citizen has positive duties toward the federation, then he must also enjoy the individual rights that make it possible to perform those duties without interference from his own government, as well as the right to due process in his transactions with the federation.

Let us concede reluctantly that freedom of speech, assembly, and publication; universal suffrage; liberty of conscience and religion; unrestricted residential and occupational choice; the right of emigration; equality before the law; private property; and immunity from arbitrary search and seizure need not be required of member states. They need only have lawful governments that claim to represent their citizens. But how is the federation, which is obliged to protect the governments of its member states against invasion or armed rebellion, to determine whether a government is lawful and representative? That issue, when raised, would have to be settled by legal process, which implies that every member state—whether it has a parliamentary, one-party, military, or even a feudal regime—must also have a written constitution by reference to which the federation would extend or withhold recognition to a government claiming to be lawful and representative. Nearly all states with parliamentary or one-party systems already have written constitutions (Great Britain is a conspicuous exception). So do most states under military rule. The only feature that would have to be common to the written constitutions of all the member states, aside from those clauses acknowledging federation rights and powers, would be a nonviolent method of amendment.

Contemporary nations show no clear preference for multiparty—i.e., parliamentary—regimes over one-party regimes, or for civil over military rule. They oscillate continually among these forms. Hannan and Carroll found that of the 39 states that had multiparty systems in 1950, 17 had changed systems one or more times by 1975. Of 43 new states that began their national existence under military rule during the same period, 15 had changed to multiparty systems and 7 to one-party systems by 1975.[16] These changes were not always accomplished peacefully. The typical mode of transition from one-party or multiparty rule to military rule is a coup, with or without bloodshed. The transition from military to multiparty rule is often accomplished by a popular uprising that shows itself in street demonstrations. The transition from multiparty to one-party rule typically involves a combination of demonstrations and parliamentary maneuvering.

The right of revolution is too highly regarded by contemporary peoples to be suppressed. What possibly can be suppressed is the initiation of armed rebellions by foreign states, amounting in many instances to invasion by proxy.

Most of the states that now have Communist regimes display the forms, if not the substance, of representative government, and claim to be democratic in their own fashion. Their written constitutions specify the rights and duties of citizens and make provision for amendment. The major obstacle to the participation of a Communist state in a peacekeeping federation would be its theoretical commitment to the encouragement of proletarian revolutions in non-Communist states. Giving up that commitment might not be too high a price to pay for the guarantees of internal and external security offered by such a federation.

Protecting the government of a member state against rebellion would be a stickier point for a peacekeeping federation than protecting it against external aggression. If a federation insisted that no constitutional changes could be effected in member states except by constitutional means, it might make the transition from a one-party to a multiparty system more difficult than the transition from a multiparty system to a one-party system, since access to the amendment process is more restricted under a one-party regime. In recent practice, the change from a one-party to a multiparty system has most commonly occurred in response to popular unrest expressed by demonstrations and strikes. These procedures should be no less effective under a federation.

Nearly all changes of regime take the form of a shift of coalitions in the triad government-army-populace. Regimes fall when the army sides with the populace against the government, as in the Philippines in 1986. Regimes resist change when the army sides with the government against the populace, as in China in 1989. These configurations would be absent in a peacekeeping federation, in which the military forces of member states consist at most of police and lightly armed militia. The elimination of military establishments would have large, not entirely predictable, political consequences for parliamentary as well as nonparliamentary governments. It is difficult to guess, for example, whether the military neutralization of member states would lead to a cessation of diplomatic relations outside of the common assembly, as among the American states after the adoption of the U.S. Constitution, or to an increase of diplomatic transactions, as among the cantons of the Swiss Confederation.

One of the most difficult tasks in establishing a representative federation would be to find a satisfactory formula for the representation of member states that differ greatly in population and wealth. The framers of the U.S. Constitution, after several false starts, settled on the device of a bicameral legislature with equal representation in one house and representation proportional to population in the other. The disparity between the most populous and the least populous American states (now California and Wyoming) was 50 to 1 in 1980; it has not exceeded that order of magnitude since 1790. The disparity in per capita income between the richest and poorest states (now Alaska and Mississippi) is just under 2 to 1; that ratio too has never been significantly exceeded. By contrast, the disparity between the most populous and the least populous member states of the United Nations, China and St. Kitts, is 25,000 to 1; the disparity in per capita income between the United States and Ethiopia is more than 90 to 1. Both the Covenant of the League and the Charter of the United Nations coped with the gross disparities of population and wealth among their member states by means of a bicameral arrangement, with equal representation of all member states in one house and the other house divided between the major military powers, equally and permanently represented, and a smaller number of temporary members.

In a peacekeeping federation whose members had given up their armed forces, military strength would no longer be a basis for representation, but other measures might have to be combined with population size to arrive at a fair estimate of a state's relative importance. A bicameral scheme, with member states equally represented in one house and represented according to their relative importance in the other, might be called for, but the rules of representation would not be easy to settle for either house. As to the upper house, beyond a comprehensible level of disparity among member states—say 250 to 1 in population—equal representation becomes absurd. A ratio of 250 to 1 would fix the minimum population to qualify for representation at around 4 million and would exclude more than half the current members of the United Nations—to their certain displeasure. As to the lower house, the allocation of one representative for every 4 million of population would produce a body of unwieldy size in which India had more delegates than the United States, the Soviet Union, Great Britain, and Japan combined.

All things considered, the arrangement that developed spontaneously at the Congress of Vienna and at subsequent peace conferences, and that was copied in the Covenant and the Charter—an upper house in which each major power has one vote and a lower house in which each member state has one vote—may be the most practicable. At least it has the advantages of custom, familiarity, and simplicity. But the addition of rotating, temporary members to the upper house—as in the Councils of the League and the United Nations—is an aberration flowing from the rule of unanimity in those bodies. With that rule in force, the only votes that matter are vetoes, and since the temporary members do not enjoy the privilege of a veto, their presence makes no difference when votes are counted. The inclusion of temporary members on a rotating basis is more of a public relations device than a constitutional necessity. In a more serious federation, the upper house would probably be limited to the major powers, if there were a consensus about which they were. There are presently only two states that qualify by economic and demographic weight—the United States and the Soviet Union—four that qualify by economic weight, with gross national products over 0.5 trillion— Japan, West Germany, France, the United Kingdom—and two that qualify by demographic weight, with populations of 1.0 and 0.7 billion respectively—China and India. One glance at this roster shows why the establishment of a worldwide federation is not a viable possibility for the time being: the United Stats and its close allies would have 5 votes out of 8. But since we are playing peace games, it is interesting to note how much more manageable the representation of major powers in a federation would be after the merger of West Germany, France, and the United Kingdom into a West European Union. The number of major powers would then be reduced to six and no faction would have an automatic majority.

As previously noted, both parliamentary and authoritarian regimes would have to impose internal changes upon themselves in order to enter a peacekeeping federation. The abolition of military establishments would have far-reaching economic and political effects that are not easily predictable. For example, it is hard to know whether authoritarian regimes are more likely to be democratized by the removal of their military props or to become more tyrannical when they no longer have to placate their armed forces. It is even harder to know if the dismantling of the military-industrial complex would have a stimulating or a depressing effect on national economies. Moreover, these effects may vary from one country to another.

A newly formed federation would have to anticipate that changes in the political and economic structures of its member states would extend over a considerable period of time, accompanied by crises of various kinds. But it would have to insist that the transfer of military power to the federation be abrupt. The retention of any substantial military capability by any member of a peacekeeping federation would be a clear and present danger to all the other members, not only because that power might be turned against them but also because it might be used to challenge the federation's authority.

Whether the total abolition of war is sociologically feasible must remain for the time being an unsettled question. Whether it would be desirable is a question on which there can be no general agreement. Armed conflict is so interwoven with national identity, economic progress, and social justice that its abolition might bring a train of baleful consequences to balance the obvious benefits. The human condition would not be unequivocally improved if armed resistance to injustice became impossible and no rights could be vindicated by force.

But the abolition of large-scale industrial war and the prohibition of "scientific" weapons—nuclear explosives, mass poisoning, artificial epidemics, death rays from space—may be necessary for human survival. If a federation that is able to suppress the use of scientific weapons is founded, it will have to be itself heavily armed. That requirement will not disappear on the distant day when the last outside nation joins a universal federation. The uncancelable technology that makes it possible to produce scientific weapons would leave a disarmed authority at the mercy of any ambitious state that secretly equipped itself with such weapons. For the foreseeable future, the same technologies put formidable military power within easy reach of criminal gangs, political movements, and secret societies. Some of them will surely challenge the federation's authority. Sooner or later, all large polities meet with violent resistance. The technology of nuclear and bacterial weapons offers at least as much scope for rebellious adventures as the technology of spears and bows. It will not be enough for the federation to be able to suppress a local uprising; it must be prepared to cope with multiple challenges that occur simultaneously either by coincidence or because one outbreak sets off others.

For the foreseeable future, it will always be possible for a group of conspirators to produce or steal weapons powerful enough to give them parity with an army. No lightly armed police force will be able to counter that threat. Any world authority will need to deploy large armed forces, and to hold scientific weapons in reserve against their possible introduction by others. To expect public order to maintain itself without an ultimate backing of force is to ignore the fundamental principles of social control.

The question of whether handicraft war might persist after scientific weapons had been brought under the control of a peace-keeping federation is intriguing. Since the federation would be obligated to protect its member states against both invasion and insurrection, it would probably not tolerate any strong military forces except its own. Handicraft war on a small scale might continue among remote tribes or between armed gangs beneath the purview of the federation and it might recur briefly in popular uprisings, but the military culture and the profession of arms would survive only in the federation's own military department, which would need troops, ships, planes, and even missiles. The maintenance of the federation's authority would depend upon its ability to organize a multinational force unlikely to be subverted into the service of any member state or group of states. Military personnel should probably be drawn in approximately equal numbers from all member states, without regard to the size of their populations, and thoroughly mixed either individually or by small units so that an infantry division, a warship, or an air base would include contingents from many nations. Promotions would be controlled by quota so that no nationality could predominate in positions of command. The soldier's transfer of allegiance from his home country to the federation would be formal and solemn and should probably be permanent.

For the time being, nuclear weapons are the most dangerous of scientific weapons. Chemical and biological weapons, however atrocious, have little strategic significance but carry various unpleasant possibilities: utilization by terrorists; an unintended but possibly universal epidemic caused by the escape or mutation of a biological agent; the discovery of a fast-acting lethal agent that becomes inert within a few hours; the discovery of a slow-acting lethal agent that can be applied undetectably to a target population. There is no doubt that scientific weapon research has other nasty surprises in store. Lasers and electron guns will not promote human felicity, nor will further nuclear miniaturization, the basing of nuclear weapons in space, or the further development of antisatellite missiles. The category of scientific weapons is necessarily open-ended, but a peacekeeping federation would discourage further development and take charge of any new devices that appeared.

As soon as the necessity for a peacekeeping federation to maintain a large military establishment is recognized, some of the political features of such a federation stand out in bold relief. The experience of modern states suggests that a military force must be commanded by a civilian head of government in order to be used effectively and kept obedient. A universal federation, like any other government, will have to be led by individuals—either one person who combines the functions of chief of state and head of government, as in the American republic, or two persons who divide these roles, as in the French republic.

The government of a universal federation could not possibly be apolitical, since its constitution would include the rules of the contest for the greatest of all prizes: the headship of the world. The social-psychological benefits of direct election are so great that even the most authoritarian of modern regimes go through the forms of direct election when it seems safe to do so. The doctrine of popular sovereignty is universally honored today, accepted without reservation by the United States, the Soviet Union, the People's Republic, and all their respective allies, and even by Islamic fundamentalists. No other method of establishing the legitimacy of a government can compare with election by a popular majority. A peacekeeping federation would benefit greatly by having its head and one or two other principal officials elected by universal suffrage. In addition to creating legitimacy, the electoral process develops public opinion, increases the flow of information between the government and its citizens, and attracts energy and talent into the political process.

The support of a global constituency would confer enormous charisma on world executives already very powerful because of their exclusive access to scientific weapons. The tendency of republics to Caesarism is as old as the republican idea. The framers of the U.S. Constitution were acutely aware that their republic might degenerate into a monarchy, like the Roman republic they took as their model. The principal safeguards they installed were control of the public purse by an elected legislature and the independence of the judiciary; these have worked reasonably well for two centuries. A peacekeeping federation whose legislature was composed of delegates from member states would certainly want to adopt the former measure, and the latter would be indispensable in an international system in which disputes could no longer be settled by war or the threat of war.

The role of political parties in a peacekeeping federation is not easy to visualize. In the politics of existing states, the maintenance of order and economic management are intertwined, but a peacekeeping federation formed by existing states would be almost exclusively concerned with the maintenance of order. The economic issues that loom so large in the politics of existing states would continue to be resolved at the national level, as they are today.

It is a nice question whether the political parties that developed in a peacekeeping federation would be willing to confine themselves to issues of international order and refrain from interference in other spheres. The federation would not be authorized to transfer territory, population, or resources among its member states, which would continue to manage their economies according to diverse and incompatible principles. Many of the major conflicts of our time stem from preferences for centralized or decentralized management, private or government ownership of production facilities, administered or market prices, protectionism or free trade. Since there is no way, short of war, to resolve these differences, a peacekeeping federation formed by existing states would have to tolerate them. Free-enterprise or state socialist economies would be under no pressure to modify themselves toward a common norm.

Most economic issues, including the preferred forms of industrial and agricultural organization, labor practices, resource management, and the regulation of imports and exports, would be national, not global, concerns. Only those aspects of economic activity directly connected with war—radioactive minerals, weapons production, space traffic—would be controlled by the federation.

The current distribution of wealth among the nations is plainly inequitable, but a peacekeeping federation would have to guarantee its members against forcible redistributions of wealth just as it guaranteed them against forcible redistributions of population or territory. Like today's international organizations, a peacekeeping federation would probably urge rich nations to assist poor nations but it could not compel them.

The federation should not only refrain from attempting to manage the global economy; it should even refrain from the regulation of international commerce, except perhaps by opening its courts to disputes over international contracts. Even that limited function might be superfluous. Today's international markets work well enough without authoritative supervision; in one way or another, they regulate themselves. The commercial disputes that arise in international trade today are settled by negotiation, arbitration, or commercial reprisal, not by threats of war or by recourse to higher authority.

The discovery that capitalist and communist economies can maintain stable and mutually profitable trading relationships has been one of the major surprises of recent decades, comparable to the discovery that Communist states are susceptible to war among themselves. Among Communists and anti-Communists alike, it was formerly an article of faith that the external relations of a Communist state would not resemble those of a capitalist state. In the event, the similarities are more striking than the differences, so that it is not implausible to suppose that states of both types could live under the same political umbrella.

Universal free trade would not be a necessary concomitant of a peacekeeping federation. It is not a practicable arrangement for collectivist states in which the government is the sole foreign trader, and perhaps no longer practicable even for nations whose commerce is largely in private hands, given the extent to which all contemporary governments manage and manipulate their foreign trade.

The question whether a peacekeeping federation would issue its own currency is easily answered. It must levy taxes to support its military and administrative operations, and equity seems to require a common monetary measure. But since the management of a world currency might draw the federation into economic issues from which it ought to abstain, it would be better to base the monetary measure used for federation taxes on metallic or energy units or on a basket of national currencies.

To say that a peacekeeping federation should not attempt to solve the problems of the global economy is not to say that those problems can safely go unsolved, but only to recognize that a global consensus on economic policy is a much more remote possibility than a consensus about the desirability of suppressing nuclear war. The capacity of national governments to cope with economic problems, separately or jointly, would be greatly enhanced by the reduction of their military commitments.

In sum, it is possible to imagine a universal peacekeeping federation that might work very well, if it existed. Indeed, in the long run, something of the kind will probably be established as the unification of the world by technology, trade, and travel increases the advantages of political unification. Playing this peace game is a useful exercise. The more carefully the details of a peacekeeping federation are visualized, the sooner it may become possible.

But there are compelling reasons why it is not possible yet, and why it is not likely to become possible before the nuclear predicament has been otherwise resolved. In the first place, a universal federation founded by mutual agreement would surely have to guarantee permanently the boundaries of its member states. No government would settle for less before disbanding its own military forces. Both the League of Nations and United Nations, weak as they were, purported to guarantee the inviolability of existing national boundaries. But past wars have left the world a rich heritage of disputed territories and territorial claims, from the division of Germany to the ownership of the Falklands. In the absence of a world authority, most territorial issues are ultimately resolved by force or the threat of force. With such an authority in place, they would become unresolvable.

There is an inherent contradiction between the integrity of national boundaries and ethnic self-determination. Modern nations were built by consolidating smaller political entities whose separate identities were never completely obliterated. Six hundred years after the incorporation of Wales into England and almost three hundred years after the amalgamation of England and Scotland into Great Britain, separatist movements flourish in Wales and in Scotland. Brittany and Provence are not totally reconciled to French rule. Lithuanians and Estonians are actively working to recover their independence. Such issues are normally settled by force or the threat of force because there is no principled way of overcoming the contradiction between national integrity and ethnic self-determination. The contradiction becomes even sharper when ethnic groups within a nation are locked in permanent conflict, as in Ireland, South Africa, Sri Lanka, Israel, and Lebanon.

Another serious impediment to the formation of a peacekeeping federation is that by undertaking to protect the governments of its component nations, it must deny the right of revolution so highly regarded by good Marxists, and, in appropriate circumstances, by good capitalists too.

Both of these problems are grave but probably not insuperable.

Armed revolution is not the only way that changes of regime are accomplished today. Social movements routinely topple unpopular regimes. Popular demonstrations have led to new constitutions in countries as diverse as France, Iran, and the Philippines. Even under the tight management of the Soviet Union in Eastern Europe, quite diverse political systems are evolving, for example, in Hungary, Poland, and East Germany.

A much more formidable obstacle to the voluntary formation of a peacekeeping federation is the apprehension that a powerful member state or bloc of states might seize control of the machinery and use it to dominate the world. The Soviet delegates at San Francisco were keenly aware of the possibility that the United Nations, if it were made independently powerful, might be used by the Western powers to destroy the Soviet system. American public opinion today would surely not consider surrendering the military power of the United States to a federation that might, by a few shifts of coalition partners, come to be dominated by a bloc of Communist states. Such apprehensions may eventually be overcome if the End Game fades away, but not any time soon. We must look elsewhere for a peace game that offers a practicable way out of the nuclear predicament.

The beginnings of a *nuclear consortium* can already be seen in the Non-Proliferation Treaty of 1968, the International Atomic Energy Agency, and the 1987 Treaty on Intermediate Nuclear Forces. The transaction intended by the multilateral Non-Proliferation Treaty, whereby the weapon states promised to move toward the abandonment of nuclear arms and the nonweapon states promised in return not to acquire any, was blocked by bad faith on both sides. The weapon states made no move to reduce their arsenals, and some of the nonweapon states continued to develop their nuclear capabilities. Two weapon states, France and China, and half a dozen potential proliferators—India, Israel, South Africa, Pakistan, Argentina, Brazil—remained outside the non-proliferation regime. The safeguards imposed by the International Atomic Energy Authority are generally recognized as inadequate, and the nuclear capabilities of nonweapon states have grown enormously since the treaty was signed, with considerable help from the weapon states. More than eighty nations have nuclear reactors within their borders, and nearly a third of these already have the means of reprocessing spent fuel into plutonium.

The superpowers, speaking jointly, have the last word in nuclear matters, as the INF negotiations of 1987 so clearly showed. Together they could put a stop to nuclear proliferation, reduce the threat of nuclear terrorism to a tolerable level, and eliminate most of the existing nuclear weapons. It is the only combination able to remove the sword of Damocles that hangs over human civilization.

The obstacles to the establishment of an international agency that would have final authority in nuclear matters may not be insuperable. In this peace game, the United States and the Soviet Union form a consortium for the limited purpose of suppressing nuclear weapons, and they use the irresistible influence which they enjoy when acting jointly to persuade or coerce other nations to join the consortium.

The replacement of the End Game by a working partnership for limited purposes is not as implausible as it may at first seem. The two nations are fairly well balanced in population and resources. Their recent antagonism has no deep historical roots and no memories of bloodshed. Russians and Americans look somewhat alike and think somewhat alike. The ideological pressure that each can exert on the other has been much reduced. Marxism-Leninism has lost the hypnotic appeal it used to have for many Americans. Soviet citizens envy our rock music and household appliances but seem to be sincerely convinced of the superiority of their own society. A strong nuclear consortium jointly sponsored by the superpowers would have more than half a chance.

This is the same device that suggested itself to responsible statesmen when the atomic bomb was invented and that was formally proposed by the United States and rejected by the Soviet Union just before the End Game got under way. Some of the blame for the failure can be apportioned to the negotiators on each side: Bernard Baruch, who dismissed quite reasonable Soviet concerns without serious consideration; Andrei Gromyko, who refused to recognize any good intentions in the American proposals. The breakdown of the 1946 negotiations on international control of atomic technology made the End Game possible, if not inevitable, and led by stages to the present situation in which 50,000 nuclear warheads are in place and not one of them can be fired without insane risk. Returning to the starting point may be the only way out of this historic cul-de-sac.

The project of a nuclear consortium was almost fully developed when it made its first official appearance in a joint declaration by President Truman and the prime ministers of the United Kingdom and Canada, Clement Attlee and Mackenzie King, in November 1945. They had met together, the declaration said, to consider the possibility of international action to prevent the use of atomic energy for destructive purpose and to promote its use for peaceful ends, and they proposed that the United Nations Organization establish a Commission to make specific proposals for the international exchange of atomic information, the control of atomic technology to ensure its use only for peaceful purposes, the elimination from national armaments of atomic weapons and other weapons adaptable to mass destruction, and the development of safeguards against violations.[17] Two months later, the General Assembly of the United Nations adopted a resolution that had been drafted at Moscow by the foreign ministers Byrnes, Bevin, and Molotov establishing the Commission and charged it to make specific proposals on each of these points. The first draft of an American proposal to the Commission was the Acheson-Lilienthal report, completed in March; it was more accommodating to the Soviet view than the plan Baruch put before the Commission in June 1946, which proposed the creation of an International Atomic Development Authority that would have managerial control or ownership of all atomic activities "potentially dangerous to world security," the power to inspect and license all other atomic activities, an obligation to foster the beneficial use of atomic energy, and responsibility for atomic research and development. Baruch promised that once this control system was in effective operation and "condign punishments" had been set up to punish violations of its rules as international crimes, the manufacture of atomic bombs would stop, existing bombs would be disposed of, and the Authority would be given full possession of atomic technology. The condign punishments would apply to the illegal possession or use of an atomic bomb or any of its components, and to defiance of or interference with the Authority. It was not clear who would apply the punishments but very clear that they would not be subject to veto in the Security Council.

It is arguable that no agreement could have been reached at the time even if the American plan had taken more account of the Soviet leaders' apprehension that the United States might use the proposed Authority to perpetuate rather than to end its monopoly of atomic weapons, and of the motives they had for retaining the veto in the face of the automatic majorities the United States then commanded in both the Security Council and the General Assembly. The Soviet counterproposal, presented only five days later, addressed both these points. They wanted the existing atomic bombs and stockpiles destroyed and the exchange of technology initiated *before* the Authority assumed control of atomic activities.[18] They were unwilling, and remained unwilling for more than forty years, to allow any intrusive inspection of Soviet facilities by foreigners. And, of course, they refused to budge on the veto. Henry Wallace, then Secretary of Commerce, put the Soviet case better than they had in a July 1946 memorandum to Truman: "Is it any wonder that the Russians did not show any great enthusiasm for our plans? Would we have been enthusiastic if the Russians had a monopoly of atomic energy, and offered to share the information with us at some indefinite time in the future at their discretion if we agreed now not to try to make a bomb and give them information on our secret resources of uranium and thorium?"[19] When the memorandum was published, Baruch demanded and got Wallace's resignation. The American negotiators did almost nothing to explore possible compromises, and the Russians were no more conciliatory. It was a time when Stalin's provocative actions in Eastern Europe were dissipating whatever goodwill remained from the wartime alliance. By September 1946, Baruch was reporting to Truman that the situation was hopeless and recommending a step-up in the production of atomic bombs.

A modern version of the Baruch Plan might look like this:

1. The establishment of an International Nuclear Authority by a multilateral treaty initially negotiated by the NATO and Warsaw Pact governments but intended eventually to include all national governments.

2. The Authority to inspect and license all the nuclear facilities of signatory states, and to control directly all stocks of enriched uranium, tritium, and plutonium.

3. Existing stocks of nuclear warheads and components to be destroyed under the direct supervision of the Authority.

4. The manufacture or possession of nuclear explosives by anyone other than the Authority to be absolutely prohibited.

5. The further development of nuclear explosives to be absolutely prohibited.

6. Each government adhering to the treaty to enact domestic legislation imposing severe punishments on violators of the foregoing bans.

7. The Authority to retain, for a period of at least twenty years, a small number of nuclear weapons under the joint operational control of the NATO and Warsaw Pact commands, to deter national governments from violating the foregoing bans.

8. Each government adhering to the treaty to agree to the free international exchange of nuclear technology.

9. The Authority to administer a set of parallel restrictions on chemical and bacterial weapons, with the object of putting a permanent stop to their military use.

This nine-point program differs only marginally from the original Baruch Plan. It places less emphasis on the Authority's role in the development of nuclear technology for peaceful purposes, overcomes the ambiguity in the original plan about who was to punish violations of the ban on atomic bombs, and provides for the Authority to retain a small number of nuclear weapons to deter violations by national governments who would not be subject to ordinary legal penalties.

The Soviet objections to the original plan have very little current relevance. The United States no longer has a monopoly or even a clear advantage in nuclear technology and weapons. The Soviet Union has recently agreed, in the INF Treaty of 1987, to submit to intrusive inspection of its nuclear facilities by Americans in return for similar Soviet rights in the United States. Stalin's fear of an "assault on the socialist homeland by monopoly capitalism" is hardly remembered.

Does this mean that the plan is now feasible? Not necessarily.

The End Game is firmly rooted in the political cultures of East and West, and supported on each side by a military-industrial complex that has much to lose and little to gain by a peaceful resolution. The paranoid mind-set required by the End Game is not easily shaken. We expect the Soviets to massacre us without a qualm if they get the opportunity, and we imagine them to be on the alert for the creation of such an opportunity by a carelessly drawn agreement or a lapse in our vigilance. Their vision of us is no more trustful. Exhortation will not remove these mutual suspicions, but new experiences, like the sight of Mr. Gorbachev wooing Washington citizens on a street corner, have begun to do so.

There are more tangible factors too. An international authority to control nuclear proliferation already exists in the International Atomic Energy Agency. It is not very effective or well organized,[20] but it does in principle have the right to inspect nuclear facilities in the 136 countries that have signed the Nuclear Non-Proliferation Treaty and to control their supplies of fissionable materials. At present, the IAEA's powers are too limited and its resources too scant to provide much real protection against the diversion of nuclear facilities and materials to military purposes. Moreover, it is excessively exposed, through the General Assembly of the United Nations, to political pressures from would-be proliferators. Yet the precedent is there, and it is not a very long step from preventing the proliferation of nuclear weapons to banning them altogether. Indeed, the IAEA was founded with the expectation that the weapon states would reduce and ultimately abandon their nuclear arms as a quid pro quo for the continued restraint of the nonweapon states.

The peace game outlined above does not imply general disarmament or the abolition of conventional war, but only the abolition of nuclear and other atrocious weapons. From the standpoint of feasibility, that is one of its strongest features. But since the United States and the Soviet Union must be the joint protagonists, and as their military establishments would be so drastically restructured, it is unlikely that such a plan could ever be adopted unless they had first agreed to disengage from the central front and to negotiate the parity of their conventional forces.

The suggested provision that the Authority would retain, for at least twenty years, a small number of nuclear weapons to deter national governments from violating the nuclear ban is not intended as a concession to the paranoid mind-set inherited from the End Game. No new institution works exactly as planned, and it would be imprudent to anticipate that every government, much less every armed gang, will comply voluntarily with the proposed ban. Even one or two nuclear weapons might present a difficult challenge to the Authority if it had no superior force at its disposal. On the other hand, the Authority is to be merely the creature of the governments that establish it, not a power in its own right, and it will not require troops or ships or planes of its own. Its nuclear reserve might consist of four batteries in widely separated neutral locations, each consisting of perhaps twenty-five independently targetable cruise missiles with single one-megaton nuclear warheads. This would be trifling compared to the existing nuclear arsenals but more than enough to inflict unacceptable damage on any nation in the world.

The joint operational control of deployed nuclear weapons by binational chains of command is a procedure that has proved extraordinarily safe and reliable in the course of the End Game. The nuclear weapons of the Authority should clearly be under the joint operational control of NATO and Warsaw Pact authorities, and the forces that guard the missiles batteries (in locations far away from the main forces of either bloc) should be mixed units drawn from both NATO and Warsaw Pact forces. It would also seem appropriate to put the decision to fire under the joint personal control of the presidents of the United States and the Soviet Union in much the same way that such decisions are reserved to them separately today.

After the prescribed twenty years, the Authority's nuclear deterrent may become superfluous if the conscience of humanity, reinforced by the criminal laws of every nation, comes to regard high-technology weapons as abhorrent and their use as unthinkable. The lack of recent experience with nuclear explosions of any kind and the age and uncertain condition of the few weapons in the possession of the Authority might make it possible to dispense with them altogether. The object, after all, is to remove this particular threat from human experience. Men and women are frequently cruel, but they do not commit every technically feasible cruelty, preferring those that have been incorporated into institutional practices and expectations.

The peace games founded on the old Baruch Plan, or something like it, seem to play better than the others considered so far.

The one peace game I have not mentioned is the continuation of the status quo in nuclear deterrence. This is the approach to permanent peace embodied in current U.S. policy. The vision of preventing nuclear war by means of a perpetual confrontation of thousands of nuclear weapons poised in hair-trigger readiness is surely an hallucination. Even if the status quo were stable, this game would be too dangerous. In fact, it is highly unstable, given the momentum of weapons technology and the diminishing influence of the United States and the Soviet Union. "Use them or lose them" is a catch phrase that appears in nuclear war games to justify a first strike. A similar line of reasoning argues for the joint development of a serious plan for the abolition of nuclear weapons by the two superpowers while they still have enough joint influence to do it. That influence is likely to decline as the Soviet Union struggles to reform its unproductive economy without losing control of its restive minorities and satellites and as the United States wrestles with its intractable budget and trade deficits and promotes, with no sense of irony, the rearming of Japan and Germany. New superpowers are emerging on the world scene: Japan is already an economic colossus; allied or merged with the rapidly industrializing nations of the Pacific Rim, it may eventually outweigh the United States. China, with its vast population, may soon outweigh the Soviet Union economically. Meanwhile, the economic and political unification of Western Europe has been steadily advancing. Some day soon, the dyad that conducts the End Game will be replaced by a much less stable configuration, ripe for divisive coalitions.

We cannot know what the future holds, but it surely will not be the status quo. Whatever new order develops in the world will be subject to the normal malfunctions of organizational systems. It will be far from perfect, but if enough peace games are played in high places in the next few years, it may not be mad.

Notes

Chapter 2. End Game—The Unfought Nuclear War

1. For nuclear hawks, the "overwhelming superiority of the Warsaw Pact in conventional forces" is axiomatic; it sustains the whole structure of nuclear deterrence. Nuclear doves tend to see the balance of conventional forces on the central front as approximately equal. Since nearly all the experts are biased in one direction or the other, it is nearly impossible to find an objective estimate, but Jonathan Dean in *Watershed in Europe*, 1987, comes as close as anyone.

2. In January 1989, John Tower, who had just been nominated as U.S. Defense Secretary, went to a NATO conference at Munich to warn the allies against Gorbachev's "charm offensive" and to insist that the modernization of short-range nuclear forces was more essential than ever to Western defense after the agreement to remove intermediate-range missiles. *Washington Post*, 29 January 1989.

3. The construction by social scientists of the intellectual foundations of the End Game began almost at the dawn of the atomic age with the publication in 1946 of *The Absolute Weapon: Atomic Power and World Order* by Bernard Brodie and his Yale colleagues, which introduced the concepts of nuclear deterrence and mutual assured destruction. The subsequent elaboration of these ideas is admirably described by Gregg Herken in *Counsels of War*, 1985.

4. For these and other operational details see Paul P. Craig and John A. Jungerman, *Nuclear Arms Race: Technology and Society*, 1986, or Ashton B. Carter, John D. Steinbruner, and Charles A. Zraker, *Managing Nuclear Operations*, 1987.

5. Paul Bracken, *The Command and Control of Nuclear Forces*, 1983, 122–123.

6. Theodore Caplow, Howard M. Bahr, and Bruce A. Chadwick, *Analysis of the Readiness of Local Communities for Integrated Emergency Management Planning*, 1984. The policy of combining civil defense with the management of fires, floods, earthquakes, and other nonmilitary emergencies has enabled the federal government virtually to abandon civil defense planning in recent years.

7. The strange history of the Crisis Relocation Policy is well presented

by Jennifer Leaning and Langley Keyes, *The Counterfeit Ark*, 1984. Some large corporations have imitated the government and set up underground headquarters in caves and salt mines, from whence they expect to conduct their business operations after a nuclear attack. These exotic arrangements are described in detail in Edward Zuckerman's *The Day After World War III*, 1984.

8. Early in 1989, a panel of the National Research Council reported to the Pentagon that the development of nuclear reactors or alternative power sources needed to operate the computers and weaponry called for by SDI might require another forty to sixty years of development.

9. *Statesmen's Year Book, 1986–1987*, 12.

10. For a somewhat dated account of the world's armaments and military forces see Michael Kidron and Dan Smith, *The War Atlas, 1983*. A geographical inventory of potential battle areas is found in John Keegan and Anthony Wheatcroft, *Zones of Conflict: An Atlas of Future Wars*, 1986.

11. Statistical Abstract of the United States 1988, 826.

12. The shift of policy was highly intentional, at least on the Soviet side. Toward the end of 1988, Gorbachev foreign policy advisers were quoted as saying that "instead of looking at the third world as a zero-sum game, both superpowers . . . should support efforts aimed at 'national reconciliation' in regions torn by conflict," and "What we need in the third world is not superpower disengagement from the conflicts but positive engagement to contain and end them." Helena Cobham, "Ending Bloodshed in the Third World," *World Monitor*, December 1988, 66–70.

Chapter 3. Social Science and the Nuclear Predicament

1. A much fuller account of this typology, using slightly different terms, may be found in T. Caplow, *Principles of Organization*, 1964, 317–356.

2. William James, "The Moral Equivalent of War," in his *Memories and Studies*, 1912, 281–282. No one else has had so clear a view of the sociopsychological elements that make war perennially attractive to the citizens of modern states.

3. Tom Bethell, "Losing Ground in Europe," *National Review*, December 19, 1986, 32–36.

4. Adam Ulam, director of the Russian Research Center at Harvard, quoted by Bethell, ibid. The signing of the INF treaty in 1987 was viewed in some European circles as leading toward the shock to which Ulam refers. It was followed within weeks by an announcement that France and West Germany would begin to merge some of their military forces on an experimental basis, and in January 1989 the French Information Service announced jubilantly that a joint

Franco-German brigade had been officially commissioned in a bilingual ceremony under the joint command of the French and West German chiefs of staff. Delivering the same speech written alternately in French and German, the two officers noted that "the creation of a unit of soldiers from our two countries represents a major event in the light of the many conflicts that have marked our past."

5. Graham T. Allison, *Essence of Decision*, 1971, 3–5.
6. General Groves, quoted in Ian Clark, *Nuclear Past, Nuclear Present*, 1985, 39.
7. Bruce Bueno de Mesquita, *The War Trap*, 1981, 8.
8. The full implications of the Prisoner's Dilemma for superpower strategy, together with a variant game called Chicken, have been worked out in loving detail by Steven J. Brams in *Superpower Games*, 1985. But since Brams takes the End Game as given, his elegant analysis leads only to a labyrinth of paradoxes.
9. Tony Ashworth, *Trench Warfare, 1914–1918*, 1980, 19.
10. See especially Edward N. Luttwak, *The Pentagon and the Art of War*, 1984; Gary S. Hart and William S. Lind, *America Can Win: The Case for Military Reform*, 1986. The latter work presents the views of the "military reform movement" in a systematic way.
11. Luttwak, op. cit., 166–167.
12. "In the case of the C-5A transport aircraft, just one of the three bidders submitted a total of 1,446,346 pages weighing in at 24,917 pounds. . . . [In] the Advanced Helicopter Improvement Program . . . one contractor's proposals (all required copies) exceeded the takeoff weight of the helicopter." Norman R. Augustine, *Augustine's Laws*, 1986.
13. Bertrand Russell, *Portraits from Memory and Other Essays*, 1956, 31.
14. Roland N. Stromberg, *Redemption by War: The Intellectuals and 1914*, 1982. A comparable account for France is Jean-Jacques Becker's *The Great War and the French People*, 1985. See also Peter Buitenhuis, *The Great War of Words: British, American, and Canadian Propaganda and Fiction, 1914–1933*, 1987.
15. Marianne Weber, *Max Weber: A Biography*, 1975 [1926], 183.
16. Stromberg, op. cit.
17. Jean-Louis Crémieux-Brilhac, "L'Opinion publique française, l'Angleterre et la guerre," in *Français et Britannique dans la drôle de guerre*, 1979. For the broader picture, see also Gury Rossi-Landi, *La drôle de guerre*, 1971.
18. "L'Evolution de l'opinion publique anglaise à propos de la guerre . . ." in *Français et Britannique dans la drôle de guerre*, 1979.
19. In a long oration, "The War System of the Commonwealth of Nations," delivered before the American Peace Society at Boston in 1849. Published in Charles Sumner, *Orations and Speeches*, 1850.

Chapter 4. Changing the Rules of War

1. The doctrine of the just war was rejected by the Vatican II Council of 1964–1965, which concluded that the development of scientific weapons called for war to be considered in an entirely new spirit. In this new formulation, only defensive war on a limited scale is accepted as just. The tactics of total war are anathematized. "Any act of war intended to destroy entire cities or regions with their inhabitants is a crime against God and man." For an elegant summary of Vatican II's deliberations on war, see Robert Bose, "Le problème de la guerre au Concile du Vatican II" in Norberto Bobbio (ed.), *La Guerre et ses theories*, 1979.

2. Leon Friedman, *The Laws of War*, 1972, 1509. Unless otherwise noted, Friedman's compendium is the source of the treaty texts quoted in this section.

3. In December 1987 after an eighteen-year moratorium, the Pentagon resumed the production of poison gas, and as of January 1989 was planning to produce more than 1 million binary nerve gas shells at a cost of $3 billion over the next decade. Production of an even deadlier agent is scheduled to begin in 1990 (*Washington Post*, 15 January 1989). Nobody knows quite why. A good account of the contradictory CBW policies of the Reagan administration is Susan Wright's "The Buildup That Was," *Bulletin of the Atomic Scientists*, January–February 1989, 52–56. See also Eliot Marshall, "Progress on a Chemical Arms Treaty," *Science*, 23 October 1988, 471–472.

4. Country-by-country estimates of civilian casualties in World War II are found in Robert Goralski, *World War II Almanac: 1931–1945*, 1981.

5. Max Weber, *Economy and Society*, 1968 [1921], 919.

6. Henry Barbera makes good use of this perspective in an analysis of the Thirty-One Year War in *Rich Nations and Poor in Peace and War*, 1973.

7. Ian Clark, *Nuclear Past, Nuclear Present: Hiroshima, Nagasaki and Contemporary Strategy*, 1985, 35 et seq. The incident was mentioned in another context in chapter 2 above.

8. Charles Horton Cooley, *Social Process*, 1918, 262.

9. A similar viewpoint was eloquently expressed by George F. Kennan in a 1985 essay on "Morality and Foreign Policy" in *Foreign Affairs*. He sketches "the outlines of an American foreign policy for which moral standards could be more suitably and naturally applied than to that policy which we are conducting today," 217.

10. F. S. Northedge, *The League of Nations: Its Life and Times*, 1986, 114.

11. Benjamin B. Ferencz, *Enforcing International Law—A Way to World Peace*, 1983, 858–860.

12. Particularly difficult to answer in the light of recent findings that—contrary to a widespread belief—arms races do not necessarily lead to war. A 1985 study of twenty-two arms races concludes surprisingly that "Military buildups were found to exercise little direct impact on the escalation of militarized disputes into war." Paul Diehl, "Arms Races to War: Testing Some Empirical Linkages," *Sociological Quarterly*, 26:3, 331–345, 1985.

Chapter 5. The Peace Game Called the Grand Design

1. The best modern edition of the *Project de paix perpetuelle* is that edited by Simone Goyard-Fabre and published in 1981 by Editions Garnier.

2. Jean-Jacques Rousseau, *Jugement sur la paix perpetuelle*, in the Vaughan edition of his writings, John Wiley & Sons, 1962, note 2. It was written around 1756 but first appeared in print in 1782. The related piece Rousseau wrote around 1756 on the St. Pierre project was the *Critique de paix perpetuelle*. It too was published posthumously.

3. Ibid., 392.

4. Susan Mary Alsop, *The Congress Dances*, 1984, 89. This lively and worldly account of the Congress is nicely supplemented by Hilde Spiel (ed.), *The Congress of Vienna: An Eyewitness Account*, which presents verbatim excerpts from the reports of the Austrian police spies assigned to surveillance of the foreign delegates.

5. Quoted in Walter Allson Phillips, *The Confederation of Europe: A Study of the European Alliance, 1813–1823, etc.*, 1914, 34–35. Phillips's *obiter dicta* about the sufficiency of conventional diplomacy for keeping the peace in Europe strike a poignant note in this splendid piece of diplomatic history written just before the unexpected outbreak of the First World War.

6. Ibid., 177.

7. Ibid., 187.

8. Ibid., 280.

9. Ferdinand Czernin, *Versailles 1919: The Forces, Events and Personalities that Shaped the Treaty*, 1964, 98. For another view of this issue see Charles L. Mee, Jr. *The End of Order: Versailles 1919*, 1980.

10. Elmer Bendiner, *A Time for Angels: The Tragicomic History of The League of Nations*, 1975, 92.

11. Ibid., 209.

12. F. S. Northedge, *The League of Nations: Its Life and Times*, 1986, 243–44.

13. James MacGregor Burns, *Roosevelt: The Soldier of Freedom*, 1970, 129–130. It is amazing how clearly Roosevelt and Churchill saw the

danger of casting the United Nations in the same mold as the League of Nations and how helpless they were to avert it.

14. Evan Luard, *A History of the United Nations*, Volume 1, 1982, 21–22.

15. Thomas M. Campbell, *Masquerade Peace: America's UN Policy, 1944–45*, 1973, 186.

16. Luard, op. cit., 96.

17. Thomas M. Franck, *Nation Against Nation: What Happened to the UN Dream and What the US Can Do About It*, 1985, 72.

18. David Pitt and Thomas G. Weiss (eds.), *The Nature of United Nations Bureaucracies*, 1986, 13. The management practices of the United Nations have been much criticized and the essays in this volume are almost uniformly unfavorable. For a more hopeful discussion of the same problems see *Administrative and Budgetary Reform of the United Nations*, the report of a 1987 conference of UN insiders convened by the Stanley Foundation.

19. Arthur Rovine, quoted in John F. Murphy, *The United Nations and the Control of International Violence: A Legal and Political Analysis*, 100.

20. See chapter 3 above, "Coalitions in Triads," and T. Caplow, *Two Against One: Coalitions in Triads*, 1968 and later editions.

21. J. A. R. Marriott, *The European Commonwealth: Problems Historical and Diplomatic*, 1918, 74.

22. Phillips, op. cit., 87.

Chapter 6. Options for Peace Games Today

1. Pierre Gallois and John Train, "When a Nuclear Strike Is Thinkable," *Wall Street Journal*, editorial page, 22 March 1984.

2. *Statistical Abstract of the United States*, 1988. "Comparative International Statistics."

3. But other Europeans are more trusting. In a November 1987 survey, 41 percent of the French population expected the U.S. to use nuclear forces if Western Europe were attacked by the Soviet Union. *News from France*, 87, 17.

4. For an interesting analysis of the background of these negotiations see Jonathan Dean, "Military Security in Europe," *Foreign Affairs*, Fall 1987, 22–40.

5. The foreign policy issues associated with the relative decline of American economic power are discussed at length by David P. Calleo in *Beyond American Hegemony*, 1987.

6. The idea of a European defense force began to revive in response to the signing of the 1987 U.S.–Soviet agreement to abandon intermediate-range nuclear missiles. Plans for mixed Franco-German military units were announced in Paris and Bonn only a few weeks later.

7. The front-line soldiers of that war were aware that the institution of war had come to grief, as appears from such participant accounts as Robert Graves's *Goodbye to All That*, 1929.
8. Charles Sumner, "The War System of the Commonwealth of Nations," in *Orations and Speeches*, 1850, 381–382.
9. I am indebted to Charles Denk for the suggestion that the status systems of the German Federal Republic and the German Democratic Republic may have grown so far apart since the Second World War as to call into doubt the possibility of their eventual reunification.
10. An excellent account and explanation of the disintegration of the United Arab Republic was presented in Amitai Etzioni's *Political Unification*, 1965.
11. Edward Bellamy, *Looking Backward*, 1888, 345.
12. Among the numerous empirical studies of intentional communities that show a high incidence of internal conflict, Benjamin Zablocki's *The Joyful Community*, 1971, is particularly interesting.
13. Napoleon in exile on St. Helena claimed to have been pursuing a master plan that contemplated the unification of Europe, the introduction of uniform laws and civil rights, and the ultimate abolition of war.
14. Although Hitler was reported as saying in 1941 that "the Roman Empire was a great political creation, the greatest of all." John Keegan, *The Mask of Command*, 1987, 281.
15. Joseph Stalin, "The Foundations of Leninism," in A. F. Mendel, ed., *Essential Works of Marxism*, 1961, 267. The phrase occurs in a long passage explaining that true internationalism must lead to the voluntary amalgamation of socialist nations.
16. Michael T. Hannan and Glenn R. Carroll, "Dynamics of Formal Political Structure," *American Sociological Review*, February 1981, 19–35.
17. U.S. Department of State Publication 2520, *Treaties and Other International Acts*, 1076–1078.
18. U.S. Department of State Publication 2702, *The International Control of Atomic Energy: Growth of a Policy*, 209–216.
19. Quoted in James Grant, *Bernard M. Baruch*, 1983, 314–315.
20. "Even IAEA inspectors themselves have reported that they probably would not have detected any bomb-making activity if it were being conducted. . . . Under the U.N. system . . . the rules on safeguards are being decided by the recipients of nuclear technology who have every incentive to make them as loose as possible." Robert Ehrlich, *Waging Nuclear Peace*, 1985, 339. For a summary of recent progress and setbacks in non-proliferation efforts, see Leonard S. Spector, *The Undeclared Bomb*, 1988.

Bibliography

Abt, Clark. 1985. *A Strategy for Terminating a Nuclear War.* Boulder, CO: Westview Press.

Allen, Thomas B. 1987. *War Games.* New York: McGraw Hill.

Allison, Graham T. 1971. *Essence of Decision: Explaining the Cuban Missile Crisis.* Boston: Little, Brown.

Alsop, Susan Mary. 1984. *The Congress Dances.* New York: Harper & Row.

Arkin, William M., and Richard W. Fieldhouse. 1985. *Nuclear Battlefields: Global Links in the Arms Race.* Cambridge, MA: Ballinger Publishing.

Armstrong, Elizabeth H. 1942. *French Canadian Opinion on the War.* January 1940–June 1941. Toronto: Ryerson Press.

Aron, Raymond. 1959. *On War,* tr. T. Kilmuntin. Garden City, NY: Doubleday.

Ashworth, Tony. 1980. *Trench Warfare, 1914–1918: The Live and Let Live System.* London: Macmillan.

Augustine, Norman R. 1986. *Augustine's Laws.* New York: Penguin Books.

Axelrod, Robert. 1984. *The Evolution of Cooperation.* New York: Basic Books.

Ayalá, Balthasar. 1912 [1582]. *De jure et officiis belliciis et disciplinia militaria,* 2 vols. Washington, DC: Carnegie Institution.

Barbera, Henry. 1973. *Rich Nations and Poor in Peace and War.* Lexington, MA: Lexington Books.

Becker, Jean-Jacques. 1985. *The Great War and the French People,* tr. A. Pomerans. Leamington Spa: Berg.

Bell, P. M. H. 1979. "L'Evolution de l'opinion publique anglaise à propos de la guerre . . ." in *Français et Britannique dans la drôle de guerre.* Paris: CNRS.

Bellamy, Edward. 1888. *Looking Backward.* New York: D. Appleton.

Bendiner, Elmer. 1975. *A Time for Angels: The Tragicomic History of the League of Nations.* New York: Alfred A. Knopf.

Bentham, Jeremy. 1843. *Plan for an Universal and Perpetual Peace.* Edinburgh: W. Tait.

Bethell, Tom. 1986. "Losing Ground in Europe." *National Review,* December 19, 32–36.

Bierstedt, Robert. 1985. "Sociology and the Atom." Unpublished paper read at a plenary session. American Sociological Association.

Bobbio, Norberto. 1984. *Il Problema della guerra e le vie della pace.* 2nd ed. Bologna: Il Mulino.

Boëne, Bernard, and Michel Louis Martin. 1987. *L'Amérique entre Atlantique et Pacifique. Essai de prospective stratégique.* Paris: Fondation pour les études de défense nationale.

Boyer, Paul. 1985. *By the Bomb's Early Light: American Thought and Culture at the Dawn of the Atomic Age.* New York: Pantheon Books.

Bracken, Paul. 1983. *The Command and Control of Nuclear Forces.* New Haven: Yale University Press.

Brams, Steven J. 1985. *Superpower Games: Applying Game Theory to Superpower Conflict.* New Haven: Yale University Press.

Brierly, James. 1963. *The Law of Nations: An Introduction to the International Law of Peace.* Oxford: Clarendon, 6th ed.

Brodie, Bernard (ed.). 1946. *The Absolute Weapon: Atomic Power and World Order.* New York: Harcourt Brace.

Brucan, Silviu. 1982. "The Establishment of a World Authority: Working Hypotheses." *Alternatives,* 209–223.

Bueno de Mesquita, Bruce. 1981. *The War Trap.* New Haven: Yale University Press.

Bundy, McGeorge. 1988. *Danger and Survival: Choices about the Bomb in the First Fifty Years.* New York: Random House.

Bureau of the Census. 1988. *Statistical Abstract of the United States.* Washington, DC: Government Printing Office.

Burns, James MacGregor. 1970. *Roosevelt: The Soldier of Freedom.* New York: Harcourt, Brace, Jovanovich.

Calleo, David P. 1987. *Beyond American Hegemony: The Future of the Western Alliance.* New York: Basic Books.

Campbell, Thomas M. 1973. *Masquerade Peace: America's UN Policy, 1944–45.* Tallahassee: Florida State University Press.

Caplow, Theodore. 1964. *Principles of Organization.* New York: Harcourt Brace.

———. 1968. *Two Against One: Coalitions in Triads.* Englewood Cliffs, NJ: Prentice-Hall.

———. 1975. *Toward Social Hope.* New York: Basic Books.

———. 1977. *A Feasibility Study of World Government.* Des Moines: Stanley Foundation Occasional Paper #13.

———. 1979. "The Contradictions between World Order and Disarmament." *Washington Quarterly,* July, 90–96.

———. 1986. "Sociology and the Nuclear Debate," in James F. Short, Jr., ed., *The Social Fabric.* Beverly Hills, CA: Sage Publications.

Caplow, Theodore, Howard M. Bahr and Bruce A. Chadwick. 1984. *Analysis of the Readiness of Local Communities for Integrated Emergency*

Management Planning. Washington, DC: Federal Emergency Management Agency.

Carter, Ashton B., John D. Steinbruner, and Charles A. Zraker, eds. 1987. *Managing Nuclear Operations.*

Clark, Ian. 1985. *Nuclear Past, Nuclear Present: Hiroshima, Nagasaki and Contemporary Strategy.* Boulder and London: Westview Press.

Claude, Inis L., Jr. 1964. *Swords Into Ploughshares: The Problems and Prospects of International Organization,* 3rd ed. New York: Random House.

Cochran, Thomas B., William M. Arkin, and Milton M. Hoenig. 1984. *Nuclear Weapons Databook,* Vol. 1. *U.S. Nuclear Forces and Capabilities.* Cambridge, MA: Ballinger Publishing.

Cohen, Stanley. 1983. *Visions of Social Control: Crime, Punishment and Classification.* Cambridge: Polity Press.

Congressional Quarterly. 1983. *U.S. Defense Policy,* Third Edition. Washington, DC: Congressional Quarterly, Inc.

Cooley, Charles Horton. 1918. *Social Process.* New York: Charles Scribner's Sons.

Craig, Paul P., and John A. Jungerman. 1986. *Nuclear Arms Race: Technology and Society.* New York: McGraw Hill.

Crémieux-Brilhac Jean-Louis. 1979. "L'Opinion publique française, L'Angleterre et la guerre," in *Français et Britannique dans la drôle de guerre.* Paris: CNRS.

Crucé, Eméric. 1972 (1623). *The New Cineas (Le Nouveau Cynée),* tr. C. F. and E. R. Farrell. New York and London: Garland Publishing Co.

Cuzzort, R. P. 1989. *Using Social Thought: The Nuclear Issue and Other Concerns.* Mountain View, CA: Mayfield Publishing Co.

Czechoslovak Academy of Science. 1964. *The Universal Peace Plan of King George of Bohemia, 1462–1464.* Prague: Czechoslovak Academy.

Czernin, Ferdinand. 1964. *Versailles 1919: The Forces, Events and Personalities that Shaped the Treaty.* New York: G. P. Putnam's Sons.

Dean, Jonathan. 1987. *Watershed in Europe: Dismantling the East-West Military Confrontation.* Lexington, MA: Lexington Books.

———. 1987. "Military Security in Europe." *Foreign Affairs,* Fall, 22–40.

Diehl, Paul F. 1987. "Arms Races to War: Testing Some Empirical Linkages." *Sociological Quarterly,* Fall, 26:3, 293–344.

Dikshit, Ramesh Dutta. 1975. *The Political Geography of Federalism: An Inquiry into Origins and Stability.* Delhi: Macmillan.

Douglas, Mary. 1985. *Risk Acceptability According to the Social Sciences.* New York: Russell Sage Foundation.

Drouet, J. 1912. *L'Abbé de St. Pierre: l'homme et l'oeuvre.* Paris.

Dubois, Pierre. 1972 [1306]. *The Recovery of the Holy Land,* tr. W. I. Brandt. New York: Columbia University Press.

The Economist. 1986. "NATO's Central Front," August 30.

Ehrlich, Robert. 1985. *Waging Nuclear Peace.* Albany: SUNY Press.

Eichelberger, Clark. 1977. *Organizing for Peace: A Personal History of the Founding of the United Nations.* New York: Harper & Row.

Elcock, Howard. 1972. *Portrait of a Decision: The Council of Four and The Treaty of Versailles.* London: Eyre Methuen.

Elias, Norbert, and Eric Dunning. 1986. *Quest for Excitement: Sport and Leisure in the Civilizing Process.* Oxford: Basil Blackwell.

Erasmus, Desiderius. 1946 [1517]. *Querela pacis: The Complaint of Peace.* New York: Scholars' Facsimiles & Reprints.

Etzioni, Amitai. 1965. *Political Unification: A Comparative Study of Leaders and Forces.* New York: Holt, Rinehart and Winston.

Ferencz, Benjamin B. 1983. *Enforcing International Law—A Way to World Peace: A Documentary History and Analysis,* 2 vols. London: Oceana Publications.

Ford, Daniel. 1985. "The Button." *The New Yorker.* In two parts, April.

Foreign Policy Research Institute. 1981. *The Three Percent Solution and the Future of NATO.* Philadelphia: Foreign Policy Research Institute.

Forsyth, Murray. 1981. *Unions of States: The Theory and Practice of Confederation.* New York: Holmes & Meier.

Franck, Thomas M. 1985. *Nation Against Nation: What Happened to the UN Dream and What the U.S. Can Do About It.* New York: Oxford University Press.

Friedman, Leon (ed.). 1972. *The Laws of War: A Documentary History,* 2 vols. New York: Random House.

Fromm, Hermann. 1982. *Deutschland in der öffentlichen Kriegszielddiskussions Grossbrittaniens 1939–1945.* Frankfurt am Main: Peter Lang.

Gabriel, Richard. 1985. *Military Incompetence: Why the American Military Doesn't Win.* New York: Hill and Wang.

Gallois, Pierre, and John Train. 1984. "When a Nuclear Strike Is Thinkable." *Wall Street Journal,* March 22.

Glassner, Martin Ira, Harm J. de Blig, and Leon Yacher. 1980. *Systematic Political Geography,* 3rd ed. New York: John Wiley & Sons.

Gochman, C. 1975. *Status, Conflict and War: The Major Powers, 1820–1970.* Ph.D. Dissertation, University of Michigan.

Goralski, Robert. 1981. *World War II Almanac: 1931–1945.* New York: G. P. Putnam's Sons.

Goyard-Fabre, Simone. 1985. *L'Abbé de St. Pierre: artisan de la paix.* Address at inaugural meeting of the Society. St. Pierre-Eglise: Society of the Friends of the Abbé de St. Pierre.

Graebner, Norman A. 1988. "Multipolarity in World Politics: The Challenge." *Virginia Quarterly Review,* Summer, 377–397.

Grant, James. 1983. *Bernard M. Baruch: The Adventures of A Wall Street Legend.* New York: Simon and Schuster.

Graves, Robert. 1929. *Goodbye to All That: An Autobiography.* London: Jonathan Cape.

Grotius, Hugo. 1901 [1625]. *The Law of War and Peace (De juri belli et pacis)*, tr. A. C. Campbell. Washington and London: M. Walter Dunne.

Hackett, General, Sir John. 1982. *The Third World War: The Untold Story*. New York: Macmillan.

Hackett, General, Sir John and others. 1976. *The Third World War: August 1985*. New York: Macmillan.

Halperin, Morton H. 1987. *Nuclear Fallacy: Dispelling the Myth of Nuclear Strategy*. Cambridge, MA: Ballinger Publishing.

Hamilton, Alexander, James Madison, and John Jay. 1952 [1787]. "The Federalist," in *American State Papers*. Chicago: William Benton.

Hannan, Michael T., and Glenn R. Carroll. 1981. "Dynamics of Formal Political Structure: An Event-History Analysis." *American Sociological Review*, February, 46:1, 19–35.

Hart, Gary S., and William S. Lind. 1986. *America Can Win: The Case for Military Reform*. Bethesda, MD: Adler & Adler.

Harwell, Mark A. 1984. *Nuclear Winter: Human and Environmental Consequences of Nuclear War*. New York, Berlin, etc.: Springer-Verlag.

Hemleben, Sylvester John. 1943. *Plans for World Peace Through Six Centuries*. Chicago: University of Chicago Press.

Hennessey, Jean, and J. Charles-Brun. 1940. *Le Principe federatif*. Paris: Presses universitaires de France.

Herken, Gregg. 1985. *Counsels of War*. New York: Alfred A. Knopf.

Hobbes, Thomas. 1952 [1651]. *Leviathan*. Chicago, Encyclopedia Britannica Press.

Hocart, A. M. 1970 [1936]. *Kings and Councillors: Essays on the Comparative Anatomy of Human Society*. Rodney Neidham (ed.). Chicago: University of Chicago Press.

Holloway, Harry, and John George. 1979. *Public Opinion: Coalitions, Elites, and Masses*. New York: St. Martin's Press.

Horowitz, Irving Louis. 1973. *War and Peace in Contemporary Philosophical Theory*, 2nd ed. New York: Humanities Press.

Ignatius, David. 1987. "Cheering the World's Dullest Treaty." *Washington Post*, 3 August.

Irvin, Dallas B. 1938. "The Origin of Capital Staffs." *Journal of Modern History*, June, 161–179.

James, William. 1912. "The Moral Equivalent of War," in *Memories and Studies*. New York: Longmans, Green.

Janowitz, Morris. 1978. *The Last Half-Century: Societal Change and Politics in America*. Chicago: University of Chicago Press.

Jervis, Robert. 1984. *The Illogic of American Nuclear Strategy*. Ithaca: Cornell University Press.

Jones, Donald M., and Lawrence J. Hill. 1988. *International Considerations Associated with Economic Planning for Recovery from a Generalized Disaster*. Oak Ridge, TN: Oak Ridge National Laboratory, June.

Joyce, James Avery. 1978. *Broken Star: The Story of the League of Nations (1919–1939)*. Swansea: Christopher Davies.

Kant, Immanuel. 1917 [1795]. *Zum ewigen Frieden (Perpetual Peace: A Philosophical Essay)*, tr. M. C. Smith. London: Allen & Unwin.

———. 1952 [1795]. *Rechtslehre (The Science of Right)*, tr. W. Harrie. Chicago: Encyclopedia Britannica Press.

Keegan, John. 1977. *The Face of Battle: A Study of Agincourt, Waterloo and the Somme*. New York: Vintage Books 1977.

———. 1987. *The Mask of Command*. New York: Viking Penguin.

Keegan, John, and Andrew Wheatcroft. 1986. *Zones of Conflict: An Atlas of Future Wars*. New York: Simon and Schuster.

Kennan, George F. 1982. *The Nuclear Delusion: Soviet-American Relations in the Nuclear Age*. New York: Pantheon Books.

———. 1985–1986. "Morality and Foreign Policy." *Foreign Affairs* 64:2, 205–218.

Kennedy, Paul. 1987. *The Rise and Fall of the Great Powers: Economic Change and Military Conflict from 1500 to 2000*. New York: Random House.

Kennedy, Robert F. 1971. *Thirteen Days: A Memoir of the Cuban Missile Crisis*. New York: W. W. Norton.

Kidron, Michael, and Dan Smith. 1983. *The War Atlas: Armed Conflict—Armed Peace*. London and Sydney: Pan Books.

Kim, Ilpyong J. 1987. *The Strategic Triangle: China, the United States and the Soviet Union*. New York: Paragon Publishing.

Laird, Robbin F. 1986. *The Soviet Union, the West and the Nuclear Arms Race*. New York: New York University Press.

Landsheer, B., et al. 1971. *World Society: How Is an Effective and Desirable World Order Possible?* The Hague: Martinus Nijhoff.

Larson, Arthur. 1963. *A Warless World*. New York: McGraw Hill.

Leaning, Jennifer, and Langley Keyes. 1984. *The Counterfeit Ark: Crisis Relocation for the Nuclear Age*. Cambridge, MA: Ballinger.

Leventhal, Paul and Yonah Alexander (eds.). 1986. *Nuclear Terrorism: Defining the Threat*. Washington, DC: Pergamon-Brassey.

Lifton, Robert Jay, and Richard Falk. 1982. *Indefensible Weapons: Political and Psychological Case Against Nuclearism*. New York: Basic Books.

Litwak, Robert S., and Samuel F. Wells, Jr. 1988. *Superpower Competition and Security in the Third World*. Cambridge, MA: Ballinger.

Luard, Evan. 1982. *A History of the United Nations, Vol. 1: The Years of Western Domination, 1945–1955*. New York: St. Martin's Press.

Luttwak, Edward N. 1984. *The Pentagon and the Art of War*. New York: Simon and Schuster.

MacIsaac, David. 1976. *Strategic Bombing in WW II: The Story of the U.S. Strategic Bombing Survey*. New York and London: Garland Publishing.

Macrae, Norman. 1985. *The 2025 Report: A Concise History of the Future*. New York: Macmillan.

Maniruzzaman, Talaukder. 1987. *Military Withdrawal from Politics: A Comparative Study.* Cambridge, MA: Ballinger.

Mann, Michael. 1986. *The Sources of Social Power, Vol. One: From the Beginning to A.D. 1760.* Cambridge: Cambridge University Press.

Mantoux, Paul, tr. J. B. Whitton. 1946. *Paris Peace Conference 1919: Proceedings of the Council of Four.* Geneva: Droz.

Marriott, J. A. R. 1918. *The European Commonwealth: Problems Historical and Diplomatic.* Oxford: Clarendon Press.

McKernan, Michael. 1980. *The Australian People and the Great War.* Melbourne: Thomas Wilson.

McLeod, Kirsty. 1983. *The Last Summer: May to September 1914.* New York: St. Martin's Press.

McNamara, Robert S. 1986. *Blundering into Disaster: Surviving the First Century of the Nuclear Age.* New York: Pantheon Books.

McNeill, William H. 1982. *The Pursuit of Power.* Chicago: University of Chicago Press.

McPhee, John. 1983. *La Place de la Concorde Suisse.* New York: Farrar Straus & Giroux.

Mee, Charles L., Jr. 1980. *The End of Order: Versailles 1919.* New York: E. P. Dutton.

Melko, Matthew, and John Hord. 1984. *Peace in the Western World.* Jefferson, NC: McFarland & Co.

Mendel, A. P. (ed.). 1961. *The Essential Works of Marxism.* New York: Bantam Books.

Meurant, Jacques. 1876. *La Presse et l'opinion publique de la suisse romande face à l'Europe en guerre, 1939–1941.* Neuchâtel: Editions de la Baconnière.

Meyer, John. 1980. "The World Polity and the Authority of the Nation-State," in Albert Bergesen, ed., *Studies of the Modern World Order.* New York: Academic Press.

More, Thomas. 1964 [1516]. *Utopia.* New Haven: Yale University Press.

Moskowitz, Max. 1980. *The Roots and Reaches of United Nations Actions and Decisions.* Alphen aan den Rijn, Netherlands: Sijthoff & Noordhoff.

Mueller, John E. 1973. *War, Presidents and Public Opinion.* New York: John Wiley and Sons.

Murphy, John F. 1982. *The United Nations and the Control of International Violence: A Legal and Political Analysis.* Totowa, NJ: Allanheld, Osmun.

Nacht, Michael. 1985. *The Age of Vulnerability: Threats to the Nuclear Stalemate.* Washington, DC: The Brookings Institution.

Northedge, F. S. 1986. *The League of Nations: Its Life and Times.* Leicester, England: Leicester University Press.

Nowak, Karl Friedrich. 1929. *Versailles.* New York: Payson and Clark.

Olson, Mancur. 1982. *The Rise and Decline of Nations: Economic*

Growth, Stagflation and Social Rigidities. New Haven: Yale University Press.

Paret, Peter (ed.). 1986. *Makers of Modern Strategy: Machiavelli to the Nuclear Age.* Princeton: Princeton University Press.

Penn, William. 1693. *An Essay Towards the Present and Future Peace of Europe.* London.

Perkins, Merle L. 1959. *The Moral and Political Philosophy of the Abbé de St. Pierre.* Geneva: R. Droz.

Perrow, Charles. 1984. *Normal Accidents: Living with High-Risk Technologies.* New York: Basic Books.

Phillips, Walter Allson. 1914. *The Confederation of Europe: A Study of the European Alliance, 1813–1823, etc.* London: Longmans, Green.

Pitt, David, and Thomas G. Weiss (eds.). 1986. *The Nature of United Nations Bureaucracies.* London: Croom Helm.

Poggi, Gianfranco. 1980. *The Development of the Modern State: A Sociological Introduction.* Stanford, CA: Stanford University Press.

Pufendorf, Samuel. 1934 [1672]. *De jure naturae et gentium,* tr. C. H. and W. A. Oldfather. Oxford: Clarendon Press.

Ravenal, Earl C. 1984. *Defining Defense: The 1985 Military Budget.* Washington, DC: Cato Institute.

Reston, James Jr. 1984. *Sherman's March and Vietnam.* New York: Macmillan.

Riesman, David. 1964. "John F. Kennedy and After." *The Correspondent,* No. 30.

Rosenbloom, Morris V. 1953. *Peace through Strength: Bernard Baruch and a Blueprint for Security.* New York: Farrar, Straus and Young.

Rossi-Landi, Gury. 1971. *La Drôle de guerre.* Paris: Armand Colin.

Rousseau, Jean-Jacques. 1962 [1756]. *Jugement sur la paix perpetuelle.* Vaughan Edition. New York: John Wiley & Sons.

Rovine, Arthur W. 1970. *The First Fifty Years: The Secretary-General in World Politics 1920–1970.* Leyden: A. W. Sijthoff.

Russell, Bertrand. 1956. *Portraits from Memory and Other Essays.* London: Allen and Unwin.

St.-Pierre, Charles Irenée Castel de. 1763. *Political Annals* translated from the last French edition. London: Henry Woodgate.

———. 1981 [1713]. *Projet pour rendre la paix perpetuelle en Europe,* ed. Simone Goyard-Fabre. Paris: Editions Garnier.

Schell, Jonathan. 1982. *The Fate of the Earth.* New York: Alfred A. Knopf.

———. 1984. *The Abolition.* New York: Alfred A. Knopf.

Schwartz, William A., and Charles Derber. 1986. "Arms Control: Misplaced Focus." *Bulletin of the Atomic Scientists* 42:3, 39–44.

Scowcroft, Brent, John Deutch, and R. James Woolsey. 1987. "The Survivability Problem." *Washington Post,* 3 December, A23.

Singer, J. D., and M. Small. 1972. *The Wages of War: A Statistical Handbook, 1816–1965.* New York: John Wiley.

Smoke, Richard, with Willis Harmon. *Paths to Peace: Exploring the Feasibility of Sustainable Peace.* Boulder and London: Westview Press.

Snyder, Jed C., and Samuel F. Wells, Jr. (eds.). 1985. *Limiting Nuclear Proliferation.* Cambridge, MA: Ballinger.

Spaulding, Oliver Lyman, Hoffman Nickerson, and John Womack Wright. 1937. *Warfare: A Study of Military Methods from the Earliest Times.* Washington, DC: Infantry Journal Press.

Spector, Leonard S. 1988. *The Undeclared Bomb.* Cambridge, MA: Ballinger.

Spiel, Hilde (ed.). 1968. *The Congress of Vienna: An Eyewitness Account.* Philadelphia: Chilton.

Stanley Foundation. 1986. *U.S. Policy and Radical Regimes: Report of a Vantage Conference.* Muscatine, IA: The Stanley Foundation.

———. 1986. *Redefining Arms Control: Report of a Vantage Conference.* Muscatine, IA: Stanley Foundation.

———. 1987. *Administrative and Budgetary Reform of the United Nations: Report of the 18th United Nations Issues Conference.* Muscatine, IA: Stanley Foundation.

Starr, Harvey. 1972. *War Coalitions: The Distribution of Payoffs and Losses.* Lexington, MA: Lexington Books.

Steel, Jonathan. 1987. "Military Security in Europe." *Foreign Affairs,* Fall.

Stockman, David A. 1986. *The Triumph of Politics: The Inside Story of the Reagan Revolution.* New York: Avon Books.

Stoetzel, Jean. 1983. *Les Valeurs du temps present: une enquête européene.* Paris: Presses universitaires de France.

Storr, Anthony. 1968. *Human Aggression.* New York: Atheneum.

Stromberg, Roland N. 1982. *Redemption by War: The Intellectuals and 1914.* Lawrence: The Regents Press of Kansas.

Sumner, Charles. 1850. "The True Grandeur of Nations," in *Orations and Speeches,* 2 vols. Boston: Ticknor, Reed and Fields.

———. 1850. "The War System of the Commonwealth of Nations," in *Orations and Speeches,* 2 vols. Boston: Ticknor, Reed and Fields.

Thompson, William Irwin. 1976. *Evil and World Order.* New York: Harper & Row.

Trudeau, Pierre Elliott. 1985. "The Nuclear Imperative." *World Press Review,* January, 25–30.

Tuchman, Barbara. 1985. *The March of Folly: From Troy to Vietnam.* New York: Alfred A. Knopf.

Ungar, Sanford J. (ed.). 1985. *Estrangement: America and the World.* New York: Oxford University Press.

Union of Concerned Scientists. 1987. *The Strategic Defense Initiative: Briefing Paper.* Cambridge, MA: Union of Concerned Scientists, June.

United Nations Library. 1983. *The League of Nations in Retrospect (La Société des nations retrospective).* Proceedings of the Symposium. Berlin: Walter De Gruyter.

Urquhart, Brian. 1987. *A Life in Peace and War*. New York: Harper & Row.

Van Creveld, Martin. 1985. *Command in War*. Cambridge: Harvard University Press.

Vaněček, Václav. 1964. *The Historical Significance of the Project of King George of Bohemia and the Research Problems Involved*. Prague: Czechoslovak Academy of Science.

Victoria, Franciscus de. 1981 [1565]. *Relectio de iure belli relectiones*. Madrid: Consejo Superior, tr. (into Spanish) L. Perena et al.

Voltaire, François Marie Arouet. 1761. "Rescript de l'empereur de Chine à l'occasion du projet de paix perpetuelle." *Journal Encyclopédique*, May.

Warner, Edward L. III and David A. Ochmanek. 1989. *Next Moves: An Arms Control Agenda for the 1990s*. New York: Council on Foreign Relations.

Weber, Max. 1968 [1921]. *Economy and Society: An Outline of Interpretive Sociology*. New York: Bedminster Press.

Webster, Graham. 1985. *The Roman Imperial Army of the First and Second Centuries A.D.* Totowa, NJ: Barnes & Noble.

Weinberg, Alvin M., and Jack N. Barkenbus. 1988. *Strategic Defenses and Arms Control*. New York: Paragon House.

Weinberger, Caspar W. 1986. *Report of the Secretary of Defense to the Congress, FY 1987*. Washington, DC: Department of Defense.

Weston, Burns H. 1984. *Toward Nuclear Disarmament and Global Security: A Search for Alternatives*. Boulder, CO: Westview Press.

Wieseltier, Leon. 1983. *Nuclear War: Nuclear Peace*. New York: Holt, Rinehart and Winston.

Williams, Robin M., Jr. 1987. "Sociological Analysis of International Relations." Paper presented at the 1987 meetings of the American Sociological Association.

Wilson, Woodrow. 1929. "The Fourteen Points," in *Famous Speeches by American Statesmen*. St. Paul: West Publishing Company.

Woolsey, R. James (ed.). 1984. *Nuclear Arms: Ethics, Strategy, Politics*. San Francisco: ICS Press.

Yankelovich, Daniel and Sidney Harman. 1988. *Starting with the People*. Boston: Houghton Mifflin.

Young, David, and others (Oxford Analytical). 1986. *America in Perspective: Major Trends in the United States through the 1990s*. Boston: Houghton Mifflin.

Zablocki, Benjamin. 1971. *The Joyful Community*. Baltimore, MD: Penguin Press.

Zuckerman, Edward. 1984. *The Day After World War III*. New York: Viking Press.

Index

About the Author

As a young soldier, Theodore Caplow saw the smoking ruins of Hiroshima. This book is, in a sense, a legacy of that experience. The idea for *Peace Games* occurred to him when most of his students in an undergraduate seminar at the University of Virginia in 1986 said they expected to die in a nuclear war.

Caplow, who is Commonwealth Professor of Sociology at the University of Virginia, has been chair of the department of sociology and also of the department of anthropology. He is the author of nine books, among them, *Two Against One: Coalitions in Triads, The Sociology of Work, Toward Social Hope,* and *Principles of Organization;* and he is coauthor or editor of seven other books.

A graduate of the University of Chicago (A.B. 1939) and the University of Minnesota (Ph.D. 1946), Caplow has taught also at Minnesota and Columbia and has been visiting professor at Stanford and at universities at Bordeaux, Aix-en-Provence, Utrecht, Bogotá, Paris, Rome, and Oslo. He has held various offices of the American Sociological Association, most recently, secretary (1983–1986). His home is in Earlysville, Virginia.

About the Book

Peace Games was composed on the Mergenthaler 202 in Trump Mediaeval, a contemporary typeface based on classical prototypes. Trump Mediaeval was designed by the German graphic artist and type designer Georg Trump (1895–1986). It was initially issued in 1954, by C. E. Weber Typefoundry of Stuttgart, in the form of foundry type and linecasting matrices. This book was composed by WorldComp of Sterling, Virginia. It was designed and produced by Kachergis Book Design of Pittsboro, North Carolina.

Wesleyan University Press, 1989